KEANU

To Lex

Sheila Johnston, a writer and film critic, studied Modern Languages at the University of Southampton and Film at University College, London, where she wrote her thesis on Rainer Werner Fassbinder. She lives in London.

I tried to get Shearer
But Keanu will do
Have a happy birthday
Best wishes to you

From Simon
6th June 1997. 33

SHEILA JOHNSTON
KEANU

PAN BOOKS

First published 1996 by Sidgwick & Jackson

This edition published 1997 by Pan Books
an imprint of Macmillan Publishers Ltd
25 Eccleston Place, London SW1W 9NF
and Basingstoke

Associated companies throughout the world

ISBN 0 330 34382 3

9 8 7 6 5 4 3 2 1

A CIP catalogue record for this book is available from
the British Library

Typeset by CentraCet Limited, Cambridge
Printed and bound in Great Britain by
Mackays of Chatham plc, Chatham, Kent

CONTENTS

PICTURE CREDITS

ACKNOWLEDGEMENTS

Many dozens of people made *Keanu* possible, first and foremost all those, named and unnamed, who agreed to be interviewed and gave me so much of their time. Thanks also to Paul Aaron, Keanu's stepfather, who confirmed some of the factual information (any surviving errors are of course entirely mine).

The staff of the following libraries did their best to satisfy my endless demands for material: the Film Reference Library, Toronto; the Central Reference Library, Toronto; the Museum of Modern Art Department of Film, New York; the New York Public Library; the British Film Institute Library, London; and the British Newspaper Library, Colindale, London.

Sleuthing the early film and television work took me to a range of sources. Paul Lynch and Steven H. Stern very kindly sent me cassettes of the films they directed with Keanu. Others were tracked down thanks to Chris Higgs at ITFC, the National Film and Television Archive, London, the Museum of Television and Radio, New York ... and the Montague Street Video Store, Brooklyn.

Catherine Hurley, my editor at Sidgwick, and her colleagues

Claire Evans, Nicholas Blake and Ingrid Connell, were tireless in tinkering with the nuts and bolts of the manuscript; thanks, too, to my agent, Michael Shaw, for his suggestions.

Among my friends and colleagues who provided advice, practical information, help and encouragement in various combinations were: Anne Billson, Barbara Burge, Sharon Churcher, Pam Cuthbert, Hugo Davenport, Derek Elley, Graham Fuller, Steven Gaines, Peter Johnston, Paul Kerr, Winfried and Evelyn Kretz, Michael McDonough, Robert Murphy, George Perry, Gerald Pratley, Steve Rosier at Public Eye, Chris Savage-King, Denis Seguin, David Thompson, Maggie Todd at Twentieth Century-Fox and Jim Whitty.

I am most especially grateful to Gaylen Ross and the McQueen family for their hospitality while I was reseaching this book in North America; to Nigel Andrews, John Glatt and Michael Shnayerson for generously making available unpublished interview material; to Alexander Walker – a far more experienced biographer than I – for his constant moral support and sound counsel; and above all to Bernard Martinez for the late night drives.

Sheila Johnston
London, June 1996

1 THE MAN IN THE MICKEY MOUSE SUIT

Keanu: at first the name seemed a liability but it became a magnet. As he nudged into the public eye, magazine profiles endlessly supplied handy pronunciation guides (Kee-AH-noo) and explained that it was Hawaiian for 'a cool breeze over the mountains'. A nice story – almost too good to be true. Liana Iaea-Honda, a consultant at Hawaiian Language Resources in Honolulu, thought that 'cool breeze over the mountains' should translate as Keanuhea. An abbreviated Keanu meant, she said, simply 'the coldness' or 'the coolness'. Nothing, but *nothing* about the man was straightforward. Still, a name which meant 'the coolness' and which could be used by either gender ... perhaps, on reflection, it was just right for this most distant and androgynous of stars.

Keanu became a teenage hero thanks to Ted, the dim protagonist of *Bill and Ted's Excellent Adventure*. But he also attracted heavy-duty directors – Bernardo Bertolucci and Stephen Frears, Francis Ford Coppola and Gus Van Sant, Kenneth Branagh and Kathryn Bigelow, Lawrence Kasdan and Jon Amiel. Contemporaries like Charlie Sheen seethed with envy. 'Emilio [Estevez] and I sit around and just scratch our heads thinking, "How did this guy get in?" How does

Keanu work with Coppola and Bertolucci and I don't get a shot at that?' Sheen grumbled (for a start he could try looking in the mirror). Finally, in the summer of 1994, *Speed* anointed Reeves a mainstream star.

The same twelvemonth which brought Keanu his international success also dealt him a triple whammy of hard personal blows. First there was the death of his friend and colleague River Phoenix in the morning of 31 October – Hallowe'en – 1993. It emerged that Phoenix had for some time been involved with hard drugs, an addiction which had probably begun as a professional experiment while playing a male prostitute in *My Own Private Idaho*. Keanu had been his co-star in that movie and he too had been dogged by rumours of drug abuse. The following July, there was the arrest of Samuel Nowlin Reeves in Hilo, Hawaii, for possession of large amounts of heroin and cocaine. The irresponsible and neglectful father whom Keanu had not seen for seventeen years was now suddenly bobbing back from the past to rain on his son's parade at the very moment when his big breakthrough film was about to roll out across America. Finally, that autumn the *annus horribilis* ended with a wave of rumours about his sexuality, climaxing in reports that he had 'married' the media mogul David Geffen in a secret New Age ceremony (a story which both men firmly denied).

The most extraordinary thing was that all this did not have the remotest impact on Keanu's popularity. He continued to command a huge following, of a breadth that no other modern film star could match. Even mildly progressive public figures confessed to Keanu-fever. Judith Church, the forty-one-year-old Labour MP for Dagenham, was pictured in her office with a poster of *Speed* prominently displayed on the wall. Liking Keanu was cool: a sign that Church was of the New Left, sexy, hip and populist. 'I'm hoping when he's next over from Hollywood he will come and have dinner at the House of Commons,' she said.

Meanwhile fans from all over the world were flocking to the frozen wastes of Winnipeg in Central Canada to see his Hamlet. A group of Japanese women bought seats for ten consecutive shows; others made the pilgrimage from as far afield as Australia, China and Argentina, many without a ticket. There were more sold-out houses (quite possibly to the same people) for his extensive American and international tour that summer and autumn with Dogstar, the 'folk thrash' band in which he played bass guitar. Turning thirty had not diminished his appeal for teenage admirers: Keanu, the turbo-dreambabe, still smouldered across the pages of *Sugar*, *Sky* and *Just Seventeen*, which commemorated the star on a natty, neon-green keyring (he reacted with a typical Keanu-ism: 'What's a keyring?' he wanted to know).

The artistic community was producing more ambitious memorabilia. For years he had been a cult icon for insiders (or Keanu-seurs, as they liked to be known). Keith Mayerson drew portraits of him in the naive manner of a teenage girl trying to get close to her idol, and immortalized him in a 1993 show called *Pinocchio The Big Fag*, a 'pictorial representation of the original folktale', which featured Keanu as Lampwick, the puppet's best friend and lover: one image had him holding Pinocchio as if to kiss him, both characters with donkey ears sprouting from their head. The most obsessional project was *Keanu Sightings*, a collection, compiled over a period of six or seven years, of about 200 carefully annotated occasions when Mayerson's friends had spotted the actor out and about.

Richard Hawkins was creating collages featuring Keanu, and was taping his photograph onto Chinese lanterns along with other stars whom the artist found desirable. The writer Dennis Cooper put him in a novel, *Frisk*, in which a Keanu look-alike got killed by an actor from *The Twilight Zone*. Keanu himself had never died in any of his movies unless you counted *Bill and Ted's Bogus Journey*; nor, for that matter, had he killed more than a couple of people (one of whom was Charles Bronson, who probably deserved it). Indeed, his gentle persona was at the heart of his appeal.

From the beginning of his career he had tried to avoid bloodshed and, according to the director Oliver Stone, declined the lead role in the 1986 film *Platoon* – a naive young volunteer who undergoes a terrible baptism of fire in Vietnam. 'I offered *Platoon* to Keanu but he turned it down on the basis of its violence,' Stone said. 'He was a bit of a pacifist at that time. He was very sweet, very nice, but he just had a real thing about guns.' It was, perhaps, not a prudent decision, since the film was to garner four Academy Awards, including Best Picture. The central character was played instead by . . . (the Oscar-nominated) Charlie Sheen.

In early 1994 the artist–lecturer Stephen Prina launched a course on 'The Films of Keanu Reeves' at the Art Center College of Design in Pasadena, California, a few kilometres down the road from San Dimas, Ted's stamping ground. It became a minor media event and numerous reporters descended on the classroom, mainly to poke fun at it as just the sort of totally bogus course you might find at the Bill and Ted University featured in the second Bill and Ted movie. 'Pre-*Speed* he was just customarily and ceremoniously written off,' Prina said. 'He was always reduced to Ted. That was the mass media's shorthand way of dealing with him. Six months later, no one was making jokes about Keanu any more. Even the way they would treat him and would edit his comments changed drastically. They were forming him into a different kind of figure.'

He had been drawn to Keanu's enigmatic screen presence. 'There seemed almost a reluctance or a holding back, never giving full characterization to any character he was playing. I didn't find that a deficiency, I found it very particular.' To explore his ideas, Prina set his students 500 pages of required reading including Roland Barthes, Walter Benjamin, Andy Warhol and Michel Foucault. Keanu dealt with the course gracefully when it came up in interviews, saying simply, 'I hope the kids learn something worthwhile.'

In a similar spirit, in the spring of 1995, London's Institute of Contemporary Arts asked its members to name any one person they would like to hear give a lecture. Keanu topped the poll by a comfortable margin; the runner-up was Slavoj Zizek, a Lacanian philosopher and intellectual arch-guru based in Ljubiljana. One other film star was nominated: Norman Wisdom. Members' tastes were eclectic.

The enormity of this interest, and its frequently bizarre manifestations, were all the more puzzling in view of the many enigmas surrounding Keanu. Was he, as colleagues in the theatre and film communities maintained, an underrated actor of impressive versatility? There must, his defenders said, be some reason why so many eminent directors – directors, moreover, so different from each other – had sought out his services. If he sometimes failed, then that was just because he was prepared to try odd and difficult roles at the risk of taking a tumble. Or was he, as his detractors argued, just a pretty himbo, known round Hollywood as 'Keanu act' and cast cynically for his box-office appeal: an actor of small talent who always played, despite superficial differences, fundamentally the same character – a variant on himself – and who became a downright embarrassment when he got uppity and took on Hamlet?

Was he smart and witty, as his collaborators claimed, with a voracious appetite for literature and art, or, as interviewers often painted him, a Ted-like airhead with nothing of consequence to say? Was he a straightforward, easy-going guy, friendly and smiling, unspoiled by fame; or secretive, consumed by self-directed anger and emotionally remote – unable, outside his immediate family, to form lasting relationships of any intimacy or to sustain a long-term love affair?

Perhaps the answers to these questions were irrelevant to the fascination Keanu exercised – perhaps, indeed, it depended on their remaining unresolved. At the peak of his fame, Keanu made a sharp comment about himself and his admirers. 'I'm Mickey [Mouse],' he said. 'They don't know who's inside the suit.' His friend retorted, 'But you're a movie star!' To which Keanu, laughing, replied, 'So's Mickey.'

His origins reveal nothing and everything of the mystery. The individual details are sparse and contradictory, but a strong pattern emerges from the general contours which were to form the man Keanu became. His parents met in Beirut, Lebanon which, before the country was torn apart by Arab–Israeli conflict and civil war in the Seventies, was a major commercial, financial and cultural centre on the Eastern Mediterranean. In the early Sixties, tourism was peaking. The city's lush climate, its lovely setting and cosmopolitan atmosphere made it a popular destination both for wealthy Arab families and for Western back-packers on the hippy trail towards India. Beirut was also a crossroads for the narcotics trade of the Middle East.

One story (discounted by sources close to the family) held that Keanu's British-born mother, Patricia, known as Patric, and his Chinese-Hawaiian father, Samuel, were both students at the American University in the city. A second version of events claimed Patric was working in a local club when she met Samuel, who was vacationing there. The Reeves had money: Samuel's mother's second husband, Colman Abrahams, had made a small fortune developing a children's edition of the *Encyclopaedia Britannica* for Canada and investing in property – money which his stepson spent on such items as a purple Jaguar XKE, one of the first E-types made. Samuel himself maintained that he was working as a clerk in a publishing company, while Patric was a dancer at a casino. According to yet other accounts, Samuel's presence in Beirut was connected with drugs, and possibly other business activities of dubious legality. Keanu himself was vague on the subject, explaining when asked that he guessed his parents were 'just hanging out' and 'doing their thing' in the Middle East.

Patric and Samuel married in 1964, and their first child

arrived on 2 September of that year: Keanu Charles Reeves. Kee-AH-noo was a Reeves family name. The actor thought one reason his mother made sure he was born abroad was so that he could avoid the draft (the Vietnam War was hotting up); he eventually acquired dual Canadian and American citizenship. Shortly afterwards they went to Australia where a daughter, Kim, followed two years later – but soon Samuel was gone. 'There were fights about Sam's drug-taking,' said Keanu's cousin, Leslie Reeves, many years later. 'My aunt grew out of the hippy phase. My uncle didn't. In fact he couldn't give up drugs.'

Patric took her family on again, to New York, where she met and, in 1969, married Paul Aaron, an American stage and film director. The following year they moved again to Toronto, which seemed to her a better place to raise her children. Here Keanu grew up in a neighbourhood which he described as 'safe and sheltered' – the sort of place 'where you could still be out playing at 11.30 at night'. The kids would build go-carts and pelt their teachers with chestnuts. One of his friends lived in the east end of Toronto, where the houses were separated by narrow lanes, and at nights they would egg each other on to leap across them.

The family remained rootless, changing houses almost out of a compulsion to keep on the hoof; certainly there was no reason that the children could divine. 'It's not like the houses got *bigger* or anything,' Kim said. Keanu was unsettled too, and hyper-active. He would get up to tricks like dismantling the furniture with his tool set. He was left-handed and dyslexic, and this, combined with the fact that he kept switching schools, meant he was no academic high-flyer. Teachers remembered him as good-humoured, bright and likeable but also scatty, often arriving late or minus his homework.

Patric and Aaron split up after the move to Toronto (although, unlike Samuel Reeves, who 'sort of disconnected' around this time, as his son put it, Aaron remained close to Keanu). By the mid-Seventies a new husband, Robert Miller, a local rock promoter, and another daughter, Karina, were on the scene. Patric had also built up a business of her own designing theatrical and rock 'n' roll costumes. Her clients included David Bowie, Dolly Parton and Alice Cooper, who stayed *chez* Reeves while he was recording *Welcome to My Nightmare* and proved a cool dude who was game for a spot of floor-wrestling with Keanu and planted fake vomit and dog turds to freak out the housekeeper. Later, when he was fifteen, Keanu went with a friend of his mother's to see Emmylou Harris in concert, an occasion which imprinted itself on his memory because he got to stay up all night and observed a man emerging from the lavatory with cocaine on his moustache.

For the most part they were latchkey kids, left to their own devices. 'We never had anyone to play with us, to watch me riding horses or Keanu playing hockey,' said Kim. '[But] you can't miss what you never had.' Her brother hung out instead with Shawn Aberle, one of his classmates at Jesse Ketchum, which he attended until the age of fourteen. It was a mildly progressive inner-city school whose pupils were a strange social mix of children from rich bohemian families and kids on welfare. Shawn and Keanu were thrown together partly by expediency: they lived close to each other in Yorkville, a fashionable, artsy neighbourhood near Jesse Ketchum where there were few other children around. There was, Aberle believed, also a shared sense of 'our families not being there for us'.

Aberle bought a newspaper route from Keanu (a common practice in North America where these were in short supply), who cannily sold it on just after reaping all the juicy Christmas tips. They lived the life of typical city kids, playing ball in the street or playground because their back yards were too small, or going to movies. At other times they took in a hockey game to cheer on the Toronto Toros, their local team in the World Hockey League. Some days they would just knock around shopping malls. 'Keanu and I used to be very famous riders,' said Aberle. 'We'd go skidding and skate-boarding down the malls. Downtown was our playground. Cars were not a problem for us, which might be one reason for his fearless nature later when he got his motorbike.'

Later, a myth was to build up around Keanu as a solitary, rather pathetic child. But those who knew him during this period recall things otherwise. Donald Mason, who taught him at Jesse Ketchum and remembered him well, said, 'He was a fun kid, good at sports and quite popular with his classmates. I enjoyed teaching him; he always had a smile. Sometimes I would be working late and get out at 5.00, 5.30, and Keanu would frequently be out there shooting hoops by himself. He'd been there for an hour or two, just playing with the basketball. But he may have been waiting for his sister. I never pictured him as a sad, forlorn type. I think he was alone a fair bit, but I'm not sure whether you'd call it a loner or a lonely side. There's quite a difference there.'

Patric (and this also later became a subject for great

disapproval in the tabloids) refused, like many women of her generation, to conform to the fading stereotype of a 'good mother'. 'Sometimes I thought she was strange,' said Aberle. 'One time I did a sleepover at his house. We said, "Let's see if we can stay up all night," and ordered pizza, watched TV, played chess. His parents didn't come home at all that evening. They'd be off all the time at rock parties. Once they had driven over the border from Buffalo and the Canadians did a six-hour search of the car and a strip-search of his parents. Keanu was very upset at the violation of his mother.'

But their home was kept in immaculate and fashionable order: not a place for unruly small boys. 'It was very particular, stylish, neat. His mother wouldn't allow newspapers lying around the house. The living room had a white leather sofa, white carpets and a glass dining table. Even the chess set he played on was an elaborate marble set. In his mother's bedroom everything was white too: white television, white king-size bed. If Keanu came in with muddy shoes or left his baseball glove lying around, that didn't fit into the scene.

'She didn't really care about the social norms of raising a family. I don't remember seeing her at school, at parent–teacher evenings or even at graduation. Keanu had to fend for himself, feed his sister and feed himself. He and Kim were inseparable. He was very much the elder brother and felt very strongly about her. So it was not an apple-pie American upbringing. But,' Aberle continued, 'they are only good memories that I have. We were in this world and happy enough about it. He seemed very able to cope on his own.'

Friends remembered them as settled, if unconventional.

Another acquaintance who saw the Reeves daily in the mid-Eighties, by which time Patric had a new partner, a hairdresser named Jack Bond, was impressed by this magnetic and dramatic-looking woman with her white skin and very short cropped hair dyed platinum. Keanu had inherited her eyes, and his elegant bone structure came from her rather than from the coarser-featured Samuel.

Patric was evidently not a keen cook. They – she, Jack, Karina and, more rarely, Kim and Keanu – would eat every evening at Arlequin, a small, chic but informal Mediterranean-French restaurant in Yorkville, almost directly opposite Bond's salon; sometimes they would drop in at lunchtime too to get take-out. Perhaps this was because Patric had been contending with illness and was painfully thin, even frail-looking, although she smoked Gitanes incessantly. This observer found the family polite and pleasant and Patric in particular reserved and 'pretty much inaccessible – a bit of a tough cookie. She didn't strike me as the maternal type, I must say.'

Alan Powell, a friend of Keanu's while the two young men were at theatre school together in their late teens, remembered Patric as 'a pretty neat lady' and supportive of her son, but also somehow intimidating. 'She seemed to know a lot and she was very perceptive,' he said. 'And she never considered herself a mom. It was Mothers' Day once and she said, "I am not a mother, I'm standing by and watching these children grow up." But the atmosphere in his home was warm. Everyone had duties, so I'd hang out in the kitchen, help chop the salad and shoot the breeze.'

Keanu himself spoke of Patric with great affection. Her

design skills meant that, come Hallowe'en, her kids always had the coolest costumes in town. And, if the earth-mother qualities were not much in evidence, in other ways she was, he said, 'ahead of her time. She surrounded my two young sisters and myself with culture and art. We learned to love ideas, even if I was hating high school.' She had a taste for the stylish and the fashionable and had the celebrated photographer Richard Avedon take Keanu's portrait when he was six. When asked later, just after he had moved to Hollywood, what he missed most about Toronto, he replied without missing a beat, 'My mom.'

His feelings towards his father were less filial. Friends remembered Keanu as bitterly resentful at the way he believed Samuel had deserted the family – on the rare occasions, that was, when he was prepared to talk about him at all; often, when his name came up, his son would brusquely change the subject or dismiss it with a sarcastic comment.

That applied in spades when Keanu was quizzed about his father by journalists. In unguarded interviews at the beginning of his career he had referred to Samuel half-jokingly as 'the Sixties burn-out guy' and 'an acid-taking goofball'. Gradually, the references petered out. He shared a fleeting, rather sad little memory with one journalist. 'The last time I saw him was when I was thirteen. It was at night. We were in Kauai. And I remember him speaking about the stars. Something about how the world is a box. And I looked up, and I had no clue what he was talking about. "No, Dad, the earth is round. It's not a rectangle, man." No, I'm sure he didn't say that. But I remember him speaking about the stars as we looked up.' More typical of his feelings was his tight-lipped response when the subject of Samuel was broached a few months later. 'He isn't anyone I really know,' he said tersely.

'He's a very angry guy, although you wouldn't know it when you met him; he's very happy-go-lucky,' said Powell, making an observation that Keanu's colleagues in the cinema and in the theatre would later echo, even if they were not always able to guess at that anger's source. Most of them assumed it to be self-directed and linked with a compulsive perfectionism, which gave the impression that he was never entirely satisfied with his own performance. The actor himself liked to put it down to astrology: he was born, he often pointed out, under Virgo, the sign of order and control.

But friends thought they saw a connection between what seemed like a deep-seated lack of self-esteem and the lack of paternal love, support and approval in Keanu's early life. 'It has to do with his father,' Powell said. 'He was an uncaring bastard, a sonuvabitch.' With his mother and two sisters, especially Kim, as his main emotional anchors, and a succession of surrogate fathers many of whom remained, for him, on the shadowy side, it was a childhood shaped by women with few significant men in his early life. 'He didn't have a male role model,' Powell continued. 'There have probably been dozens of ropes that have come down the hole to help him out. But he's never taken them, I don't think.'

Later, once Keanu had moved to Los Angeles, he fell back under the tutelage of Paul Aaron and a colleague of Aaron's, Erwin Stoff, who became his manager. But for the moment that continuity eluded him. His stepfather, whose directing career kept him in the United States, had been much less present since the family had relocated to Toronto. And, after leaving Jesse Ketchum in 1978, Keanu bounced around a series of high schools in quick succession, making it difficult for him either to find a teacher-mentor or to build long-term friendships with his classmates – even if, as seemed unlikely, he had been temperamentally inclined to do so.

He found the North Toronto Collegiate, which he attended between the ages of fourteen and fifteen, uncongenial, with its conservative teaching methods and emphasis on academic achievement, and teachers had the impression that he was not really happy there. But it did have an acting programme. Paul Robert, who taught the Grade 10 introductory drama course, noticed that Keanu was now definitely interested in the theatre, but after his own fashion. He needed to be encouraged to join in the group exercises: 'It wasn't a negative thing, just that he was an independent, freewheeling guy, relatively a loner.' Keanu did not audition either for that year's main stage play, a production of *HMS Pinafore*, or for a more experimental, student-written piece called *Angel*, which was open to anyone who wanted to be in it. 'He didn't really like working with the others,' Robert said. 'He wanted to get into something a little meatier.'

But Keanu was pursuing his new passion indirectly. He would fly over regularly to spend school vacations with Paul Aaron in New York or Los Angeles, hanging around and watching him at work on various film and television projects, including an Emmy Award-winning production of *The Miracle Worker*. These trips also gave him a vicarious taste of stardom, and visits to the homes of people like Chuck Norris mightily impressed the teenage boy.

In 1980 suddenly, although not to Aaron's great surprise, Keanu announced that he would like to change schools yet again and to audition for the High School For The Performing Arts. This was a new place, privately run along free, experimental lines; traditionalists sniffed that it was 'loose and druggy' (it closed after a couple of years). Despite his total lack of experience, Keanu was one of only twenty-five students accepted for the first year's intake. Acting immediately became an obsession, Aaron recalled: 'I mean, every part of it – the voice, the movement, the contemporary, the classical. This was never a kid who said, "Gee, I think I'm good-looking, maybe I'd like to star in a TV series."'

But even in this supposedly progressive haven, his unruliness and independent-mindedness got the better of him: after one year he left, a credit short of graduating. 'He was booted out,' according to Evan Williams, a childhood friend, after he got into an argument with a teacher who told him he would just have to 'bite the bullet', and Keanu answered back cheekily, 'Yeah, but I don't have to eat the whole rifle.'

Ice hockey was his other great passion. Scott Barber, his coach, met Keanu at fifteen and immediately tried to recruit him for his team: he was a good sportsman and, importantly, liked to play in goal, a position that was often hard to fill on teenage teams. Even here, in a bid to combine his two hobbies, he would, to his team-mates' amusement and bemusement, suddenly take to delivering blasts of Shakespeare or snippets from movies in the dressing room and even on the rink.

But, Barber said, the other players took him in their stride.

'He was a very funny guy; everybody liked him. And goalies in Canada, sometimes people figure they've taken one too many pucks. It goes with the territory; they're a little bit odd. Goalies, they're real intense, but they're usually happy-go-lucky and a little bit off the wall, in a nice sense. They walk to a different drummer.' Goal was, in short, the perfect position for Keanu. It made him part of a team, while allowing him to retain a certain individuality and apartness.

There were various part-time jobs. Over summer vacations, he worked for a landscaping company owned by Barber, mowing lawns and trimming shrubs. In the winter, he manned a shop at the hockey rink, sharpening skates and selling sticks. He briefly ran a small outpost of a franchise called Pastissima where he sold fresh pasta and made 100 pounds of the stuff a day, advising customers with great authority on which wine to drink with which sauce. 'The ladies sure loved him,' recalled his boss, Dick Butti. 'The guy had pizzazz – he brought in traffic. When he was there.' But Keanu was not cut out for a career in consumer sales. 'He wasn't a very good manager. He spent most of his time outside the shop going to auditions.' This job ended after a couple of months by mutual agreement.

Barber had got Keanu into De La Salle, a private Roman Catholic college where he was the rink manager, in order to secure him for the school team. He fared no better there academically, flunking every class except Latin, which he liked for some reason. He also appeared in a production of *The Crucible*, in which his character posed the question, 'What am I?' Out of the audience came the reply from an early fan: 'A hunk.' Keanu still managed to fail his Grade 12 exams twice, and though he vaguely considered trying to catch up on the missing credit, never quite got around to graduating.

But he flourished on the hockey team, where he earned the nickname 'The Wall' and was voted the Most Valuable Player. He even considered going professional: talent-spotted by another coach at a summer camp for goalies, he was sent to a tryout for the Spitfires, a team in the Junior Hockey League based in Windsor, Ontario. 'Keanu was all ready to go,' Barber recalled. 'But that weekend, before the camp started, he was going down to spend the week with his stepfather, Paul Aaron, in New York, and he phoned me from there the night before the training camp and said, "Scott, I've decided I'm going to be an actor."' Barber was disappointed. But Keanu kept up his passion for hockey and it later turned out to be of practical use in his acting career, helping him land his first film role.

His life took a new, more decisive direction when he applied for Leah Posluns, a respected acting school with a 500-seat theatre attached to it in suburban Toronto. Rose Dubin, the Head, was much taken by the lanky kid auditioning for her in her tiny office, enthusiastic, single-minded and oblivious to the phone's ringing and other interruptions. 'He was very engaging and charismatic,' she said. 'There was innocence combined with a macho quality in Keanu. And he thoroughly convinced us that that was what he wanted to do.' Tom Diamond, a teacher who sat in on the session, was also impressed. 'We were both arrested by him. He was quite timid and almost couldn't believe that we liked his work. Which we did very much.'

So certain were they that Keanu was taken directly into the

advanced acting class, where students eyed him curiously. 'We'd all been studying there for quite some time, at least two years, and he was green,' said Tirzah Lea Tward, a classmate. 'Boiling over with potential, though. He was this bundle of energy, very hyper. The big challenge for our teachers was calming him down a little bit. But he was not at all an airhead, or spacey, just sort of a free spirit.' The female members of the class also took a keen non-professional interest in the new arrival. 'He wasn't perfectly coiffed, he was wearing beat-up clothes, it wasn't like a *GQ* model walked in or anything,' Tward said. 'But there was an air about him. I remember people saying at break, "Did you see the new guy? He's *gorgeous*."'

He hadn't yet lost the raw edges and the spirit of rebellion, the mistrust of authority figures which teachers had already noted at his previous schools. Alan Powell's initial impression was that Keanu was something of a joke. 'I didn't think he was serious about acting at first. Once he was thrown out of the classroom for doing something silly. I thought, "Jeez, what's he doing here?" He was opposed to a lot of things. "This is ridiculous", it was that kind of attitude.' But soon Powell had changed his mind.

Keanu had a style all his own. Shael Risman, another colleague, remembered an open casting for one of the school's end-of-year shows. 'Everyone had learned these cheesy prepared monologues from things like *The Dark at the Top of the Stairs*. We all sat around in a circle and everyone went into the centre and did his audition. Keanu came in, threw his bag to the side and started this unbelievable, off-the-top-of-his-head rambling monologue about driving a motorcycle down

the road and meeting famous people along the way. It was
based loosely on some stand-up comedy routine he'd heard
sometime, but it was all over the place. He was making it up
as he went along, but he was absolutely mesmerizing and so
committed emotionally to what he was doing. It was so
genuine that everyone was totally taken aback.'

The workshop production, staged in May 1983, was called
For Adults Only and was based on a series of real-life
abductions of young women which were then occupying the
Toronto news headlines. Colleen Murphy, who wrote up the
play based on student improvisations, found Keanu riveting
but also a little inarticulate. 'I don't know if we're talking a
great actor here,' she said, 'but we're talking a great personality who's very open with his feelings, who has a face
audiences can project a lot of stuff on to. There's a mystery –
when he doesn't speak too much.' It was an observation made
by many others after her: Keanu was a superb physical actor
but not always as sure a verbal one.

But *For Adults Only* attracted attention and also netted
Keanu his first agent, Tracy Moore, who managed the child
and teenage clients at Noble Talent. Moore had gone to the
production to see another student who was already on her
books, but Keanu caught her eye and she called him the
following day. He quickly began to get work, at first in a
number of commercials and later on television: he co-hosted
a CBC young people's magazine show and got guest spots on
other programmes including *Night Heat*, *The Comedy Factory*
and *Hangin' In*, a series based in a drop-in centre for teenagers
with problems.

'I sent him out on a lot of casting calls for commercials,

just to get him started,' Moore said. 'And every time he went out he seemed to get something. He was a sure sell in a way. He was always extremely intense – he took his work very seriously. At times he drove me crazy, but he had a direction in his head and he went for it.' He was already displaying his later obsession with research and preparation. Up for a Coca Cola ad in which he would play a racing cyclist, he bounded into Moore's office proudly to show her his shaven legs: he had discovered that this was what Italian Grand Prix racers did to take a few seconds off their time. 'He really got into every role, even for something as simple as a commercial.'

Keanu had a boundless disdain for things he considered unimportant. Perhaps as a reaction against his immaculate home or, more likely, simply out of a typical teenage boy's indifference, he often looked a scruff. His wardrobe contained a few stylish items, thanks to Patric who made him the odd shirt and a smart leather jacket. But most of it was culled from thrift shops (one Christmas he gave Alan Powell a present of a second-hand suit jacket). He would be seen around in ripped jeans or, in summer, cut-off track pants, favouring in particular a dog-eared army jacket. He had also acquired his first car, an ancient and beat-up green 1969 122 Volvo which friends had to keep jump-starting; the stereo system was probably its best working part. This he would treat like a school locker, slinging clothes and belongings in at random.

Grunge was not yet fashionable in eighties Toronto, and Keanu's look did not always impress. Moore had to remind him to smarten up from time to time. 'He was not the tidiest of people and he didn't like to get dressed up in his Sunday whites. It was like, "Keanu, clean up your act, make sure that you've had a bath, don't go in there looking like a slob." We always had to babysit him a little bit at the beginning. But in the long run it didn't make any difference at all because he'd still get the roles. He wasn't a problem; it wasn't to the point where he smelled or was really offensive.'

Rose Dubin remembered his leaving to audition for a cornflakes commercial in torn jeans and T-shirt. 'At that time, people didn't dress that way. It was very conservative. [But] everyone was taken with him. It was something that he had. Lots of students come through theatre school and you think, "maybe, maybe", but somehow with Keanu you figured "yes, it will happen for him".'

In fact, many people in the business found his lack of pretension refreshing and rather endearing. 'He always looked like this kid who lived out of a knapsack,' said the casting director Lucinda Sill, who later picked him for the male lead in the Toronto-based film *Flying*. 'I never recognized him in a suit. He wore khakis, an old army jacket, gloves with the fingers out, plaid flannel shirts. It looked like he never brushed his hair. He was very laid back and never appeared to be super-ambitious. If he talked to the executive producer he would never try to put on airs.'

The class at Leah Posluns was a close-knit group and would often hang out together after rehearsal, at McDonald's or in a ravine behind the school. Keanu was always game for a laugh. Once, at a student's house, he dived into the swimming pool from a second-storey window on a dare. Another time, for the same reason, as friends were dropping him off at a busy street corner, he pulled down his trousers and walked naked from the car into the subway. 'There were memories of laughter and fun,' said Powell, who would often be woken up at 2 a.m. by a tap on his bedroom window: Keanu was on the roof, wanting to go out and play. They would spend all night at the bowling alley, movie house, pool hall or even the local playground, horsing around on the pulleys and swings.

Others remembered him as outspoken and at times surprisingly perceptive. 'He could really put you on the spot if you were full of shit,' said Diane Flacks, also a student at Leah Posluns and now a Toronto-based actress. 'Once, we went out to the theatre and I was wearing a dress although I was very much a tomboy. I was making a joke about wanting to be macho and he just looked at me and said, "Diane! You've got tits!" And he was right. I was so uncomfortable with my own femininity as a teenager that I was always making jokes about it and he was able to say, "You're just afraid of being a woman, basically." I'll never forget that because he was so right. He just nailed me.'

He would go out of his way to avoid fights and proved adept at defusing awkward situations. Once, at dinner with friends, one of the women was suddenly taken ill and threw up spectacularly across the table. The group sat there for a minute or so in horrified and embarrassed silence. Then Keanu eyed the splodge of vomit, which had landed in front of him, looked at her and said, 'That's not bad, but it's not quite a metre.'

Another time, Shael Risman went out with him after a party. 'I was just loaded, ripped to the gills. And he wasn't.

We were in the middle of a busy street, it was maybe two o'clock in the morning. I remember saying to him, "I wanna f-f-f-fight you, right now." He started laughing, doing a little dance around me, touching me on the head. And he called me a wood nymph. Don't know where it came from, never heard it since,' recalled the chunky and hardly sylph-like Risman, still tickled by the whimsical description. Those incidents revealed a personality trait which later endeared Keanu to his fans: a consistent policy of non-aggression.

There was a stream of girlfriends, none of them serious. 'He's not a committed person; he wasn't committed to a long-term relationship when I knew him,' recalled Shael Risman. 'That wasn't his style. He was always with a different woman.' And even close friends felt at times they barely knew him. 'He was a very private guy,' said Alan Powell. After several years, he would suddenly be introduced to another of Keanu's close friends whom he had never heard of before. It was as if there was a large chunk of his life which he was keeping secret. Once, they quarrelled when Reeves asked to borrow $500 and Powell accused him of only calling him up when he needed something: he felt in the end frustrated by what he saw as Keanu's remoteness. 'On the outside he's a great guy. But in my perception of him, he was afraid of being close to anyone.'

Popular and fun to be with, he seemed, on one level, a regular guy: what you see is what you get. But friends also detected an elusiveness to him. 'One of the jokes about Keanu was that, if you asked him where he came from or what his roots were, he was anything you wanted him to be,' said Tirzah Lea Tward. Leah Posluns was attached to a Jewish

Footprints

One night a man had a dream. He dreamed he was walking along the beach with the LORD. Across the sky flashed scenes from his life. For each scene, he noticed two sets of footprints in the sand; one belonging to him, and the other to the LORD.

When the last scene of his life flashed before him, he looked back at the footprints in the sand. He noticed that many times along the path of his life there was only one set of footprints. He also noticed that it happened at the very lowest and saddest times of his life.

This really bothered him, and he questioned the LORD about it. "LORD, you said that once I decided to follow you, you'd walk with me all the way. But I have noticed that during the most troublesome times in my life, there is only one set of footprints. I don't understand why when I needed you most you would leave me.

The LORD replied, "My precious, precious child, I love you and I would never leave you. During your times of trial and suffering, when you see only one set of footprints, it was then that I carried you."

                              Ref 1013

community centre (although it was open to students of all denominations) and Tward remembered it being said, either by Keanu or by someone else, that he too was Jewish. That quality was hardly surprising in someone who had moved around so much, and who had been required so many times to start afresh and to fit in with a new crowd. Adaptability had become one of Keanu's great virtues, if only by force of circumstance. And his chameleon-like skill in reflecting and blending in with his surroundings – and being all things to all men (and women) – was something else which, when he became a star, lay at the core of his appeal.

2

A BABE IN HOLLYWOOD

In February of 1984, six students from Keanu's class at Leah Posluns joined forces for another student-written show called *Holding Someone Holding Me*, which they produced in a converted morgue in the downtown area. 'It was not too memorable as a play,' said Rose Dubin tactfully. 'But the kids were really great in it.' Shael Risman, who was one of the group, was more outspoken: 'It was terrible. Keanu played a character who was a total preppy and he was completely convincing. He hated doing it, there's no question about it. But he did it. And people went to see it. It was a milestone for him, though he probably never talked about it again.'

That spring, however, Keanu was cast in his first professional stage production, *Wolfboy*, a play by Brad Fraser, at a fringe theatre called the Passe Muraille. It was to be directed by John Palmer, who had a reputation for provocative work: among his previous credits was a show named *Charles Manson aka Jesus Christ*. He described *Wolfboy* as 'about the survival of love in the Eighties [which] is going to come from the streets', adding ominously, 'and it's going to be violent.' Wanting untrained actors for his two leading roles, he cast his net outside the usual channels. 'I asked around and put ads in underground papers. I made them sound slightly salacious, sort of grimy. All kinds of strange people turned up – and Keanu, who wasn't strange but absolutely right for what I wanted. He was gorgeous. He turned everybody on instantly. I don't mean just sexually: he had "It", which is a very old expression. He had a glow about him.

'To begin with, this kid was very insecure. He had no technique whatsoever; he was bouncing all over the stage. But that had its pluses and its minuses. He was very good to work with. He understood what he didn't know and his sincerity and desire to learn were enormous. We'd go for lunch a lot and walk around and talk for hours. About girls. Movies. Acting, theatre. Clothes to some extent. He was really smart and interested in discussing all kinds of things, philosophers or artists or whatever.'

Also on the agenda was *Wolfboy*'s raw subject-matter. Keanu's character was a suicidal middle-class youth sent to a mental hospital. There, a disturbed male prostitute who believed he was a wolf (played by Carl Marotte) seduced him and ended up sucking his blood. The connotations were unmistakable. In one scene, for instance, Marotte strapped Reeves to a bed and threatened to strangle him. Then, abruptly, the two characters started talking about *The Wizard of Oz*, calling each other Dorothy and Toto.

'We discussed the homosexuality implicit in the play, Carl, Keanu and myself,' Palmer recalled. 'But because it was not overt – they never actually made out; they kissed at one point, but it was ambiguous – we did not have to deal with whether you could play a homosexual if you were a heterosexual. We talked about the character's age and illness allowing him to be carried along by the other boy and Keanu was intelligent enough to see that that was quite possible.' In fact, Palmer was struck by his lack of inhibitions. 'A lot of young actors do have problems with something like this; it's back-breaking work to get them to deal with what they have in themselves. But it didn't bother him. Even if he'd been playing a drag queen, I think he would have put the costume on and done it.'

The publicity for *Wolfboy* highlighted its eroticism which, Palmer knew, would be a powerful selling point. David Hlynsky, who was hired to photograph the production, sprayed the two bare-chested actors with water 'for a sweaty glow' and suggested they caress each other. He remembered Keanu as nervous but professional. 'If I took any pair of eighteen-year-old men off the street, whatever their sexuality, and asked them to assume a soft-core erotic pose, they would be very reluctant, to say the least. But he wanted to make sure we had a successful image and didn't baulk at it; he played the role for the camera. He was giddy about it, in a way. It was naughty and silly; something they just had to get into. I respected the way he was able to do that.'

The poster which emerged from this session was striking. Reeves and Marotte were pictured in close up and in profile, their eyes closed, their lips almost, but not quite touching; the black and white still was enclosed in a shocking pink frame. 'The image was really quite hot; there was a lot of tension, a lot of sensuality to it,' said Hlynsky. 'It was definitely a gay image at a time when there weren't a great many of those around.' Eleven years later, the Passe Muraille sold a few copies for $200 (CA) apiece. However, the theatre resisted attempts by collectors to buy what were rumoured to be 'salacious' unpublished production stills.

Wolfboy opened on 4 April 1984 to withering reviews. 'A real howler', sniffed the *Toronto Globe and Mail*, which dubbed it (in a mocking reference to Peter Brooks' *Marat-Sade*) 'The Theme of Possession, as Worked Out Through Homosexuality and Demonism and Hinted Incest, with Digressions into the Letter Page of *Penthouse* Magazine, as Performed by the Inmates of the Moose Jaw Asylum for the Terminally Goofy'. The *Toronto Sun* liked it no better; its review, headlined 'Bloody Awful: Awful Bloody', concluded, 'my rating is the lowest – one star.' Neither critic commented on Keanu's performance, although at least it earned him his first Equity card.

'The play was a flop commercially, in the sense of getting large mainstream audiences,' Palmer admitted. 'But, because it was flirting with homosexuality at a time when that was more of a big deal, it became a cult for punk teen types, gay and straight.' On-stage attractions included the spectacle of Keanu, his body oiled and gleaming, doing push-ups in white shorts. 'The first couple of performances we had leather boys comin' out,' Keanu recalled. 'You know, caps and the whole deal. And they were walking out at intermission because there weren't enough shoes flying.' It was probably here that the later rumours about the actor's sexuality began.

Keanu had auditioned for *The Breakfast Club*, directed by that one-man factory of halfway decent roles for teenage actors in the Eighties, John Hughes, and was bitterly disappointed not to be chosen. But in July he landed his first film, a small part in *Youngblood*, an ice hockey flick being shot locally. The director was Peter Markle, whose main previous claim to fame was a broad but mildly successful comedy about ski bums called *Hot Dog: The Movie. Youngblood* was something of a one-man-band: he had also written the story and the script and was the camera operator on the scenes shot in the United States.

The film was to be a vehicle for Rob Lowe, then a teen idol, who played an American farmboy recruited to a Canadian Junior League team. At first teased for his 'pretty boy' looks and bullied by a thug from a rival team, he eventually found acceptance and gave his enemy a thorough thrashing. His co-star, Patrick Swayze, had trained as a figure skater but had no ice hockey experience; Lowe himself had to learn how to skate. Many of the minor roles were, therefore, filled by actors who already knew how to play and could help them learn the ropes. Keanu's hours at the rink now stood him in good stead: he was cast as the team's goalie, the position he favoured in real life. 'He seemed like a real natural and definitely had a quirkiness to him that was right for the character he was playing,' Markle remembered. 'He was very easy to work with and I got a kick out of him. We played a lot of hockey together up there; we'd drive to practice in his very funky old Volvo.'

Youngblood turned out to be a coarse, violent film which gloated on the players' animalistic behaviour. Its motto was enshrined in the embroidered samplers hanging in the team's locker room: 'winning isn't everything, it's the only thing' and 'when the going gets tough, the tough get going'. Comedy scenes involved dunking false teeth in a girl's drink or getting caught in possession of a pornographic book. The best thing in it was the energetic skating scenes, for which the low, fast-moving camera was mounted in a wheelchair on the ice. It garnered lousy reviews: 'Superficial' (*Variety*); 'a hack movie' (the *New York Post*); 'aimless' (the *New York Times*); 'absolutely nothing surprising in this hunk of dry ice' (the *Boston Globe*); 'the only team one could possibly imagine [Lowe] skating with would be a *Vanity Fair* summer-league squad' (the *Los Angeles Times*). Keanu himself was later crisply to declare it 'awful'.

It was not his finest hour, although not an embarrassment either; his role was too small for that. He could be glimpsed briefly in early segments, in a bar and at a match, before seeming to disappear from the movie, and delivered less than half a dozen lines in a peculiar French Canadian accent. As goalie (and hidden, moreover, behind a protective face mask) he barely figured in the hockey sequences. 'Some of his scenes would have been more extended, but a lot of his part was cut out,' Markle said. 'It was basically for time.'

But almost immediately Keanu began to attract much more substantial roles. That October he appeared in *Flying*, another film with a sporting theme: it was about a young gymnast (Olivia D'Abo) determined to overcome an injury she had sustained in the car crash which had killed her father. Because it was a Canadian production based in Toronto rather than a Hollywood movie, local actors were in with a chance for major roles, and Keanu was cast as Tommy, a schoolfriend of D'Abo's who was in love with her. 'It was a toss-up between two actors,' recalled the director, Paul Lynch. 'Keanu was impressive but unconventional. When he came in, he was more like the character he played in *Bill and Ted's Excellent*

Adventure, as opposed to being a conventional leading man. It was a very tough decision between the two. Finally everybody agreed that the guy with the ability was Keanu.'

Sporting a selection of loudly patterned shirts, he managed to breathe life into a character written essentially as a nice-but-dull boy next door. He was supposed to be less good-looking than his romantic rival ('I guess I'm not pretty enough for you,' he told D'Abo) but since this strained at the limits of plausibility, the film distinguished between the two boys by making Tommy a little eccentric. It was a sweet role which gave Keanu several major speeches, including a long, theatrical monologue about working as a fairground barker, as well as his first bedroom scene.

'The part evolved in that direction when Keanu joined the company,' Lynch said. 'What you see up there on screen is basically him; that's what we liked about him. He would just show up and act. I don't think he actually got real serious about it until a couple of pictures after *Flying*. This was just a guy having fun, like acting was an alternative to hanging around. He was totally relaxed about it. I wouldn't have guessed he would be the megastar he became but you could see in every day's rushes that he would have a future somewhere.'

The melodramatic story – a dying mother, a wicked stepfather and a crowd of catty classmates – turned critics off when the film was eventually released in Toronto in December 1986 (it went straight to video in the United States under the title *Dream to Believe*). 'Altogether a minor effort that deserves little attention,' sniffed *Variety*. But Keanu earned the odd favourable comment in the Toronto press. 'When *Flying* isn't working up gloom or functioning as a metaphor for redemption, Reeves and D'Abo get to show a touch of insouciance,' wrote the *Toronto Globe and Mail*. 'Toronto actor Keanu Reeves as boyfriend Tommy and Jessica Steen as best pal Carly manage to breathe life into characters which threaten to asphyxiate without them,' said the *Toronto Star*. The *Toronto Sun* called the film 'embarrassing and inept' but added, 'two members of the cast shine through. One is Jessica Steen as D'Abo's best friend; the other is quirky Keanu Reeves. A movie about *them* might have produced some real chemistry on screen.'

In spring 1985, the senior student production at Leah Posluns was *Romeo and Juliet* with a guest director, Lewis Baumander, then the Artistic Director of another small theatre called the Skylight. Keanu had set his sights not on the lead but on Mercutio, Romeo's high-spirited, reckless and tragic best friend. Baumander, a young but serious and intense man, liked this: unlike many of the other hopefuls auditioning, the actor before him was not simply in love with the idea of appearing in a play.

'Most of the kids coming in wanted to get any part at all,' he said. 'The ambitious ones tried for Romeo. Then in walked Keanu with a passion, a hunger and a zeal: he said, "I *need* to play Mercutio." He did the Queen Mab speech, and was extraordinary. Only twice or three times in my life have I cast someone there on the spot, but I did it with him. It struck me that he had an understanding of the piece, and of the soul of Mercutio. There was no question to me that he was a very special young man.' Once cast, Keanu attacked the play with a dogged single-mindedness. 'He was so committed to that role,' said Shael Risman, who played Friar Laurence. 'He talked about it night and day, he worked on it consistently, he was always thinking about it, he would call Lewis in the middle of the night.'

The production ran for just one week, from 28 May to 2 June, but staff and students retained vivid memories of his performance. 'For his age he was a brilliant Mercutio,' recalled Rose Dubin. 'He was very exciting to watch. We sat there and wondered how someone that young could do such a super job. He had such a range of feeling from comedy to despair and a note of cynicism. At the time you really felt he was Mercutio. Possibly it was all the things Keanu was going through himself, I don't know.'

Baumander had a similar impression. 'There was something essential about himself that he needed to express through Mercutio,' he thought. 'There's a profound sadness ultimately to that character that manifests itself in a kind of manic energy.' Keanu, for his part, was left with a passion for Shakespeare and the desire to become a classical stage actor. Even though the next few years took him down a very different route, he was, time after time, to cite Mercutio as his favourite role, 'so full of passion and wisdom and anger'.

That spring Keanu was to get his first real entrée into Hollywood. As *Romeo and Juliet* went into production, Steven H. Stern, a Toronto-born film director based in Los Angeles, was in town to audition for a television movie he was setting up at Disney called *Young Again*. The story was a forerunner of the wave of body-swap comedies that swept through Hollywood at the end of the Eighties (of which *Big*, starring Tom Hanks, was to be the most successful). Stern's sister was the Artistic Director of Leah Posluns; Tirzah Lea Tward, his niece, was one of the students. As they were having dinner together one night the talk turned to Keanu.

Stern was only looking for bit players, 'the one- and two-liners'. Disney wanted big names for the principals and they were to be cast in Los Angeles. But when Keanu walked in, the director took to him instantly. 'There was something about him that I liked a lot. He actually reminded me a lot of myself at that age, wanting to be something, and hoping and wishing that someone would come along to give him the opportunity. I told him to take the script home with him and read for the lead.' At the audition a couple of days later, Stern was, like Keanu's colleagues at Leah Posluns, struck by the actor's inexhaustible vitality. 'He had an enormous, excessive energy level; he was like the prototype for ADD [Attention Deficit Disorder]. I'm sure he must have been really coming off the walls when he was a little kid, although by that time he was pretty focused. He was funny and full of life. And there was a kind of sweet innocence about him. He wanted desperately to be liked, or loved.'

The director knew he would have a struggle to get Disney to agree to his unknown protégé. When the first response was "no way", he flew Keanu to LA so that executives could see him in person. When they still demurred, Stern decided to go to the top, and sent a videocassette of the actor to Michael Eisner, then newly installed as the Chairman of the studio. 'Eisner thought he was very good. And I told him that, after all, I was guaranteeing the picture; I was producing as well as directing and if it didn't work out I would have to recast and reshoot and pay for it myself. He said that if I was prepared to take that risk he would go along with it.'

The story began with a forty-year-old unmarried business-man, played by Robert Urich, being thrashed by his young squash partner and wishing he were seventeen again. Magi-cally granted his wish, he then turned into Reeves as his teenage self. The first part of the film remained strictly in the realm of wish-fulfilment fantasy, as a jubilant Keanu went on a shopping, skateboarding and disco-dancing spree: as in all the other body-swap movies, the child-man just happened to be extremely wealthy, combining the boons of golden youth with the more tangible assets of a Gold Card. But when he went back to high school, and ran into his childhood sweetheart, now forty herself, the story developed in a more unexpected direction. Keanu gave a layered performance, suggesting the maturity, sensitivity and life experience that set him apart from his schoolmates (berating them for their cholesterol consumption and lack of respect towards women) as well as the inner solitude that had often marked him out. It was also the first of a string of films to team him romantically with a much older actress.

Young Again was billed as 'introducing' Keanu Reeves – the actor had kept quiet about his two local movies, leaving Stern with the impression that this was his screen debut. In the end credits he was 'K. C. Reeves'. He had been informed, to his vast dismay, that Reeves was good and solid, but Keanu was too 'ethnic'; the lilting, vowel-laden name would deter casting agents from even agreeing to see him. 'That freaked me out completely,' he said. 'I came up with names like Page Templeton III. And Chuck Spidina. My middle name is Charles. Eventually they picked K. C. Ugh, terrible. When I would go to auditions I'd tell them my name was Keanu anyway.'

It was a delicate moment in his career. In Toronto, Keanu had never seemed like a handicap; on the contrary. 'It was actually more intriguing,' said his first agent, Tracy Moore. 'Like, how could you upstage that name? That was never, ever an issue with us.' Both *Youngblood* and *Flying* had traded on the actor's unusual looks and faint sense that he was not like the rest of the pack. 'There are times when you do see that Keanu is not the all-American boy,' said the Canadian casting director Lucinda Sill. 'But his Hawaiian background is not that evident. He looks like the kid next door. He could have been typecast as ethnic, Native American, but I don't think many casting directors looked at him that way.'

But now, in Hollywood, where newcomers were expected to fit into an existing template, it was feared that, if he were to seem even slightly different, he would end up in the same pigeonhole as actors like Jason Scott Lee. Lee was an instructive point of comparison. Born in Oahu, Hawaii, in 1966 – two years after Keanu – he too came from mixed-race Chinese-Hawaiian parentage (although his features were more asiatic than Reeves'). And he was invariably cast as an all-purpose ethnic minority hero, playing everything from Inuit to Indians to characters from assorted South-East Asian countries. That was a pattern Keanu would do well to avoid.

It was true that there were few precedents: when Keanu eventually made it on to Hollywood's A-list of top male stars, there might have been others on it with foreign-sounding handles – Schwarzenegger being the prime example – but they were always reassuringly Caucasian. Nobody else had a name that evoked Asia and the Pacific Rim. Combined with the plain no-nonsense surname, it was a brilliant combination.

Young Again was the first film to get him seriously noticed. When it was broadcast on American television in May 1986, *Variety* gave his performance a rave: 'Teenager K. C. Reeves steps in with terrific success as Urich the youth. Without imitation of a lookalike face, he conveys the Urich essence to uncanny effect . . . Reeves' open-faced, exuberant study of the boy who turns into a young man in love goes a long way towards keeping the fantasy in the realm of reality.' Stern remembered his young protégé with affection and telephoned him in the summer of 1986 to offer him another role. But by then Keanu was off filming in Munich and his career was well underway.

He had been having a good time in Toronto. His mother was renovating their house and he had moved out into a friend's basement, 'a cool pad in a cool neighbourhood'. He would drive across the border to gigs in the ancient Volvo and stay out dancing all night at alternative music clubs. But Keanu was also becoming frustrated. He had applied twice to act in Ontario's prestigious theatre seasons devoted to Shaw and Shakespeare – and had been twice rejected. 'I didn't fit,' he recalled later. 'I was too young and unruly by their standards.' And it was becoming clear to him that what he described as 'steak and potatoes roles' were never going to come his way while he was still based in Toronto.

The Canadian film industry was not buoyant enough to keep him in work, and any stray Hollywood productions that came to town would only consider him, as a local actor, for the hero's sidekick, or else, as he put it, for Thug Number One or Thug Number Two. 'One of the problems in Canada is that the roles don't open up for hometown boys until they've gone and made a name for themselves in the American market,' said Lucinda Sill. 'When the local Toronto boy was here, it was "Keanu who?"'

He thought his stepfather might be able to help him get a green card. And so he packed up his battered car and headed West with $3,000 in his pocket. It was a route that many an ambitious Canadian actor had travelled before him, and the only surprise was that Keanu had left it relatively late. 'I procrastinated for a year,' he said. 'But I knew I wanted to go for it. I guess there was a part of me that wanted to be a movie star.'

He stayed for a while at Paul Aaron's house, then rented his own apartment at Fairfax and Beverly. Aaron took him in charge and steered him towards Erwin Stoff at 3 Arts Entertainment, a long-time friend of the family whom Aaron had met some years earlier at the University of Washington. Stoff became and remained his manager. He quickly found an agent too, Hildy Gottlieb Hill, then Head of Talent at ICM. 'In twenty minutes I was crazy about him. He was very fresh,' Hill told a colleague. 'I've just signed a new client, and I don't even know if he can act.' Like any new kid on the block, Keanu found the cattle market demeaning. 'He used to call me every three months,' remembered Alan Powell back in Toronto. 'We'd talk for hours. It was hard. He was trying to get auditions, and actors with résumés longer than his leg were walking in and grabbing the parts. He said, "All they do is talk here. Talk, talk, talk. Every actor round here is writing a script." He was yelling, "SHUT UP, shut the fuck up and just do it." He was getting so fed up.'

In fact, Keanu was doing extremely well compared to other

struggling young actors in Hollywood and was cast in four television movies in short order. The best, a big meaty role which allowed him to show his mettle, dramatically speaking, came up that autumn in Thomas Carter's *Under the Influence*, the cautionary tale of an alcoholic (played by Andy Griffith) whose denial of his problem nearly destroyed his family. Each of his four children tried to cope in different but always inadequate ways. There was the over-achieving business-woman who could never do well enough to satisfy Daddy; the self-sacrificing youngest daughter, tempted to give up a longed-for art scholarship at her parents' insistence; and the wisecracking elder son who left home to turn his dysfunctional family into a glib and bitter stand-up comedy routine.

Keanu played the black sheep, the younger son who, out of complex motives – rebellion against his father mixed with a desperate desire to please him – was all set to follow in Griffith's boozy footsteps. Offering his father a consolatory bottle of liquor as he lay in hospital, expressing his love and grief at his death in a long, eighty-second single take, emptying a shotgun in anger and self-loathing into his grave, he was touching, volatile and impressive. It was the first, and the most intense, of a series of films in which Keanu's character railed against an inadequate or over-bearing father (he would do so again in *The Prince of Pennsylvania*, *Bill and Ted's Excellent Adventure*, *Parenthood*, *My Own Private Idaho* – even, actually, as Prince Siddhartha in *Little Buddha*). Of course, most young actors find themselves pitched into this sort of Oedipal role at some point. But Keanu was cast in these parts repeatedly and brought to them an intensity fuelled by personal experience.

Under the Influence suffered from an earnest, disease-of-the-week didacticism (its working title was the plodding-sounding *Adult Children of Alcoholics*). A friendly doctor kept popping up to say things like, 'What I see here is a very sick family.' But the film contained a full house of powerful performances, and it earned Keanu both his Screen Actors Guild card and some high praise. The *Hollywood Reporter* found him 'outstanding' and *Variety* and the *Los Angeles Times* also commended his performance. However, Keanu remembered the production chiefly for its 8 a.m. morning calls. 'I thought this was . . . unfair,' he grumbled. 'It's hard to act in the morning. The muse isn't even awake.'

His next role took him straight back to Canada. *Act of Vengeance* was based on the true story of Jock Yablonski, a United Mine Workers official who, along with his wife and daughter, was murdered in 1969 for challenging the corrupt union boss. Although the action was set in Pittsburg, like many low-budget Hollywood films a number of scenes were actually shot in Toronto. The twist in an otherwise standard scenario was to cast Charles Bronson, an actor best known as the vigilante hero of the *Death Wish* movies, as the victim, Yablonski. Keanu was also cast against type, as one of the baddies. 'I was the second guy [on film] ever to kill Charles Bronson,' he later joked.

It was a very minor distinction. His character showed up some seventy-eight minutes into the movie, a babyfaced assassin brought in after the original hitmen had repeatedly botched the job. It was a Thug Number Three role. Unshaven, beer-swilling, his voice hoarse with panic, he had one big moment, a wonderfully ridiculous speech explaining that his mother had spent two weeks in a coma while she was carrying him: 'It's not to boast,' croaked Keanu, 'but it shows I was made for something special.'

'It was just a cough-and-spit – I mean, a good part, but it was small,' remembered the director John Mackenzie, respected for his British gangster movie *The Long Good Friday*. 'But we took a while casting it because I wanted this quality of a guy who would be crazy. And that's the quality Keanu had, this slightly weird, wayward, off-the-wall thing which I liked because that was the character.'

It was, all the same, an odd and atypical role for Keanu to take, given his dislike of violence, and Mackenzie was one of the few film-makers who found him difficult to work with (or who admitted to it – which is not the same thing at all in an industry where massaging egos is a means of survival). 'He turned out to be unnecessary trouble. Disorganized, never there, generally anarchic, always hard for the assistant to find, self-absorbed. Not getting things right because he wasn't listening.

'He was always tripping over and hitting things; at that time he was like one of those puppies with big feet that fall all over the place. When he broke into the house in the middle of the night to do the murder, he fell up the stairs, he tripped over things. I said, "Keanu, the entire fucking house-hold is now awake, would you mind trying to keep it quiet?" Then he delivered his lines in a whisper which wasn't a whisper at all. He wasn't concentrating on the job. "I haven't got my beer-can" . . . all that went on. He was all over the place.

'He was a pain in the arse and no one else was, I may say,

even Old Stoneface. So it was a bit annoying to have this little upstart. I took him round the block and gave him a real wigging. He didn't quite know what I was talking about at first. Then he realized and was very contrite and after that he was perfectly adequate; good, actually.

'His character had to have a manic, slightly mad unpredictability about him, and he may have been carrying that over while he sat around the set. Maybe he didn't like being a killer, maybe someone talked him into doing it. Or it may have been that he was taking drugs. He wasn't doing it on the set. Charlie Bronson would go crazy if someone started smoking a cigarette in front of him, practically.

'But,' Mackenzie added, 'despite all this, I said, "I bet that guy's a star in five years." I cast him as soon as I saw him. The instant you put him on film, he burns up the celluloid. He's not consistent; I don't think he's a very good actor. But when he hits the moment, he's just got a God-given thing.'

Act of Vengeance was poorly reviewed by the *New York Times*, but liked by *Variety*, which deemed it 'powerful, suspenseful, even obscene'. Perhaps by way of divine retribution for his misbehaviour, Reeves' name was misspelled Keannu in the closing credits.

Another undistinguished early project was *Brotherhood of Justice*, a vigilante picture about a group of youths (two of the other members were played by Kiefer Sutherland and Billy Zane) who banded together to combat drugs and crime in their high school. As they began to enjoy their roles as 'baby pigs; equalizers', as one of them put it, Keanu was the kid who began to have second thoughts about the whole idea. It was not much of an acting stretch for him; his role was a passive one, calling mainly for him to register anxiety and confusion; 'I was just bad in it,' he later said.

The film itself was attacked for claiming to expose the problems of vigilantism, but actually revelling in its own violence. The *Los Angeles Times* review was typical: 'What's missing is any real understanding of the phenomenon ... [Reeves] eventually begins to doubt the wisdom of the gang's efforts, but inasmuch as this concern weighs less heavily on him than the distress of losing his girlfriend, it hardly makes for compelling viewing.'

In July 1986, Keanu flew to the Bavaria studios just outside Munich. His mission: to play another juvenile lead, in *Babes in Toyland*, a remake of the operetta by Victor Herbert and Glen MacDonough which had been previously filmed in 1934 with Laurel and Hardy, and again in 1961 with Tommy Kirk and Annette Funicello. The new version was directed by Clive Donner and written by the playwright Paul Zindel; much of the original score was to be replaced by seven additional songs by Leslie Bricusse.

Drew Barrymore played a young girl pitched by a car accident into a fantasy world where people she knew reappeared as fairy-tale characters: Keanu was the boyfriend of Barrymore's elder sister, who was transformed into Jack Nimble, resplendent in a leather jerkin, knee britches and what looked suspiciously like highlighted hair. His nasty boss resurfaced as the evil Barnaby Barnacle, who plotted to take over Toyland. The only hope of thwarting him was if Barrymore, whose character was 'never really a child' and was old beyond her years, reaffirmed her belief in toys. There was a certain poignancy to all this since Barrymore, a child star catapulted into precocious adulthood, was in real life entering a period of serious alcohol and drug addiction.

Keanu dances! Keanu sings! (Actually, like most of the other actors, he mimed to playback.) It was the first and (at the time of writing) the last time he had appeared in a musical and he performed both functions with as much dignity as he could muster. He had some frightful lines to deliver. In a high-camp early scene, for example, he had teasingly to call his girlfriend (Jill Schoelen) 'The Delilah of the Five-and-Dime', while twirling the pom-pom on his red Santa Claus cap.

'It was terribly difficult to cast that part,' Donner remembered. 'It required somebody who is grounded in some way in his own personality and character and does not find it embarrassing to say, "Hey! I'm Jack!" Most young actors would have been too knowing. But there was a kind of natural confidence about Keanu which allowed him to be open and say "yes". He got the gaucheness of Jack, which could have been toe-curling. I was never actually sure that he'd really taken on board quite how potentially dangerous some of the lines were. There was a naiveté about his acceptance of the script, which was not bad but did have some very icky things in it.'

For Keanu's big love ballad with Schoelen (with whom he had a brief on-set fling), Donner had imagined a big *Oklahoma!* style ballet. 'He worked at it fantastically hard but he's no Nureyev and it just didn't look good; in the end we filmed it differently. But he gave it a shot, he was prancing around there like a good 'un. He had a great capacity for throwing himself into things totally without any sense of reluctance.'

Babes in Toyland was, as Donner admitted, not a success. It was rushed: the director had to shoot it in thirty-three days (short days at that, since there were restrictions on the hours he could work with his underage actors). The budget was inadequate: Toytown was the set of a coal-mining village the crew had discovered on the Bavaria backlot and transformed with a swift lick of pink paint. There was no time to plan the big production numbers properly, some of which were taught the actors in the morning and shot in the afternoon.

More fundamentally, it peddled an old-fashioned and obsolete fantasy of childhood, as the script itself seemed to recognize (the Toymaster, played by Pat Morita, regretted that kids no longer wanted his wooden soldiers; they were keener on Death Ray guns). Barrymore, the casting of whom Donner had fought against tooth and nail, was then aged eleven, like her character, but looked too old and knowing for her role, as though her real idea of fun was not skipping around with furry animals but – as the actress did just before shooting began – staying out all night and getting blind drunk at a Rod Stewart concert. 'She never gave me the impression that she really saw the magic in it,' Donner said.

It was a mistake, too, to stretch the thin material to a three-hour prime-time special (to crown it all, when the film came out a little short, television executives simply responded, to Donner's extreme displeasure, by transmitting it at a lower speed), and when *Babes in Toyland* aired in America just before Christmas, the reviews were merciless: 'Charmless ... Everyone seems to be going through his paces on automatic pilot' (the *New York Times*); 'painful to behold' (*USA Today*). 'A Christmas fantasy about Toyland ought to look like

Neiman-Marcus,' said the *Los Angeles Times*. 'This one looks like K-Mart.'

But Keanu threw himself gamely into the spirit of the enterprise and Donner respected his professionalism. 'He was never condescending about the material, or the way we were doing it, or the other kids, who sometimes drove me mad. Somebody would come and say, "The duck's piddled in her feet, can we pull her out and change her?" But he was sympathetic and supportive. There was never any question that he had committed himself to it.' Throughout his career, with a couple of exceptions, once Keanu had agreed to a film, whatever reservations he might have secretly had about it, his dedication was total.

3

EXCELLENT ADVENTURES

Bill and Ted were born in 1983. Their progenitors, Chris
Matheson and Ed Solomon, both had previous writing connections: Matheson's father was the fantasy author Richard
Matheson while Solomon had contributed to the television
sitcom *Laverne and Shirley*. They met on campus at UCLA
where they became involved in an improvisational comedy
group and developed an act about two amiable but terminally
dim teenage boys who played in a terrible rock band, were
hopeless at school and sweetly oblivious to the outside
world.

That in itself was nothing unusual. What distinguished Bill
and Ted was their slangy, florid private language, peppered
with made-up and literary words like 'bodacious', 'egregious'
and 'excellent'. In a typical interchange, Bill would ask Ted,
'Did you hear about the war in El Salvador?' and Ted would
sigh, 'Oh, bogus!': there was an element of political satire in
Bill and Ted at this stage. The two writers would hone and
act out the characters at a Westwood restaurant over burgers
and, after they left college, continued to correspond as Bill
and Ted (sample letter: 'Dear Ted, I hope you are well. I'm
excellent! Sincerely, Bill'). B&T eventually grew into a feature-

length script – their first – which they wrote in seven days and sold in 1984.

The project knocked around for a while; there was some interest from directors like Frank Oz and Rick Rosenthal but they failed to get it off the ground. Then it landed on the table of a young film-maker named Stephen Herek. Herek had studied cinema at the University of Austin under, among others, the veteran director Edward Dmytryk. He had worked for a spell at Roger Corman's New World studio, a nursery for many successful film-makers, where he had edited *Space Raiders* and *Slumber Party Massacre*. He had made one feature, *Critters*, a horror comedy about malevolent space aliens conceived to cash in on the success of Joe Dante's *Gremlins*. While no masterwork, the picture was polished and successful enough to catch the studios' attention.

Herek was offered the sequel to this, and a sheaf of similar comedies, but his fancy was taken by *Bill and Ted's Excellent Adventure*, as the film was called. He was captured by the characters: their energy, their blindingly simple philosophy of life and their sharp, colourful rap. Bill and Ted reminded him of his brothers and some of his former flatmates – indeed, of the kids he could observe daily hanging out in the burger bars and shopping malls of the Los Angeles Valley suburbs.

However his enthusiasm was not shared by the brass at Warner Brothers, which owned the rights. There, the feeling was that the wave of teen comedies of the early Eighties, spearheaded by films like *Porky's* (1981), had spent itself as the core cinema audience began to age. And the *Bill and Ted* script, which by then had been gathering dust for two years, was, they said, hopelessly dated; if it were to be made at all, it would have to be a very cheap production. Herek was unable to secure the budget he thought he needed and in mid-1986 the studio dropped the project altogether.

Six months later Dino De Laurentiis's company DEG picked up the option and Herek buckled down to the task of finding his Bill and Ted. It was a long haul: Keanu presented himself for seven auditions. 'We did an enormous talent search to find Bill and Ted,' recalled the film's co-producer, Scott Kroopf. 'We got it down to sixteen finalists and mixed and matched people together. The most striking thing was that at the audition, every time we would walk out into the waiting room to call the next guys in, Alex [Winter] and Keanu were sitting there talking about their motorcycles or their bass guitars, which they both played, or they had gone out together and gotten burritos to eat. It was not only evident when they sat down and read that they had the perfect chemistry for it but just by the fact that they became incredibly fast friends.' His instinct did not mislead him. The two actors clicked, striking up a friendship that was to continue long after the film was over. They looked very different, too, presenting the sharp physical contrast essential to a comedy double act.

Winter, who had acted for a spell as a teenager on and off Broadway, had studied cinema at New York University Film School and actually wanted to be a director; he had reverted temporarily to acting to pay off the debts he had racked up as a student. While Keanu was tall, dark and lanky, with the uncoordinated body movements of a teenager who had shot up too fast, Winter was much shorter and chunkier, with blond, curly hair, a hooked nose and sardonic, hooded eyes. With the casting of these two, rather than, say, the broad comic Pauly Shore, who was also one of the finalists, Bill and Ted, who could have been unpopular, spotty geeks, turned definitively into cool, good-looking dudes. 'There was some stuff in the first movie about them being ostracized by high-school athletes, and we shot it,' Kroopf said. 'But we eventually cut it way, way back because we discovered that it was a little too conventional. The fun of Bill and Ted was that they were in their own world as opposed to being rooted heavily in the realistic world of high school.'

They were, however, incorrigible slackers, in danger of flunking – 'most egregiously', as they would say – their history class. Ted, played by Keanu, faced the prospect of being sent by his overbearing father to a military academy in darkest Alaska. Their sole hope was to excel in their end of term project, which set the question: what would historical celebrities make of the West Coast *anno* 1987? Fortunately help was at hand from a mentor from the future (played by the comedian George Carlin) who supplied the duo with a machine enabling them to voyage through time. Originally a van, it was hurriedly changed into a phone booth when *Back to the Future* came out – ironically, for British viewers, this instantly sounded even louder echoes, of the television series *Doctor Who*. And off they set to round up a few dead dudes, including Socrates (pronounced 'Soh-crates'), Napoleon, Joan of Arc, Genghis Khan and Freud (pronounced 'Frude', as in 'the Frude dude'), in order to transport them to the present day.

The trip was a triumph: Beethoven discovered synthesizers, Napoleon pigged out on junk food (the waiters plying him with ice-cream were Matheson and Solomon in a guest cameo), Joan of Arc got into aerobics and Genghis Khan found new uses for baseball bats. Also a triumph was Bill and Ted's term paper, which became a flamboyant show-and-tell entertainment. It was the comic conceit of the film that the combined geniuses of history would be agreed in finding Californian shopping mall culture the summit of all knowledge (the profoundest insight Soh-crates managed to come up with on the late twentieth century was that he really dug baseball).

The film went into production in Phoenix, Arizona, in early 1987. Herek's budget, just over $8 million, was hardly lavish for a movie which involved both numerous historical settings and extensive special effects. The director decided to make a virtue out of necessity, sending up the film's cheapness: one scene cheekily and very obviously spliced in stock footage from King Vidor's 1956 film of *War and Peace* (another De Laurentiis production) to simulate the Battle of Waterloo. He also hired as his designer Roy Ford Smith who had worked on *Monty Python and the Holy Grail* and *Jabberwocky*. Herek hoped Smith would give the period sequences in *Bill and Ted* the same surreal, deliberately makeshift feel. Indeed DEG had already started promoting the movie as 'equal parts Mark Twain, Monty Python and rock 'n' roll'. Herek didn't altogether like this corny sales pitch but he was a Python fan, as were both Reeves and Winter who would keep the crew entertained by improvising Python routines.

Shooting ended in May after a couple of weeks filming castles and colosseums in Italy for the historical episodes, and Herek began editing the movie. A first inkling of trouble came when the company that had begun processing the special effects suddenly shut down after completing only basic visuals. Then, in early 1988, came a serious blow: DEG itself collapsed and its slate of completed films, which also included Julien Temple's *Earth Girls Are Easy*, was put on the market. The company had already funded a string of duds and nobody was excited about the new line-up. MGM picked up one film for distribution, a zombie flick called *Pumpkinhead*, but the rest, including *Bill and Ted's Excellent Adventure*, found no takers. It looked as though the Valley Dudes were, literally, history.

Keanu had hoped to tour Italy after completing the final scenes of *Bill and Ted's Excellent Adventure* there. But it was not to be: he was summoned back to Los Angeles to shoot some additional sequences for a comedy called *The Night Before* which he had filmed the previous autumn. The movie, he told the press soon afterwards, was having 'Hollywood technical difficulties. That means the producer and the director have artistic differences. Which means the film might be *really bad*.'

The story began with Keanu waking up abruptly in the middle of the road, dressed in a flashy but bedraggled prom suit (white tuxedo with satin lapels, pink carnation). A truck was about to run him down. Struggling to remember what had brought him there, he relived in flashback the past few hours. His high-school prom date with a spoiled rich girl, played by Lori Loughlin (who had also been his love interest in *Brotherhood of Justice*), had gone badly wrong: the couple had lost their way, fetching up on the wrong side of town in the Rat's Nest, a sleazy gangland club. There, events got out of hand and Keanu ended up selling Loughlin to a pimp and being slipped a mickey – hence the later amnesia. *The Night Before* (had it been better directed) could have been a light teen version of Martin Scorsese's *After Hours*, with the two kids bumbling through escalating disasters as they tried to find their way home.

Keanu later changed his mind about the film, defending it to all comers, and there was nothing in it for him to be ashamed of. As the hopeless nerd whose idea of impressing his date was to bring her a gift of a fridge magnet, he gave a performance which allowed him to perfect one of his most successful expressions, that of charming bafflement. A dance sequence revealed him as a neat mover; a scene in the men's room where Keanu, reeling from the mickey, tried none too successfully to pull himself together, displayed his comic flair. One of the sweetest moments came near the end where, helping Loughlin change her clothes, he conveyed a mix of desire and embarrassment with a flickering, shy glance.

No one much had a chance to appreciate him. *The Night Before* finally limped into a handful of cinemas in April 1988. The *Variety* reviewer thought the premise of the film ridiculous, but found the young leads attractive performers. He also noted that he and his companion were the only two people in the Minneapolis cinema where he caught the movie, adding, 'that was two more than attended the following showing'.

However, one movie compensated handsomely for these two setbacks: *River's Edge*. It had actually been shot in early 1986 and had also been thrust for a while on the shelf when Hemdale, its British producer-distributor, lost faith in it.

When it was finally released, in May 1987, no one was in any doubt as to why Hemdale had got cold feet.

The story was loosely based on a real-life event in the small Northern Californian town of Milpitas in 1981. There, fourteen-year-old Marcy Conrad was raped and murdered by her sixteen-year-old boyfriend Jacques Broussard. Broussard bragged about the killing to several dozen of his friends and took them to see the corpse. Some hit the body with rocks, others threw leaves on to it, but it was two days before anyone reported it to the police. The case shocked America and inspired scores of articles.

Among the many struck by this bleak little tale was Neal Jimenez, a film student in San Jose, who was preparing a project for his screenwriting class. Set over one day and night, Jimenez's version of the story unfolded from the kids' confused, stoned perspective. He earned a meagre C-plus from his teacher, but put the script on the market. It startled and impressed the studios, but the corrosive nihilism seemed to make it a non-starter commercially. Then Hemdale, which had already had some success with difficult films, notably *Platoon*, came on the scene. The choice of director was Tim Hunter, who was known for several polished films about mixed-up teens (*Tex*, *Over the Edge*) and at first turned down *River's Edge* for that reason. But he was won over and, months later, was shooting it with a cast that included Dennis Hopper and Crispin Glover on a small budget of $1.7 million and a tight, thirty-two-day production schedule.

When the film was test-screened in Seattle in October 1986, it earned great reviews and did terrible business. Hemdale was in financial difficulties and decided to postpone the release. It was only after *River's Edge* began to make a mark at festivals that it was picked up by Island, a small independent distributor, which marketed it aggressively under the slogan 'The Most Controversial Film You Will See This Year'.

It was, indeed, profoundly depressing, with its wintry landscapes, sulphurous, polluted river and blank, overcast skies: the story had been transplanted from sunny California to the Mid-West. The older people in it, from Hopper's raddled hippy to the pothead mother of Keanu's character and the class teacher, with his stream of radical-chic clichés, were shown without exception as burn-outs for whom the Sixties had changed, fundamentally, nothing. Their children, listless and amoral, did not even have the consolation of those threadbare counter-cultural ideals, or of strong emotions. 'I wasn't even mad, really,' said the young killer, trying to explain why he had strangled his girlfriend on a whim.

In short, *River's Edge* was a portrait of the blank generation, a concept which was just beginning to become a media buzzword thanks to the success of novels like Bret Easton Ellis's *Less Than Zero* and Jay McInerney's *Bright Lights Big City*, both of which vividly portrayed the moral emptiness at the heart of the Eighties economic boom, albeit in a rather more upscale social setting (as well as, a couple of years later, Douglas Coupland's *Generation X*). The way had also been paved by a cluster of films dealing with the dark side of America, including *Angel Heart* and David Lynch's influential *Blue Velvet* – which again starred Hopper, himself making something of a comeback.

At the same time there was a glib, slightly sentimental streak to *River's Edge*, a sort of tainted romanticism: Hopper had loved the woman *he* murdered, which somehow justified the act. Some of the performances were ill-judged: Hopper, for example, always an actor who veered towards hamminess, hobbled around on crutches, playing Russian roulette and smooching an inflatable sex doll, while Glover's wild-eyed, hysterical, hyperkinetic character was so overexcited that it was suggested Hunter should dub in extra dialogue, explaining that he was a speed freak, in order to justify his bizarre behaviour.

Keanu was consistently generous about his co-star. And his own work in the film excited much comment. Unshaven, defeated-looking, a skull painted on the back of his denim jerkin, he made a powerful impact as the one kid who felt uneasy enough about the murder to report it to the authorities; as often in his films, he was the moral centre of the story, inasmuch as there was one at all in *River's Edge*. One sequence crosscut between the killer reliving his deed and Keanu making love to the girl on whom he had a crush; he was the only character with a halfway healthy attitude towards women.

But he was also able to display a dark side which his later roles would rarely exploit, exploding with anger, violence and frustration when interrogated by a hostile police officer or taunted by his mother's new lover. In another strong scene, he confronted his little brother (also well-played by the bitter, pinch-faced Joshua Miller as a child old before his time) who was so angry at Keanu's betrayal he planned to shoot him.

The reviews were mixed, skewering the film's weaknesses, but also (with the notable exception of a crushing pan by Pauline Kael in the *New Yorker*) respectful of its ambitions.

David Denby of *New York* magazine found it 'the most disturbing movie I have seen in the nearly nine years I have held this job'. Keanu won kudos for his 'sly, understated performance' and 'exemplary restraint'. And, to everyone's surprise, it became a modest hit, selling particularly well on video. It was an impressive calling card film. Asked what first drew Reeves to their attention, directors would again and again cite *River's Edge*.

On his first serious outing on the promotional trail, Keanu struck journalists as much younger than his real age (twenty-two); certainly, with his pudding-basin haircut and boyish grin, he *looked* significantly younger. Accompanied by Hunter (who lent the interviews a semblance of seriousness) he appeared uneasy, or perhaps simply impatient with the whole process, writhing 'in that painful combination of insecurity and high spirits that marks the transition to adulthood'. But there was charm at work too: one female columnist found him 'so funny and energetic and attractive that we catch ourselves sort of rethinking the maternal side of the Oedipal dilemma'. And he also had the presence of mind to send himself up a little, fielding one ponderous question, in one of the odd turns of phrase that he was sometimes prone to: 'Yes, the miasma of adolescence and the pituitary gland, I'm familiar with.'

Keanu's career was definitely looking up. There was a 30-minute television play called *Moving Day*, in which his small role (under the K.C. Reeves alias), as the removal man's son, a would-be ballet dancer, was singled out as 'notable' in *Variety*'s favourable review. And that September he landed a major part in a film called *Permanent Record*, about a high-school student who inexplicably kills himself, devastating his peers. He had gone up for this role, but it went to another young actor, Alan Boyce. Instead, he was picked for the lead, the student's best friend, Chris, who plays with him in a garage band and goes to pieces after his death. The film was modelled on 'serious' teen pictures such as John Hughes' *Pretty in Pink* and *The Breakfast Club*. The success of these, and of *River's Edge*, had confirmed a market for high-school angst and helped secure *Permanent Record* studio backing (from Paramount) and a comparatively high budget, $8 million.

The film-makers issued appropriately solemn statements of their intentions: 'Today there is pressure on young people not to be left behind,' said the producer, Frank Mancuso Jnr. 'You need good grades so you can get into the right school and later get a job that pays you what you need to make a decent living. That's a lot of responsibility for eighteen-year-olds to carry. I wanted to make a movie that thoughtfully deals with these concerns.' The director, Marisa Silver (the daughter of the respected independent film-maker, Joan Micklin Silver), wanted *Permanent Record* to be 'life-affirming: to inspire others with a story about young people transcending misfortune and communicating their problems'.

Their pious manifestos failed to impress critics. Despite attempts to make the film hip by hiring Joe Strummer of The Clash to write the score and enlisting Lou Reed for a cameo (he appears in a recording studio near the start of the story), the *New York Times* sniffed at its 'implacable earnestness', while *Variety* found it 'populated by profoundly unrewarding characters doing and saying utterly uninteresting things'.

Most of the attacks fastened upon the trite finale, in which the kids come to terms with their bereavement by putting on a show (one of the songs even announced that 'life goes on'). It seemed falsely upbeat – a blatant attempt to impose a feelgood ending on a feelbad story. It started, reviewers said, like *River's Edge* and ended like *Fame*; as the *Los Angeles Times* suggested, perhaps this was due to the difference between a film made independently (like *River's Edge*) and one produced (like *Permanent Record*) for a major studio.

However, Keanu again drew favourable comment. Since his character was the only one to witness his friend's death and to know it was suicide, he had to give a tightly interior performance, carrying many scenes on his own. In a long series of heavy-duty dramatic sequences, he evolved from a likeable, beer-swilling slacker to a young man burning with hurt and bewilderment – but finally able to escape from the shadow of his more talented friend and emerge as a musician in his own right. For the *Variety* critic, 'Chris's gradual coming to grips with his sense of guilt gives the film its only point of interest, largely due to Keanu Reeves' performance which opens up nicely as the drama progresses'. The *Boston Globe* was even more complimentary: he, it said, was 'clearly a young actor of depth and remarkably sure instincts'. And the *Los Angeles Times*, in one of *Permanent Record*'s few sympathetic reviews, praised his 'relaxed vitality and unwavering honesty'.

Next up was *The Prince of Pennsylvania*, a first film for Ron Nyswaner, although he had some screenplays to his credit, including *Smithereens* and *Mrs Soffel* (it also turned out to be his only directorial outing; he later returned to writing and was Oscar-nominated for *Philadelphia*). He had grown up in the coal-mining town of Clarksville (pop. 500) and his movie, in which he used several members of his family, was set in the equally small town of Mars, a stone's throw away. Its rebellious hero, Rupert Marshetta, was besotted with the older, semi-hippy woman who ran the dilapidated local diner, and hatched with her a plot to kidnap his father and hold him to ransom. The film's title was a reference to the Marshetta family's dynastic pretensions (as the father said, he had always seen himself and his wife as a king and queen and their son as a prince), and there were elements of Oedipal drama in the plotting. But the main tone was of rueful comedy – the incongruousness of this band of semi-bohemian misfits trying, none too successfully, to survive in conformist, mid-Eighties America.

Nyswaner had seen Keanu in *River's Edge*, but wondered whether he could also be funny. A forty-five-minute meeting in a Los Angeles hotel was enough to convince him. 'I saw in him constant emotion,' he said. 'He's like a Chinese menu – he'll give you half a dozen different readings.' Nyswaner was not to know about the actor's antagonistic relationship with his own father. But, it seemed to him, 'the real Keanu is a lot like the character in the film, despite his refusal to see any resemblance'.

For his role Keanu devised a weird hairstyle, buzz cut on one side, long and floppy on the other. He had wanted to shave part of his head completely, but Nyswaner dissuaded him and Keanu was a mite disappointed when little old ladies stopped him in the street to tell him they found his hairdo 'rather cute'. But the Janus look lent Rupert an intriguing schizoid quality: in one profile he was cropped and clean-cut while from the other angle his long hair made him look almost feminine.

Hair was important. 'Oddly, one of his pet peeves was that he had to have what he considered to be Ted Hair,' recalled Scott Kroopf, of Keanu in *Bill and Ted's Excellent Adventure*. 'He and the make-up artist had this ritual, they found what Ted Hair was and they achieved it for every take. Until he looked in the mirror and saw that image he wasn't content that he had achieved full Ted-ness. Whatever exactly his technique is, setting the physicality of the character is one of the things he really likes to do.' Keanu saw Rupert in *The Prince of Pennsylvania* as 'a bit pathetic but also heroic' and played him as a likeable buffoon padding around gawkily in large, half laced-up boots. (A nutritional deficiency in his early childhood had left him slightly bow-legged, which partly accounts for his distinctive gait in these early films.) He was beginning to grow out of teenage roles, but still gave them his best shot. 'When I do a gig I try to walk the walk and talk the talk,' he said. 'I try to understand the thinking, where the kids are coming from, as much as I can.'

Even so, reactions to the film were lukewarm. *Variety* liked it, and Keanu. But it was hard to overlook the script's central flaw, the kidnapping episode, which was riddled with implausibilities. Nor was his romance with the older woman, played by Amy Madigan, and its abrupt resolution at the end, entirely convincing. Most critics were left cold by the attempts at quirky humour and found Keanu 'belligerent' and 'sulky'; the *New York Times*, for instance, commented, 'Mr Reeves, who was extremely good in *River's Edge*, appears to have been bushwacked by the sheer obnoxiousness of the character he plays.'

By now Keanu was able to be increasingly selective about his roles. He had been offered the lead in the sequel to *The Fly*, and had turned it down, a wise move in retrospect: the part eventually went to Eric Stoltz, a young actor who had been highly praised for his performance as an appallingly deformed young man in *Mask*, but whose career subsequently took a downward turn. Instead, Keanu went for the more prestigious project in preference to the commercial one, auditioning for *Dangerous Liaisons*, a film which would pay about one-tenth of what he would have earned for *The Fly II*. It was also his first costume drama.

Dangerous Liaisons was based on a hugely successful Royal Shakespeare Company stage production, which in turn had been adapted by Christopher Hampton from *Les Liaisons Dangereuses*, Choderlos De Laclos's classic novel about two decadent aristocrats plotting to seduce and destroy everyone around them against the first distant rumblings of the French Revolution. Hampton himself was to write the screenplay and the producer would be Norma Heyman. Stephen Frears, a British film-maker known for gritty low-budget work, most of it for television, was the chosen director: his budget for *Dangerous Liaisons* – $14 million – was over five times bigger than anything he had commanded before. Frears was a less eccentric choice than he at first appeared. He was known to be good with actors and with dialogue-heavy movies. And, after the British cinema revival of the Eighties had enabled him to work for the big screen, he had made a string of artily erotic films about odd couplings: *My Beautiful Laundrette*,

Prick Up Your Ears and *Sammy and Rosie Get Laid*. He later succinctly described *Dangerous Liaisons* as 'like all my films: about sex, power and money'.

There was a second factor at play. Time had become of the essence since another film-maker, Milos Forman, had contacted Hampton about directing the movie, but was now reported to be preparing a rival project. The race was on. Hampton fired off his screenplay in three weeks flat, and continued to rework it up to and during the filming. Frears therefore suddenly had another strong point in his favour: a reputation for bringing in his movies on schedule and under budget. Asked when he could start filming, he impressed the producers mightily by answering, only half in jest: 'Tuesday.'

When an early decision was made to use mainly American actors, eyebrows were raised, especially British ones: after all, when the play first transferred to Broadway, Hampton and his director, Howard Davies, had insisted on bringing over the West End company rather than recasting with US performers. But the writer was completely reworking *Dangerous Liaisons* for the screen, returning to the source novel rather than adapting the play, and it was felt better by all concerned to choose actors who would come to the characters completely fresh. John Malkovich, Glenn Close and Michelle Pfeiffer had already been offered the three principal roles by the time Frears came on board. Their names would, of course, also give the film a welcome boost in the US market.

Fortunately Frears was comfortable with this: he thought the story would seem less remote, more immediate, with American performers (to the same end, the film lost its

original French title by the time it was released). And, since
he did not want the story to be swamped by the sets and had
it in mind to shoot much of it in close-up, he suspected that
Americans would be more effective at allowing the complex
emotions the roles demanded to play over their faces (in a
slyly witty twist, the servants' roles all went to British
performers).

Keanu bounded into the New York audition, late and
dishevelled from his bike ride across Manhattan, his knees
peeping through the holes in his cut-off jeans. He was never
one to stand on ceremony: David Parfitt, the co-producer of
Much Ado About Nothing, later recalled that, when Keanu first
reported for duty in his ripped jacket and scruffy jeans, the
women in the office mistook him for a motorcycle messenger.

In *Dangerous Liaisons* he was up for the Chevalier Darceny,
an impulsive young man who became a pawn in Close's
malevolent game as she attempted to have him deflower a
beautiful virgin, played by Uma Thurman. His role, while
extremely small, was still the second male lead. It would also
give him the chance to fight a duel, a skill he had acquired
for *Romeo and Juliet*. His appearance was unlikely to faze
Frears, himself never renowned for his sartorial splendour.
But, confronted with this actor so touchingly eager to impress
the 'English dudes', the director did wonder briefly whether
he was following the right casting policy and politely asked
Reeves if he could be a little less . . . well, American.

Hampton remembered his first impression of Keanu at that
meeting as rather misleading. 'His attention span seemed very
short and he fidgeted a lot. After he'd left Stephen said, "I
think he's rather interesting. Take a look at this film called

River's Edge." That evening I watched *River's Edge* and thought he had an extraordinary quality of stillness, which he didn't have in life at all, or not at that stage. So I changed my mind. When we actually worked on the film he was charming. Slightly other-worldly, as if he'd arrived from another planet. I think very fondly of him.' A few years later Hampton suggested Keanu for the title role in an adaptation of Joseph Conrad's *Nostromo* which the British film-maker Hugh Hudson was attempting to set up after the original director, David Lean, died. The actor was interested, but this was before *Speed*, and his name was not yet big enough to secure the American share of the picture's $30 million budget.

While he was waiting to hear Frears' verdict, Keanu's passion for motorbikes caught up with him. As his career took off and his income began to improve, these were his main indulgence; otherwise he had accumulated very few possessions. At this time he was driving a Moto Guzzi, and later acquired a 1974 Norton Commando touring motorcycle, which would accompany him on many of his filming trips. 'Time goes much slower at 130 mph,' he said: he had developed a taste for roaring around cities in the middle of the night at high speed, preferably without goggles or a helmet. In the countryside, he would streak along with his headlights turned off – a pastime which he called 'canyon busting' or 'demon riding'.

It was, he said, his main way of letting off steam. But that spring he was involved in a serious crash in Topanga Canyon, just outside Los Angeles, which left him with a ruptured spleen and a long scar snaking down his abdomen (which was to cause regular headaches for make-up artists on the numer-

ous occasions he appeared bare-torsoed in his films). Keanu
was undeterred by the setback; it was by no means the last
accident he would be involved in. Indeed he would joke that
he worked in order to pay his motor insurance.

As he was recovering in hospital, he learned that he had
won the part in *Dangerous Liaisons*. Shooting began in France
on 30 May 1988. His role had shrunk considerably: most of
his character's affair with Glenn Close had been cut from the
shooting script, surviving only in a few brief glimpses and
allusions. One of his big speeches, in which he told Pfeiffer
about Malkovich's deathbed confession of his love for her,
was overdubbed with music. He also had trouble with
Darceny's soppier aspects, exasperating Frears by his difficulty in crying on cue: 'I don't cry much in real life,' he
admitted. But his climactic duel with Malkovich, a welcome
blast of action in a film otherwise saturated in dialogue,
allowed him to shine and was featured at length in the
finished film.

Dangerous Liaisons was rushed out in America just before
Christmas in order to qualify for the Academy Awards the
following spring, eventually being nominated for seven Oscars
and bagging three. It also won another important race, easily
beating Forman's film, *Valmont*, to the finishing post. The
reviews were quite divided, however. *New York* called it a
'considerable achievement of style' while *Newsweek* deemed it
'nasty decadent fun', adding, 'the surprise is how much
anguished emotion seeps through its cool marble heart'.
Pauline Kael in the *New Yorker* applauded the use of American actors. But many people thought the film oddly and
badly cast.

Most of the attacks were reserved for the silky, faintly camp performance of Malkovich, an actor whose looks scarcely equipped him to play an irresistible womanizer. But several reviewers found Keanu unconvincing in period dress: 'howlingly out of place,' scoffed the *New York Post*, 'unmistakably a gangly, lip-licking Eighties juvenile'. The criticism would re-echo throughout his career whenever he essayed historical drama; he was always perceived as a quintessentially contemporary actor. Moreover Darceny, described in the screenplay as 'colourless', 'mawkish' and 'intensely stupid', was hardly one of the more complex characters. Keanu himself declared later that he felt unhappy with his own performance: 'My Darceny, if you compare it to the book . . . it's awful,' he said. Still, his involvement with such a high-profile, highbrow and commercially successful production did his career no harm at all.

With *Under the Influence, River's Edge, Permanent Record, The Prince of Pennsylvania* and now *Dangerous Liaisons*, Keanu was acquiring a reputation for playing troubled, rebellious and confused young men and (since every actor is known at the beginning of his career as the new somebody) was being described as the new Matt Dillon. But something was about to happen which would cause a dramatic spin in his image.

4

AN ACTOR PREPARES

Meanwhile Stephen Herek had not lost heart over *Bill and Ted's Excellent Adventure*. Even as the remnants of DEG were in the process of selling off his film to Home Box Office for a direct-to-cable television airing, he organized a series of sneak previews at which audiences were highly enthusiastic. Finally a distributor bit: Nelson Entertainment picked up the video rights, selling the film on to Orion for cinema release. *Bill and Ted's Excellent Adventure* opened in America in February 1989.

The reviews were sniffy. For the *Village Voice* it was a pale copy of *Back to the Future*, while the *New York Times* called it 'painfully inept', adding for good measure in a follow-up piece, 'singularly awful'. Several critics deplored its stupidity: 'Bill and Ted is *not* a satire of mindlessness,' grumbled the *Los Angeles Times*. 'It's unabashed glorification of dumbness for dumbness' sake.' The trade papers forecast a swift disappearance from cinemas: 'should open to a tame response and peter out from there', predicted the *Hollywood Reporter*, while *Variety* concluded, 'the box-office report card will likely be average'.

They were wrong. *Bill and Ted's Excellent Adventure* went

on to gross $45 million in America alone. Far from seeming dated, it was followed by a small rash of similar movies, notably *Heathers* (1989) and *Wayne's World* (1992). There was a minor dispute with the latter over which came first: *Wayne's World* appeared as a feature film well after *Bill and Ted*, but its origins (like *B&T*'s) went back to the early Eighties where Wayne started life as a skit by the star, Michael Myers, on Canadian television. And the parallels between the two dopey duos were unmistakable.

In some ways the question was academic. As Alex Winter remarked later, 'I don't think either one came before the other. And neither is that original to begin with. They're a reaction to a certain temperament within the country. Those characters represented what people, especially overseas, saw as a kind of American type: uneducated, hopeful, unflappable – dreamers, basically.' And in any case, the similarities were superficial. *Wayne's World* had a kind of false naiveté to it: its teenagers were played by much older, sophisticated actors, Myers (aged twenty-eight) and Dana Carvey (thirty-six).

'It came out of a *Saturday Night Live* skit and it was about those two comedians poking fun at a certain archetype,' Winter said. 'They weren't actually trying to *be* that archetype; they were definitely people in wigs poking fun at it. Which was very funny on its own merits. But it's a totally different kettle of fish.' The more modest success of *Bill and Ted*, on the other hand, was largely due to the energy and conviction of its two authentically young stars. 'It's like the difference between *The Goodies* and *Monty Python*,' said Peter Hewitt, who later directed a sequel, *Bill and Ted's Bogus Journey*. '*Bill and Ted* was a slightly younger audience that maybe doesn't go to college.'

Another common criticism was that the two protagonists were virtually interchangeable. 'The two actors give spirited performances,' commented the *Hollywood Reporter*. 'But the characters behave, talk and sound alike.' Alex Winter conceded the point, but added: 'We're a little underwritten, but I'm not sure it matters. The fact that we're alike was funny because those characters are best friends. They're so close they become like one person and all the different aspects of their life just dissolve. Especially at that age when they're not dealing with the world, with the things which shape their identities. They're dealing with fantasy land, in which case they would talk the same, act the same and breathe the same. I thought that was actually a good comment to make.'

Besides the two were not identical. Apart from their physical differences, Winter as Bill came across as pragmatic, pugnacious and savvy, while Reeves' Ted was gentler, almost feminine, and more vulnerable. *Bill and Ted's Excellent Adventure* touched lightly on his stormy relationship with his martinet of a father: the Frude Dude, supplying a helpful lightning analysis, concluded, 'Ted's father's own fear of failure has caused him to make his son the embodiment of all of his deepest anxieties about himself. *Und* hence his aggression transference on to Ted.'

'Keanu has a dreamier side to him, and this overwhelming sweetness, while Alex loves cartoons and comes from this whole Tex Avery school of comedy acting,' Scott Kroopf said. (Winter's more surreal and savage sensibility would eventually find expression in his own directorial debut, *Freaked*.) 'So in some ways their approaches as actors ended up defining a little bit of difference between Bill and Ted. Alex is really, really physical and loves to do pratfalls. Keanu is equally physical but he does it in a different way – it's a little less about mechanics and more about finding the essence of the character. Steve Herek kept telling them he wanted them to be like puppies. Alex translated that into "crank up the energy" and I think that Keanu dug in and tried to figure out what it felt like to be a puppy.

'He brought to it an oddly serious sensibility for such an unserious character. That was part of what made the movie great and it's also what makes Keanu great as an actor. You'd walk into his trailer and he'd be reading Stanislavsky's *An Actor Prepares* and applying it to Ted. I know it kind of sounds ridiculous but that's what he did. I think he and Alex found a lot of their characters by blending their acting styles.'

After the *Bill and Ted* sequel, Winter drifted away from acting and swiftly shook off his fictional alter ego. But Keanu remained joined at the hip with Ted for many years. Partly, this was due to the popularity the characters came to assume as teen icons. The film spun off a cartoon series, some episodes of which were voiced by Reeves and Winter, an unsuccessful live action television sitcom with different actors, toy merchandising and a cereal ('a most awesome breakfast adventure'). Flushed with pride at its meteoric rise to fame, the town of San Dimas, California, where the films were set, even considered naming a street after Bill and Ted.

Partly it was because, until *Speed*, these films were Keanu's only major commercial hits. Partly it was that he had, perhaps, played Ted too well. 'There is an aspect of Keanu that is totally Ted, the lightest side of him,' Kroopf said. 'But the reason he ended up unfairly taking this rap of "he *is* Ted" was that he did such a great job and it's hard for any actor, when they truly excel in something, to break out of it.'

But mainly it was that Keanu seemed to identify with Ted, and even to take on some of his qualities. 'When I first played Ted it changed my life,' he said later. 'I tapped into something in myself I hadn't really seen. There's a lot of joy in that guy. Playing him for three months, every day for fifteen hours – it's like having the experience of a best friend, how you change when you hang out with that best friend, how you start sounding like him.'

At interviews, self-conscious about the delicate business of self-promotion, he would almost invariably present himself as a card-carrying airhead. 'I know what you're going to say,' he remarked in 1990. 'How do I play stupid people so incredibly well? It's easy, I guess. I'm not the most intelligent person in the world.' It gave reporters vast satisfaction but caused people who knew him some surprise. Gus Van Sant, who later directed him in two films, said, typically, 'Keanu is really well read, but he doesn't think he is. And he's very intelligent. But he's a sort of punk rocker, in a way, and has this façade.'

The screenwriter Robert Mark Kamen, who had known Keanu since he was fifteen, observed, 'What always struck me about him was how polite he was. He was a teenager, his hair was wild and his jeans were ripped and he looked like all these other kids. But he was unbelievably polite and widely read. So many of the early roles he played were inarticulate teenagers. But he's a voracious reader and can talk about any number of things intelligently. I always liked that disparity between the image and the reality. I don't think he cultivated it; it just sort of evolved.'

Some suspected that Ted *was* a pose to keep probing questions at bay. But when this was put to Keanu by *Vanity Fair* in 1995, the actor emphatically denied it. 'I've never played stupid to keep someone distant,' he said. 'Either it's been a failure on my part to articulate, or my naiveté, or ingenuousness, or sometimes it's the nature of the form.' And since his childhood dyslexia he had never had much of a way with words. Whatever, the character stuck around: when he played Hamlet in 1995, the press dubbed it 'Keanu's Excellent Shakespearean Adventure'. As Keanu said ruefully, whatever else he did in the course of his career, after his death what he'd be remembered for was playing Ted.

By 1988 Keanu was getting itchy feet. He had played a string of troubled adolescents and would now quite like to act his age at last. 'I don't want to be one of those forever boys,' he said. 'That would be very depressing.' Finally, in the fading weeks of summer, as he was just turning twenty-four, he got to play a virtually grown-up role, in an American Playhouse production, *Life Under Water.* 'It's great,' he said. 'I get to be twenty-two years old. I don't have to be eighteen *again* and lose my virginity *again*.' An added attraction for him was the piece's theatrical origins: it was adapted for television by Richard Greenberg from his own stage play.

Wordy and melancholy, the story, such as it was, followed the erotic intrigues of five bored, wealthy people vacationing in the Hamptons: Keanu, his mother, her lover, a vulnerable, depressive young woman, played by Sarah Jessica Parker, and her bitchy best friend. Lindsay Law, the executive director of American Playhouse, described Keanu's character as 'an adolescent in a one-parent household, with the parent as lost as he is. He's a sort of Holden Caulfield of the Eighties.' The literary allusions were deliberate; apart from Law's reference to *The Catcher in the Rye*, the script also quoted *The Great Gatsby*. Keanu's own summation of the plot was, typically, less pretentious: 'One night my mother grounds me. I get drunk and go walking on the beach and fall in front of two girls; we make love and then "The Future" and then I bail and I get driven home by my mom. It's a comedy.'

It was a fairly accurate assessment. In the story he seduced Parker, telling her, 'I have trouble with people too. I think unapproachable people like us have a responsibility to seek each other out.' But later, faced with the ordeal of commitment, he turned out to be as amoral and insincere as everyone else. The teleplay did not really explain his change of heart – it felt as if a scene or two were missing – but Keanu did his best with the character, displaying the rare quality of being able to listen convincingly to Parker's long, tortured monologues and carrying off several long scenes on his own. A brisk flash of frontal nudity was a bonus.

The adaptation was not altogether successful: speeches and behaviour which, on stage, might have seemed convincing looked forced and artificial in the more naturalistic glare of television. Some reviewers took a dislike to the languid Ivy League types who inhabited Greenberg's world. 'The production is soporific, and the privileged characters are self-absorbed and unsympathetic', wrote the *Los Angeles Times*.

Unsurprisingly, East Coast critics were kinder: *Newsday* liked its 'witty, snotty conversation' and the *New York Times* deemed it 'unusually sharp television'.

Keanu was beginning to be noticed by the media, and had even taken the step of hiring a publicist. He was already regretting some of the choice bloopers he had made in previous press encounters: the interview in which, for instance, he expressed an anxiety about showing up for a big date with mucky underwear, or the one where he said he would like to bed Meryl Streep because 'even if I wasn't good, she could fake it the best'.

One assignment gave particular cause for anxiety: Joe Queenan, whose star profiles in *Rolling Stone* and *Movieline* magazines were notorious for their pitiless sarcasm. But Keanu succeeded in beguiling even this fierce adversary. Noting his track record, 'a string of superb movies . . . work an actor can be proud of, work you can build a major career on', Queenan indulgently chronicled the erratic interview, concluding with the avuncular advice, 'Gee, Keanu, why don't you just try relaxing? Everything's going to be fine. Everything's going to be *just* fine.'

A film which helped bring him further into the mainstream was *Parenthood*, a sprawling multi-character comedy. The director, Ron Howard, had told his casting consultants that he wanted names with proven box-office appeal to play each of the main adult characters. It was a sign Keanu's star was rising that he headed the list of candidates for the role of Tod when he went to read for it with Martha Plimpton.

Tod was the boyfriend of Plimpton, who played Dianne Wiest's daughter (Wiest, in her turn, in *Parenthood*'s complex genealogy, was the divorced sister of Steve Martin, the movie's main character). The theme was the troubles, but mainly the joys, of parenting in Martin's extended, mildly dysfunctional family. Tod was, superficially, another edition of Ted: a likeable but, by his own admission, not overly bright slacker of whom Wiest heartily disapproved. In the course of the film he did stunts like half-shaving his and Plimpton's heads, taking nude photos of her and indulging in drag racing (emerging dazedly from a wrecked car he asked, 'Did I win?'). But his character also had a kinder, more mature side, taking Wiest's troubled younger son, played by Leaf Phoenix, under his wing. And his waywardness was revealed as springing from a low self-esteem ('That's a good job for me – crash dummy') and an abused childhood.

Keanu's character was relatively minor but, in a film that was, indirectly, about a series of long-suffering mothers and inadequate fathers, he had one of the keynote speeches: 'You need a licence to buy a dog or drive a car. Hell, you need a licence to catch a fish. But they'll let any butt-reaming asshole be a father.' He delivered the speech with an odd little shake of the head, as if half-embarrassed by the high seriousness of it all, but part of the movie's appeal was its ability to vault effortlessly between melodrama and comedy.

Parenthood took some flak for its middlebrow, soap-operatic view of family life (several reviews noted Howard's background as a child star in sunny television sitcoms like *Happy Days* and *The Andy Griffith Show*), and its markedly conservative stances towards working mothers and abortion. But many critics loved it. 'An ambitious, keenly observed and often very funny look at one of life's most daunting passages,' opined *Variety*, whose review also singled out Reeves as an 'inspired touch'. More importantly, it was also a substantial popular hit. America's post-war baby boom generation was entering its thirties, starting families and producing a new demographic blip of its own: movies like *Parenthood* and *Look Who's Talking* (a comedy with John Travolta and the voice of Bruce Willis as a wisecracking baby) spoke directly to this audience's experience.

Parenthood was followed by another film with a large ensemble cast: Lawrence Kasdan's *I Love You To Death*, a broader and much darker comedy based on the real-life case of Anthony and Frances Toto. In 1984 Frances made five unsuccessful attempts on the life of her philandering husband, an Italian-American pizza-maker – who responded by falling in love with her all over again. Kevin Kline and Tracey Ullman were to play this odd couple, with Joan Plowright and River Phoenix in supporting roles.

Kasdan had seen a number of Keanu's films and was particularly struck by him in *River's Edge*. *Parenthood* had just wrapped, and he called Howard to enquire about the actor. 'Then Keanu flew out to LA to read for me and I was delighted by him and his spirit,' Kasdan recalled. 'I thought he was an extraordinarily charismatic young actor. Very serious about acting and all the different shapes that it can take. And great-looking, like a teen idol. That combination is always intriguing.'

The part Kasdan intended to offer to Keanu was a small one. He would be one of two hitmen hired by Ullman to despatch her husband; the other was played by William Hurt. Their spectacular incompetence, which extended to taking a taxi to their murder assignment and being unable to locate their victim's heart, was also drawn from life. It was basically another Thug Number Three role, but of a superior kind.

The cast convened in Los Angeles that spring for extensive rehearsals. Keanu was a little fazed by Hurt's seriousness and his heavyweight reputation. 'I was really awed at first – William Hurt! He's such an incredible actor. But he looked at me on the first day and just went *Thththwww!*' Reeves recalled, blowing a raspberry. Hurt riposted, 'That schmuck! He acted like *I* was supposed to be intimidated by him! So what could I do? You look at Keanu's face, and you've got to do something! He's so pretty that you've got to break that mould. I'd ask him something in my language, and he'd answer in his, and I thought, "Well I guess I gotta sit back and listen, I just gotta listen to him."' It would have been amusing to be a fly on the wall while these two famously inarticulate actors discoursed together. 'He's a real serious, tense guy, you know?' commented Keanu of his partner in crime on a later occasion. 'So I went up to him and asked him, "Hey, Bill, what kind of movie do you think we're in?" And he said, "Well, Keanu, if your name is Marlon and my name is Harlan, I guess we're in a comedy."' But once the two got to know each other they would, he said, 'sit down and rap about God'.

Since Harlan and Marlon were doped and dopey hippies with not a great deal to say for themselves, rehearsals focused on their physical comedy and how they would move together. Harlan had a habit of knocking his head on overhanging lights. Marlon evolved as a stoned and mangy version of Ted with a way of walking into doors and an attention span so short he was unable to recognize his victim when they met shortly after the murder attempt. He sported a straggly beard, nose ring, too-short bell bottoms, half-shaven head *à la Prince of Pennsylvania* and a cannabis leaf tattooed on his neck. Even his dialogue had elements of Tedspeak. 'Marlon is not the swiftest person in the world,' said Keanu with characteristic understatement.

On 10 April, the team decamped to the small working-class town of Tacoma, Washington, where most of the shooting took place. It was a grim hole, permeated with the foul fumes emanating from its pulp mills. Diversions were sparse; Kline remembered many a quiet evening spent in his hotel with Ullman and Plowright. Keanu passed the time shooting baskets and sampling what nightlife he could find with River Phoenix. The two had already met while Keanu was filming *Parenthood* opposite Phoenix's girlfriend, Martha Plimpton, who now joined them in Tacoma, and his brother, Leaf. 'I liked the guy. I wanted to work with him,' River said of Keanu, whom he regarded as the older brother he never had. Kasdan and his cast remembered the shoot fondly. 'It is the most fun I've ever had on a movie,' recalled Kline years later. 'It was really trippy,' said Keanu. 'Mr Kasdan kept saying you couldn't go too far. And nobody did except Kevin Kline. He would just cheese it up too much, but we'd all be too busy laughing to try and stop him.'

Kasdan's first inkling that his audiences would not be laughing came at sneak previews where, to his dismay, most of them hated *I Love You To Death* – despised it, even. '[They] didn't like the film because they want to go and see good-looking people achieving things,' the director remembered. 'That's what American movies are about.' Instead, his story featured unglamorous losers doing seamy things in ugly surroundings. It viewed murder as, in the words of Plowright's character, a 'national pastime'. In America, she pointed out, 'people kill each other right and left'. In accepting the commission, the two hitmen were merely trying to better themselves by earning an honest buck. 'If we're gonna waste the dude, we oughtta get paid for it,' Keanu said. 'It's the American way, right?'

Preparing to shoot Kline, Hurt joked that they should perhaps read him his rights first. Then, debating where best to aim the bullet, the two remembered how they used to place their hand on their heart when swearing allegiance to the flag at school, and proceeded to recite the Pledge over their victim. None of this was calculated to appeal to righteous-thinking Middle Americans, to whom the film seemed cynical and unpatriotic. And they failed to see the funny side of a couple of junkie killers.

I Love You To Death fared no better with critics: when it opened on 11 April 1990, almost a year to the day after shooting had begun, the reviews were terrible. Kasdan had failed, they said, to carry off the difficult tone or to control his cast. 'A stillborn attempt at black comedy that wastes considerable acting talent,' wrote *Variety*. 'Kasdan has inexplicably reduced flesh-and-blood characters to cartoons,' said *Rolling Stone*. A few reviews found kind words for the Reeves–Hurt double act; others thought it overplayed. Kasdan kept a soft spot for their scenes, however. 'That part of the movie moves at its own pace, it's at their pace really,' he recalled. 'Some people didn't like it but I treasure those moments.'

During the shoot Keanu had plied Hurt and Kline, both seasoned theatrical actors, with questions, telling them that he had just taken a month-long workshop at Shakespeare and Company in Lenox, Massachusetts, to develop his verse-speaking, clowning and breathing techniques. As a result of those classes, he had been selected to return that summer, to play Trinculo – one of Caliban's bibulous sidekicks – in a production of *The Tempest* opposite André Gregory as Prospero.

Kline listened to all this cautiously. Theatre acting and verse speaking demanded very different skills from film work. And it was hard to divine if Keanu had any talent for them from his zonked-out Marlon. 'I'd not seen his other work, so all I knew was that he was eager to do it,' Kline said. 'Our connection was tenuous at best. [Anthony Toto] was near comatose or heavily drugged at the time, and his character was as far-gone as mine was, so I can't say we bonded in any serious way. It was not a meeting of the minds!' Nonetheless, he was pleased at Keanu's interest in the theatre. 'I was encouraging because it's rare to find an actor, especially a film actor, who really wants to take time off from a cinema career.'

As it turned out, Keanu's performance in *The Tempest* was a triumph. The *Boston Globe* had withering words for Gregory's Prospero, but found the production, directed by Tina Packer, 'as enchanted as enchanted gets'. The reviewer singled out the 'fluent ease' and 'shrewd timing' of the comic interludes and noted that at the performance he saw the audience was applauding Reeves' scenes 'with something like eruptive joy'.

By now Keanu's salary had hit the six-figure mark, but he could still be seen hurtling down Sunset Boulevard in the same battered 1969 Volvo that had brought him there from Toronto four years ago. He was sleeping on the floor of the West Hollywood apartment he shared with another actor. 'Did it have a swimming pool?' one interviewer wondered. Keanu laughed heartily: 'Are you kidding?' It was a lifestyle that he continued to follow, even after the success of *Speed* added another zero to his asking price.

Up until now, one image had coloured almost all his major characters. In film after film, Keanu was to be seen as tatty, scatty and eccentric. But now a very different kind of role presented itself. *Aunt Julia and the Scriptwriter* was based on the 1977 novel by the Peruvian writer Mario Vargas Llosa, about the romance between a young man and his much older aunt. The hero, too, was named Mario, and the affair mirrored Vargas Llosa's own youthful marriage to his aunt-in-law, Julia Urquidi. This relationship, however, was just the starting point for the story. Pedro, the scriptwriter of the title, was a Machiavellian author of radio soap operas who engineered and spied on Mario's affair, pillaging the lovers' intimate encounters for dialogue to fuel his fiction. As often in Latin American magical realism, the novel contained multiple layers of narrative: as the plot thickened, Mario and Julia's story was interleaved with the lurid, outrageously implausible imbroglios of Pedro's radio soaps.

The project started life at Columbia under the aegis of David Puttnam, the studio's then-head, and was entrusted to another Brit: the director Jon Amiel, who already had a track record in exploring the shifting boundaries between fantasy and reality in his acclaimed BBC television series of Dennis Potter's *The Singing Detective* and one cinema feature, *Queen of Hearts*, an imaginative melodrama set in London's Italian community. *Aunt Julia* would be his first Hollywood picture.

Both Amiel and his own scriptwriter, the novelist William Boyd, knew that the novel, with its Chinese box construction, called for very free adapting. The central romance presented few problems, but the tangle of subplots involving nine different, increasingly violent, surreal and complicated soap operas would need to be simplified into one, relatively straightforward serial. And there was something more important. 'One aspect had already been made clear to me by Columbia,' Boyd said. 'There was no way that it was going to be set in Lima, Peru. Lima, Idaho, maybe, but definitely not Peru. This film, if it were going to be made, was to be an American comedy, not Peruvian.' All cinema involves a degree of compromise, and it appeared to Boyd and Amiel perfectly acceptable to shift the story northwards – a move to which Vargas Llosa gave his blessing.

The city they hit upon as Lima's closest counterpart was New Orleans, 'the one North American city', according to Boyd, 'that seemed to reproduce, approximately, all the aspects of Lima that permeate the novel: polyglot, multi-racial, Catholic, teeming low-life slums contrasting with impossibly elegant swank and swish'. Amiel liked the idea for another reason: a great admirer of Sturges' and Hawks' screwball comedies, he felt the city had a larger than life quality to it: 'it's packed with eccentrics; everyone's doing some shtick or other'.

All this had begun back in 1987, since when Puttman had left Columbia. His successor, Dawn Steele, declared a blanket ban on period pictures (*Aunt Julia* was set in the Fifties) and the project bounced to MGM/UA. By the time it came to fruition, in the summer of 1989, it had moved on again, to an independent production company, Cinecom. The budget was just over $8 million, fairly tight for a costume film with a number of explosions, car crashes and fires, as well as over forty-five separate locations and fifty-odd speaking roles. To save time and money it would be filmed not in New Orleans but in Wilmington, North Carolina.

Amiel's first move had been to cast Peter Falk as Pedro the scriptwriter – a decision which met with some opposition at Cinecom since Falk was famous for his role in the *Columbo* television show but had few big screen credits. Keanu, too, was hardly an obvious choice. 'Most of the kids he plays are very freaky, eccentric and wild,' conceded Amiel, who was taken aback when the actor turned up for his audition sporting his bizarre coiffure from *I Love You To Death*. 'His hair was shaved bald on one side and long on the other. The hair had time to grow back before rehearsals, but on the first day he turned up swathed in bandages and he was limping after yet another tumble off his motorbike.'

Nonetheless, it took the director only one brief interview to cast Keanu as the articulate, neatly groomed Martin (as Mario was now called). 'I have', he said, 'a very peculiar auditioning technique in that I never read actors. Many good actors can read badly and many bad actors deliver their best performances in audition. What I'm looking for when I meet and talk with them is the truthful and unimpeded passage of thought and feeling through the face and body. So most often I'll end up talking about their families, their past, anything they feel strongly and passionately about.'

At first Keanu seemed distracted, but his manner changed on being asked about his family. As he talked about Kim he became animated and began, Amiel said, 'to express an intensity and warmth I hadn't seen anywhere else in his work. He'd only up until that point played wild child roles, and I saw in him an ability to feel great affection and a tremendous romanticism, actually. I felt there was more native intelligence than I'd seen used before on the screen.' He had, the director also thought, something of James Stewart's awkward grace.

Keanu prepared himself by reading Vargas Llosa's novel, working intensively with a dialogue coach and studying an oral history tape made by a lifelong resident of New Orleans, which he would fall asleep listening to at nights. Despite his efforts, when the production moved briefly to New Orleans to shoot some exteriors and he took the chance to try out his accent on a local cab driver, he was asked, 'Where are you from, New Hampshire?' Dialects were never his strong point.

A greater challenge was presented by the love scenes. Amiel had cast him and his co-star, Barbara Hershey, separately and they met for the first time at rehearsals. Amiel's work focused upon encouraging him to play 'a kid who was articulate and sexually quite confident. I think Keanu found that process quite daunting. I constantly encouraged him to work with the outgoing, almost breezy elements of his personality. He's very shy and in many ways not suited to superstardom. He's quite

A new action hero: Keanu as an undercover FBI agent turned surfer in Kathryn Bigelow's *Point Break*, the film that paved the way for *Speed*.

Early roles: Jack Nimble (third from left) with Drew Barrymore in the fairytale musical fantasy *Babes in Toyland* and (below) a troubled teen who has to come to terms with a classmate's suicide in *Permanent Record*.

Brooding with Ione Skye Leitch in *River's Edge*,
Keanu's breakthrough film. Below, battling John
Malkovich in *Dangerous Liaisons*.

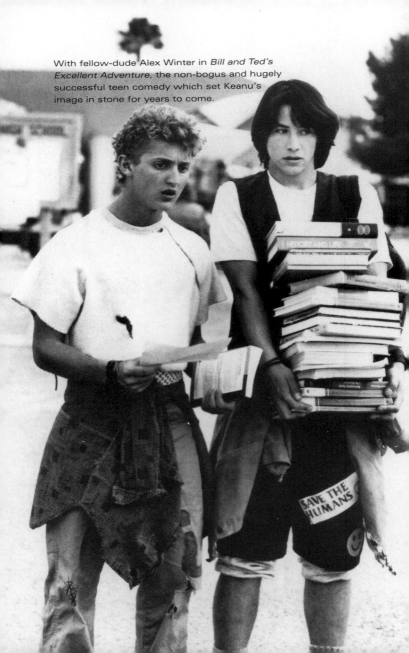

With fellow-dude Alex Winter in *Bill and Ted's Excellent Adventure*, the non-bogus and hugely successful teen comedy which set Keanu's image in stone for years to come.

With William Hurt as incompetent hired assassins in Lawrence Kasdan's *I Love You To Death* (Keanu almost never killed, or was killed, in his movies). Below, preparing to ride the waves in *Point Break*.

Opposite: Keanu reteamed with Gus Van Sant – the only director he has worked with twice – for a cameo role as a cosmopolitan Mohawk Indian in *Even Cowgirls Get The Blues.*

On the set of *My Own Private Idaho* with River Phoenix (right) and the director Gus Van Sant (second right); (below) the iconographic poster image from the film which made Keanu and River, playing male hustlers, into cult stars.

With his trusty green 1969 122 Volvo, the ancient and beat-up car which (somehow) took him from Toronto to Los Angeles.

reticent with women, which is kind of surprising for a heart-throb, but at the time I was working with him he was still a young man.'

It was the long rehearsals for a complicated scene in which the couple danced the jitterbug that broke the ice. 'That was how we started to meet each other,' Keanu said. 'Being thrust together.' Barbara Hershey declared herself happy with her partner. 'I had thought of him as a natural talent with a beautiful, Arabian prince kind of face, but I didn't know much about his range. And it takes a certain bravery for a modern young man to play someone so innocent, so naive.'

Amiel noticed something else about Keanu which had struck his other collaborators: an obsessive perfectionism which sometimes erupted in spurts of temper. 'Keanu is very hard on himself. Halfway through a take he will very often swear violently and storm off into a corner. At first it's very disconcerting, but what you gradually realize is that he's only angry with himself and has no other way of expressing it. One of the things I learned to do with Keanu was, in a sense, protect him from his own anger.'

When *Aunt Julia* was completed the following autumn, Vargas Llosa, who had been busy losing the presidential election in Peru while the film was in production, declared himself happy with the result and gave it his blessing. He was less keen on the fact that it would be released in America under the jaunty title *Tune In Tomorrow*: preview audiences had found *Aunt Julia and the Scriptwriter* 'hard to remember'. 'We were trying to find a title that fit the movie's sense of fun,' said the co-producer Jonathan Tarlov. 'While we're faithful to the spirit of the book, we want a wider audience than the book

had.' Richard Abramowitz, the head of Cinecom's distribution division, was even blunter: 'The novel's title is stodgy.'

Foremost in the company's mind was the need to avoid the
arthouse label. It claimed, with amazing confidence in the
precision of its statistics, that between 82 and 83 per cent of
the American public would be less likely to see a movie like
Tune In Tomorrow if they thought it was art. It was, therefore,
to be sold not as a romance but as a broad slapstick comedy
aimed at young men rather than at older women. The original
title would be reinstated for the European and Canadian
campaigns, 'where', Tarlov opined, 'people who go to the
movies are more intelligent'.

Amiel felt angry about the way his movie was treated.
Cinecom had been taken over during the making of *Aunt
Julia* which, he thought, 'was effectively thrown to the dogs.
It was probably never likely to be a massive broad-based
comedy hit. On the other hand, if it had been properly
handled, it could have easily developed a very strong follow-
ing. But it was never going to sell simply on those names.
Keanu wasn't a star at that point.'

Cinecom's campaign was not a smart decision. From the
opening credits, spoken excitedly in voice-over by a radio
announcer rather than printed on screen, the film was clever,
knowing and pitched at a sophisticated audience. Its theme
was the way art reflects life – which reflects art. 'You just
copied word for word what we said!' an outraged Keanu
complained to Peter Falk on discovering that his love affair
had been purloined for the latter's scripts. 'And where did
you get the words you used?' Falk riposted. 'You feed on us,
we feed on you.'

Dapper, bow-tied, his neatly cropped and parted hair polished to a patent-leather sheen, Keanu was virtually unrecognizable from the scruffs he had played in his other recent movies. The humour in the writing played to his strengths, and he and Hershey brought a playful, mischievous tenderness to their long scenes together, even if, as Amiel noted, 'it was something that was largely created on screen; it didn't exist off-screen'. In spite of an over fifteen year age gap between their characters, the match was entirely plausible. 'You could almost be my son, you know that don't you?' she said to him. 'So I've almost got an Oedipus complex,' he replied with a don't-give-a-damn smile.

The film got one or two positive American notices, from the *Hollywood Reporter*, which deemed it 'one of the most pleasurable films to come along in quite some time', and the *Village Voice*, which suggested that it might prove 'the year's best comedy: an intelligent, surprising, funny, well-acted and well-mounted pastiche of parody and romance'. But the device of intercutting the love story with long dramatized segments from Falk's fevered soap opera slowed the film down, and other critics found it repetitive ('a giddy, enjoyable tribute to its own ingenuity which by its ending has worn thin', wrote the *New York Times*) and, for all Boyd's valiant attempts to streamline the novel, it remained a little over-burdened with a surplus of plot ('lusty and full of zany characters, but so cluttered and overdone that theatrical possibilities are muted': *Variety*).

Falk garnered mixed reviews: some thought he stole the show, others that he spoiled it with his fruity, over-the-top performance. Keanu played the straight man to his antics, and

his understated manner could have easily been eclipsed, as
has often happened in his other movies, by his more flamboyant fellow actors. But he attracted almost universal plaudits.
'A breezy engaging presence and a winning hangdog lyri-
cism,' wrote the *Los Angeles Times*, while the *Wall Street
Journal* felt he conveyed, 'just the right mix of innocence and
smarts' and *Variety* called him and Hershey 'outstanding'.
Entertainment Weekly raved: 'With his short hair slicked back,
Reeves has the outrageous glamour of a Thirties matinee idol,
and he gives his most winning performance yet ... The two
actors barely have a love scene together, yet when they're on
screen *Tune In Tomorrow* crackles with romantic lust. It's the
one movie this year that makes love itself seem sexy.' Keanu
himself was proud of it too, referring to it years later as 'a
very under-appreciated picture, I felt, a good film.'

What was surprising about all this in retrospect was how
rarely he was cast in love stories. It would be another five
years before he landed his next one – and, not by coincidence,
it was another period piece in the magical realist tradition: *A
Walk in the Clouds*. There was a reticence and an old-
fashioned courtliness about Keanu's screen presence which
somehow made him ill-suited to contemporary sex scenes
and eventually a myth grew up (connected, perhaps, with the
gossip about his sexuality) that he was unable to play them.
And yet, as *Aunt Julia* proved, he could be thoroughly
convincing as a romantic leading man.

5

YOUNG, DUMB AND FULL OF CUM

Over the last two years, Keanu had been edging into a bigger league. He had built up a body of work for such respected directors as Stephen Frears, Ron Howard, Lawrence Kasdan and Jon Amiel, but always in supporting roles (the exception, *Aunt Julia and the Scriptwriter*, had not been enough of a commercial success to make a mark). Now he was about to embark on an exhausting marathon, shooting three films, and starring in each of them, in the space of seven months. These were all high profile projects and, when they came out, also within a few months of each other, they confirmed his versatility and box-office muscle, propelling him fast-forward on the road to stardom.

The first was *Point Break*, a thriller by Kathryn Bigelow, who, with *Near Dark* and *Blue Steel*, had secured a reputation as one of Hollywood's most talented and original action directors. She too had first noticed Keanu in *River's Edge* which, although completely unlike the film she planned to make, showcased his acting and also, perhaps more import-antly, his screen presence: his ability to, as she said, 'put the audience in his back pocket'.

He would, she thought, be ideal for her main character, a

young FBI agent who went undercover in order to infiltrate a group of surfers suspected of robbing banks while wearing latex masks of Reagan and other ex-Presidents. (They justified their activities on the grounds that they were merely continuing what the White House had been doing for years, namely screwing people.) The agent gradually became ensnared by the beach boys' sybaritic but spiritual lifestyle and by their charismatic leader, played by Patrick Swayze, whom Keanu had met on his first film, *Youngblood*.

There was a snag: his lack of any action-movie credentials and, Bigelow said, 'convincing everybody that he was the right person took a bit of doing. It was perceived as a stretch for him. But,' she added, 'Keanu was thoroughly dedicated to playing this part. I mean, he was already doing research and we were working together on the background to the character long before he was actually cast. He went off to Hawaii, which is probably one of the most difficult places to learn to surf, and started to teach himself, just after an initial conversation with me.'

After his parents' divorce, Keanu had kept in touch for a while with his father, travelling to Hawaii for holidays to see him. But he had never learned surfing. After much dogged practice he was finally able to keep his balance, 'depending on the wave', he said modestly: in the film it was noticeable that he seemed to spend as much time falling off his surfboard as riding on it. 'He became fairly proficient,' Bigelow said. 'You also have to appreciate that in the context of the story he does not become a great surfer. He just learns enough to get by and find himself in that milieu with some small degree of credibility.'

Even by Bigelow's standards, *Point Break* was an uncommonly action-crammed film. Keanu's other preparations included a spell with FBI agents learning to use firearms – a skill which would later stand him in good stead for his role in *Speed* – and some football training, since his character was meant to be a former star quarterback forced to leave the sport because of a knee injury. There were also two skydiving sequences, for which he would have liked to try parachuting, but the insurers were none too happy at the idea. 'The money aspect of the film was very concerned about twisted ankles and death,' he said ruefully. These scenes were shot instead on a complex system of cranes and platforms. Swayze alone was allowed up with the stunt divers to film actual footage of himself in free fall, and that only after the end of principal photography. Keanu had hoped to join him, but as soon as *Point Break* wrapped he had to fly off to Oregon to start work on Gus Van Sant's *My Own Private Idaho*.

Point Break was meant to show the moral disintegration of the FBI agent: the erosion of his resolve as he fell under Swayze's spell. 'My character is a total control freak, and the ocean beats him up and changes him,' said Keanu. 'After a while everything becomes a game. He becomes oblivious to guilt. Then he goes into what I call juggernaut mode. He becomes as amoral as any criminal. He loses the difference between right and wrong. Once he gets his eyes on something, he'll kill you to get it.'

The film did not quite pull this off; its centre of gravity kept shifting. At some moments it applauded the surfers, seeming to approve of Swayze's talk of 'accepting the wave's energy', his romantic, live-fast-die-young philosophy and his rejection of the straight world, 'those dead souls inching along the freeway in their metal coffins' (at an early stage the picture was named after The Doors' hippy anthem 'Riders On The Storm'). Then, when it suited the story, they suddenly became selfish, violent and irresponsible.

It was also unable to decide whether the young agent's progress was an enlightenment or a kind of corruption (by the end he had betrayed everyone he had grown to care for), and there remained a frustrating vagueness at his core. In any case, psychological complexity was never going to figure large in a character named Johnny Utah: it may have been a deficiency in Keanu's performance, but there was nothing in the screenplay to suggest what Swayze called at one point his 'demons'.

Keanu had some sweet love scenes with a young woman (played by Lori Petty) whom he had picked up in order to make contact with the surfing community. But the film was extremely male-dominated. In one typical scene, as the men sat around bragging of their surfing feats, Petty flounced off declaring, 'too much testosterone here'. She was soon eclipsed by Keanu's male friendships, with his older partner (Gary Busey) and, particularly, with Swayze, his friend and nemesis: their connection was already signalled in the way the two actors' names melded in the opening credits. Petty was reduced to a pawn, as Keanu became obsessive in his pursuit of his quarry. 'I know you want me so bad it's like acid in your mouth,' Swayze taunted him, just before they skydived together.

Some critics saw in all this a homoerotic subtext, although the film-makers were, naturally, disinclined to make much of that angle. Bigelow viewed the characters in more general terms: 'Together they are two halves of one person, not unlike Jamie Lee Curtis and Ron Silver [the cop and the psychotic] in *Blue Steel*. It's like the ego and the id. That's definitely there in the material.' Swayze, for his part, described the relationship as a kind of mystical union. 'We wanted to explore how intense the bond between two men can be that goes beyond macho,' he said. 'In a way you could call it a love story without sex. It's what happens between men when they become very, very, very close. It's not about sex, it's not about some level of eroticism. It's about a powerful bond between two souls cut from the same cloth.'

One thing was certain: *Point Break* suddenly confirmed Keanu as a himbo, a sex object potently attractive to both sexes, in a way that nothing he had done previously had managed to achieve. One tastefully erotic overhead shot posed him and Petty like a nude sculpture on their bed's black sheets. The widely quoted line, in which his sardonic boss described him as 'young, dumb and full of cum', seemed to sum up the essence of this new image.

Bigelow's trump card had always been her action sequences and Keanu moved gracefully through the film's sinuous, ninety-second Steadicam opening shot showing his arrival at the FBI headquarters. He displayed a kinetic energy in the various fights and chases (even if, at one point, he had to suffer the brief indignity of being beaten up by a naked woman). He proved deft, too, at the lighter moments – the ironic smile and the deadpan riposte – and also showed he could look good in a suit, not an item of clothing that he had had much occasion to wear so far in his career. For once he was playing a character whose age (twenty-five) was the same as his own.

He attracted generally warm comment ('Reeves holds the screen well as the stop-at-nothing young Fed,' said *Variety* typically) but *Point Break* itself was panned. As often in Bigelow's work, the film was let down by its weak plotting and plausibility, with much (down to the very title) left unexplained. 'An exercise in stylish lunkheadedness', said the *Washington Post*; 'It doesn't seem to be inhabited by people, thoughts or feelings', concluded the *Los Angeles Times*. *New York Newsday* put in an early nomination for it as worst movie of the year, and the *Village Voice* noted the jeers and snickers which greeted it at the press screening. However, the public disagreed, turning *Point Break* into one of the more successful independent films of the 1991 summer season.

There was no vacation for Keanu after the strenuous seventy-seven-day shoot. 'I finished *Point Break* in Hawaii at six in the morning when the sun came up,' he remembered. 'Then I got on a plane, arriving in LA at four in the afternoon. I flew to Portland the next morning and *bam*, started filming.' His next role could scarcely have represented a greater contrast with Bigelow's glossy, Hollywoodesque action movie (and nobody was contesting *its* homoerotic edge): he was to play a street hustler in Gus Van Sant's *My Own Private Idaho*.

Van Sant was building up a name on the strength of his two first features. *Mala Noche*, a very low budget film shot in black and white, was the story of a salesman in a skid-row liquor store who was desperately in love with a Chicano street kid. *Drugstore Cowboy* followed the escapades of a quartet of junkies who robbed pharmacies to fuel their habit. Bleak and painfully funny, both were set on the margins of society but were driven by a hip, poetic romanticism that had secured the director a powerful cult following.

However the industry people now beating a path to his door were a little dismayed when they read his draft script for *My Own Private Idaho*, in which one of the very first scenes involved a rent boy being fellated by a client in a motel room. Still, the liberal helpings of drugs and gay sex should have come as no surprise to anyone familiar with the director's other work. More disconcerting was the loose, free-associational structure of the story: the very look of it, cobbled together by Van Sant on his home computer with a patchwork of different-sized letters and typefaces, failed to conform to Hollywood norms.

It was short – eighty pages – and had long sections written in cod-Elizabethan English borrowed freely from Shakespeare's *Henry IV* by way of Orson Welles' film *Chimes at Midnight*. There were puzzling leaps in continuity, too: one minute the action would be set in a motel, and the next it would suddenly jump to an empty road in the middle of the country. The main character was narcoleptic, and would be inexplicably overcome by attacks of deep sleep. The brusque jump cuts reflected his blackouts.

After a chain of refusals, Van Sant was offered $2 million by an outside investor. He held out little hope at this stage of attracting name actors and planned to make *Idaho* with real street kids in the leading roles. To generate a little advance publicity he had himself photographed by Bruce Weber for *Interview* magazine together with Mike Parker, a sixteen-year-old hustler who was the inspiration for the lead character and whom Van Sant thought he would cast in the movie.

Meanwhile, however, Keanu was becoming interested. Van Sant knew the actor's work from *Permanent Record*, which had been shot in the director's home town of Portland, and from *River's Edge*. Both were tough, low-budget subjects with similarities to his own movies. He had also seen *Bill and Ted's Excellent Adventure* and was fascinated by the 'false eloquence' of the Valley Boy dialogue. This, and Keanu's theatre experience, also suggested that he would be able to cope with the stylized speeches he would be required to deliver in *Idaho*.

'Our first meeting was in the afternoon at my apartment in Hollywood,' Van Sant said. 'It was short, an hour or so. He came over on his motorcycle and we talked about the script. He resembled quite a bit the character I imagined he would be from the films. If he wanted to do it, I was ready, I didn't need an audition or anything like that. There was enough work out there that I'd seen. I was always taken with a certain spontaneity that he had and which is hard to find anywhere.

'I knew it was risky material and it was kind of up to him if he wanted to do it. I didn't try and persuade him. I don't usually do that when I'm offering a role to somebody. Because if you talk somebody into it they may want to get out of it again later. I think that one of the appealing things for him was that it was a smaller, lower-budget thing. It was a less of a showbusiness deal.'

Keanu would play Scott Favor, the son of the wealthy mayor of Portland who, as an act of defiance towards his father, was living on the streets. But he was only a sexual tourist, safe in the knowledge that he was about to come into a large inheritance. The part of the narcoleptic male prostitute was as yet uncast. 'I hadn't offered it to River [Phoenix] at that time,' said Van Sant. 'I was going to: I told him I was going to ask River to play this other character. So Keanu was in first.'

Reeves later denied that either he or his manager was ever worried the role might hurt his image. 'Hurt my *image*?' he said scornfully. 'Who am I – a politician?' Besides, he thought the sex scenes not particularly sensational, and less important than the overarching theme of the film: the two main characters' problems with their parents (the narcoleptic kid in the story was haunted by fantasies of his missing mother). River's agent, Iris Burton, remained suspicious and Van Sant and Reeves combined forces to talk to the actor and win him over. *Drugstore Cowboy* helped convince him. Matt Dillon's striking and highly acclaimed performance as a self-styled 'shameless full-time dope fiend' in that film had been, as it were, a shot in the arm for his flagging career.

Perhaps out of solidarity, the two actors contested this version of events, claiming that they had made a pact to do the movie at the same time while they were filming *I Love You To Death* together in the spring of 1989. 'We were driving in a car on Santa Monica Boulevard, probably on the way to a club, and were talking really fast about the whole idea,' River said. 'We were excited. It could have been like a bad dream – a dream that never follows through because no one commits, but we just forced ourselves into it. We said, "OK, I'll do it if you do it. I won't do it if you won't." We shook hands. That was it.' Keanu's story was the same. 'Really, I would not have done it if River hadn't done it,' he said.

Whatever the case, Van Sant would have counted himself lucky to land either one of these hot young stars. 'They were very interested themselves in doing it together,' he said. 'It was more important to them than it was to me. Had one of them said "no" and the other "yes", I would have still ventured onwards.'

The arrival of Phoenix, who had already signed up to star in Nancy Savoca's *Dogfight* – due to start filming in May 1990 – meant that *Idaho* would have to be put back by nine months. By now the original backers had disappeared, and the production had passed to New Line, an independent company which had made a mint from the *Nightmare on Elm Street* franchise and was now looking to move into more ambitious, upscale movies.

This did not mean that there was much more money in the pot: the budget was still only $2.5 million. And New Line executives who had read the script were already worrying that it might be a mite *too* ambitious for them. Several were strongly against the Shakespearean scenes and wanted to cut them altogether (although in Europe there were different priorities and the foreign distributors wanted 'as much Shakespeare in there as we could get', Van Sant said).

Before filming began both Keanu and River spent some time observing gay street life at first hand, initially accompanied by the director and then with Scott Green – a friend of Van Sant's from a well-to-do family who was then working as his personal assistant – and Mike Parker, the two people on whom their characters were respectively and loosely modelled. Their research involved visits to Portland's Old Town district, where they hung out on a strip known as

Vaseline Alley. 'I took River and Keanu down to where boys prostitute themselves and we'd sit on the corner and just watch,' said Green, who, like many before him, remembered Reeves as enigmatic and remote. 'I hung out with Keanu more, but River was easier to talk to and to make friends with,' he said. 'Keanu's kind of withdrawn and he's a confusing person.'

They met more hustlers at Van Sant's house, and also spent time at the home of Bob Pitchlynn, a former rock promoter who had fallen on hard times and now lived in an old house in the middle of the Portland ghetto; he was the prototype for the Falstaffian Bob Pigeon character in the story. All Van Sant's films had dealt with social outcasts who find solace and security in alternative 'families': the male hookers in *Mala Noche*, the junkies in *Drugstore Cowboy*, the street kids in *Idaho*, and, in the director's subsequent work, the ranchers in *Even Cowgirls Get The Blues* and the young drop-outs drawn to Nicole Kidman's weather girl in *To Die For*. During the filming of *Idaho* this theme found expression in the way the cast and crew cohered into a temporary community.

Many of the younger members bunked down in Van Sant's ten-room house on a hill overlooking Portland and, when not too tired from the day's shooting, would launch into long impromptu jam sessions far into the night: this group included River, Keanu, Flea (the bass guitarist of the Red Hot Chilli Peppers, who had a small role in the film), Van Sant, Parker, Green and others. It was an opportunity for Keanu and River to cement the relationship they had begun on *I Love You To Death*. In later interviews, Keanu described River as his best friend, and the two joked about playing *Romeo and Juliet* together (with Phoenix as Juliet). 'They were pretty close,' Van Sant said. 'They have a lot of things in common. They made a good twosome, they have a shared background. They were of similar ages and they were both champion young actors.'

In fact there was a significant age gap: when they were filming *Idaho* Phoenix had just turned twenty while Reeves was already twenty-six. But whereas Keanu had served a quiet apprenticeship in the Toronto theatre before going to Hollywood at the relatively late age of nineteen, River had been driven to California and thrust into acting by his parents as a nine-year-old child. By the time he landed his first film role (in a sci-fi adventure called *Explorers*, in 1985, just as Keanu was also entering the movies), he had already been in dozens of commercials and television programmes. He was a precocious showbiz veteran.

Perhaps for that reason, the film's producer Laurie Parker found him more outgoing than Keanu. 'River is diplomatic down to the bone; Keanu is not,' she said. 'Keanu is normally reticent about publicity and can be rude – in fact he offends people all the time, and that's caused him to develop a weird rap in the press because, I think, he doesn't like to promote himself, but he was a *joy* to work with.'

Both were the children of flower-children, from unconventional, Sixties-style families which had been constantly on the move. Neither had had much of a traditional education. But, for all his constant changes of address, school and stepfather, Keanu came from a comfortable background and his childhood and fashionably bohemian series of homes were a model of stability compared to the Phoenixes'. They had been involved with a religious sect, the Children of God, which was later accused of sexually abusing children. They had moved house forty times, including two years spent as missionaries in Venezuela, by the time Phoenix was seventeen. One reason why he and his sister had been pushed towards Hollywood was that the family was desperately short of money.

Van Sant picked up on this when he remarked that '*Idaho* is the story of a rich boy who falls off the hill and a kid on the street. I saw a bit of the hill in Keanu's personality and a bit of the street in River's. They played out those extensions of themselves.' Scott Favor, the wealthy, middle-class kid slumming it for kicks, was, the director admitted, drawn from life. 'Well, he's probably me. I can use my own background as an example for Scott's background, and I did sometimes with Keanu too. Keanu grew up with a well-off background himself and used that when he was figuring out how to play the part. We tried to work out who Scott was. At times he was maybe both of us, Keanu and me. Whereas River had a different background than I had and related more to Mike.'

Keanu had compensated for his lack of formal schooling by becoming an omnivorous reader. He had carried over this appetite for learning into his approach to acting. He would study a character almost as though taking a college course on him. 'If I sent him a book that had something to do with the film, he would read it right away,' said Van Sant, who fed his two stars different source texts: among Keanu's were *The Satyricon*, Petronius' classic satire on the vice and decadence of Ancient Rome, and *City of Night*, John Rechy's 1963 novel about drag queens and male prostitutes. 'Keanu would read

City of Night and then he would read three other books by John Rechy. And River would, like, not look at the first page of the book.'

Keanu built up Scott Favor through an accretion of small details, devising his clothes, his background – 'Once,' Van Sant remembered, 'he said he knew what house he lived in, he had chosen the neighbourhood he was from.' The actor imagined a personal history, with specific reasons why Scott and his father might have become estranged. Phoenix suspected (although the two did not broach the subject directly) that his co-star used elements from his own past in creating his character.

River, by contrast, plunged deep down the Method acting route, becoming Mike and living his life. 'He has this kind of Mozart quality of just burying himself completely in research,' Van Sant said. 'He does it through a sort of osmosis; everything you give him feeds into this plant that's growing out of the information he's got. He tape-records things, and talks to people; he has his own sources. It's more tactile: River will create something out of mixed media – films, writing, records, people talking, this whole wild thing.' Mike Parker, his real-life counterpart, found this total immersion a little alarming. 'He pulled out all the stops to get into his character,' Parker said. 'He found it so challenging that it took over his whole being. Maybe he just went a little too far.'

River was also keener than Keanu on improvisation and made one major contribution to the script (there are numerous differences between the film and the published screenplay, mostly details of dialogue or sequences which were cut or rearranged at the editing stage). This change was in the tone and the meaning of a conversation between the two characters by a campfire, during which Mike made an unsuccessful sexual overture to Scott ('Don't you ever get horny?'). The exchange, originally a brief three-page scene, grew to eight pages at River's urging: his discussions with Van Sant and improvisations with Keanu had convinced him that the difference between love and sex was the key to the film and to his character.

According to Van Sant, 'The way it was originally written, it was pretty much innocuous: Mike makes a pass at Scott very routinely because he's bored, he's in the desert.' In the final film, their encounter turned into a declaration of love. Mike answered Scott's statement that he only ever had sex with men for money with the rejoinder, 'I love you and you don't pay me.' The scene ended with (another new addition) a long and tender kiss.

Some, like Scott Green, saw the exchange as an expression not so much of gay love as of Mike's craving for an affection which he was otherwise denied. 'River thought his character loved Keanu because Scott Favor took care of him,' Green said. 'It was kind of his only family figure.' Even so, Mike, bisexual in the script (in which he had a sex scene with one of the female hookers), had now become, if not definitively gay, then at the very least a confused and lonely young man with strong gay leanings.

Keanu's character, on the other hand, had moved in the opposite direction. The film retained a snippet of dialogue from the screenplay in which Scott's father referred to his son as 'effeminate'. The word had been lifted from *Henry IV*, and Van Sant thought that in the Shakespearean context this was a reference not to the character's sexual orientation but to his youth – the fact that he had not yet reached manhood. All the same, at one point the director thought it might have worked well if that effeminacy had been carried over, in its modern sense, into Keanu's performance.

'There was always the question of why Scott Favor hangs on the streets, the attraction,' he said. 'In our movie version it became a sign of just revolting against his father, pushing away from the family. Another way to go about it would be that he had some interest down there; if he sleeps with guys, maybe he likes that. Maybe he's a gay kid who's attracted to that seamier street existence.' In that light, Scott's insistence on being paid for gay sex could be seen as a denial of his true sexuality: 'it came out of the paradox of people having sex with someone of the same sex yet refusing the label that this gave them'.

The actor also seemed a little uncomfortable with *Idaho*'s gay elements. He had had no problem with *Wolfboy*, a piece dealing with similar issues, but that was a fringe theatre production in Toronto six years ago, at the beginning of his career before he had to worry about anything as fragile as a star image. (Even today, no major Hollywood star is openly gay.) And this material was much more sexually explicit: one sequence involved a series of *tableaux vivants* showing three-way sex with a client (played by Udo Kier).

River tried to help him relax by joking, 'Just think, Keanu. Five hundred million of your fans will be watching this one day.' This remark, to Van Sant's horror, immediately had the effect of making Reeves doubly embarrassed, although he rallied sufficiently to complete the takes. Afterwards he said he didn't consider his role controversial because his character did not engage in anal sex, unlike River Phoenix's, and remarked elsewhere: 'I'm not against gays or anything, but I won't have sex with guys. I would never do that on film. We did a little of that in *Idaho* and it was really hard. Never again.'

Nonetheless, the part was still perceived as sexually ambiguous enough for a minor panic to arise when a glamour shot of Keanu heavily made up as a Japanese geisha girl, smiling coquettishly and holding his hair up on top of his head, appeared in the October 1991 issue of *Vanity Fair* magazine: the short caption commented on his 'controversial performance' in *My Own Private Idaho* which had 'raised more than a few painted eyebrows'.

It was a splash to worry his minders for several reasons. For a start, it was a reminder of just how oriental he could look when he chose to (and, moreover, anti-Japanese feeling was just peaking in Hollywood as a result of Matsushita's takeover of Universal a year ago and Sony's acquisition of Columbia-TriStar in 1989). Above all, it underlined the femininity of his delicate features and, according to one report, his publicists at the agency PMK, who had tried hard to kill the story, would rather not have questions raised over his sexual preference.

It was true that the homoerotic sex scenes sent some of Keanu's admirers scurrying for the exits (when it was released on video in the States, the sleeve artwork played safe by picturing the two co-stars each sporting a woman on his arm). Keanu declared himself unfazed. 'Every actor has his own battles,' he said, 'and mine right now is coming from a younger man trying to get more mature parts in cool films. *Idaho* is an example of "Keanu moving on", you know, a real cool part in a really great film. I heard some people in theatres were going nuts, just losing it, but I'm glad they were doing it not out of boredom. As long as they were confronted and challenged, then it's worth it.' And the film certainly helped swell the numbers of Keanu's gay fans.

There were other rumours. It was on *Idaho* that Phoenix was said to have first become seriously involved with heroin as part of his kamikaze mission to transform himself into Mike. The full extent of that addiction emerged three years later, when the actor died of an overdose. Keanu's friends in Toronto remembered him as having little interest in artificial stimulants as a teenager. 'I used to be into alcohol and drugs but when I met him I stopped,' Alan Powell said. 'Because as long as I knew him I never saw him do that. We'd go dancing in clubs a lot and when he got sweaty and ready for a drink, he'd order Coke rather than a beer.' However, Keanu had remarked himself that hash and LSD were freely on offer at school when he was in his early teens, and had later expressed curiosity about experimenting with drugs. 'I want to be on speed!' he had said in a much-quoted interview in 1990. 'I've never been on speed. I want to be a speed freak for a while. Is that a stupid thing to say?'

Colleagues on *Idaho* observed him picking up some bad habits. 'Keanu had some trouble, some serious trouble,' said Scott Green. The director Peter Hewitt, who inherited the actor a couple of months later for *Bill and Ted's Bogus Journey*, found him 'very tired. I always put it down to his not being sure whether the sequel was something he should be doing. But there could have been other reasons why he was strange and confused. All credit to him for making it through. But it was tough.' Whether it was the partying or simply his excessive workload, Keanu emerged from *Idaho* somehow disconnected from the films he was involved with over the following year.

On *Idaho*, too, he retained a core of inner discipline which seemed to make him more able to cope than Phoenix. When Matt Ebert, the production assistant, woke them both every morning by serenading them with show tunes, Keanu would rise promptly and wait down by the van, script ready in hand, but it was a much harder job to drag River from his bed. By the end of the shoot, Phoenix was drained. One journalist who visited the set described him as looking 'like crap ... He appears in dire need of a good night's rest, which the actor seems intent on getting, promptly collapsing on a bench.' River spent most of the day in a horizontal position, and it was left to a hyper Keanu to promote the film, albeit even less coherently than usual, to the visiting reporter. 'I thought it was an amazing script,' he said. 'Just in terms of narrative, man, there's cows, *bang! bang! bang!*, porno shops, salmon swimming, blow jobs, money-exchanging, and then I burst out in Idaho, *smash!* And then Shakespeare . . .'

Whatever happened on the set, when the film was completed almost all the acting kudos went to Phoenix, who won the Best Actor Award at the Venice Film Festival in September 1991. His role had become more prominent: the screenplay (which had originally started by introducing Scott) was now structured from Mike's point of view. Numerous subjective dream sequences elucidated his inner thoughts and feelings, while the revised campfire scene confirmed him as the film's emotional focus.

Van Sant might have been closer in background to the wealthy, privileged Scott, but his spiritual affinity was with the underdog and Mike was another of the appealing child-men that Phoenix had often played before, still sweet and soft with puppy fat. Scott came across as cold and hard, scorning and exploiting both his real father and, at the end, his adopted street 'family'. Keanu's insolent, ironic performance (unusually for his screen persona, which was on the whole open and unthreatening) had a dangerous edge to it. It was one of his cruellest characterizations.

The actor was aware of his character's selfish side, commenting perceptively, on the difference between Scott in *Idaho* and his counterpart in *Henry IV*, 'In the Shakespeare world, Prince Hal turned out to be a good king. To avoid internal strife he gets into these wars. All the dukes and lords were pretty happy because men were going off to die for a noble cause, and people were being fed. But in *Idaho*, Scott is not connected to the people. He's got his own agenda. He just dogs everybody and goes his own way. So he doesn't have the noble aspect. Perhaps that's what makes it a modern tale.'

The other reason why River scooped all the attention was that his was an impressively passionate and detailed, but much more conventionally naturalistic screen presence. With an Oscar nomination already under his belt (for Best Supporting Actor in the 1988 film *Running On Empty*), he invited, and earned, comparisons with classic Method actors like the

young Brando and, especially, James Dean whom, with his
raggedy quiff, he slightly resembled. 'His sublime performance . . . takes Dean's arithmetic into a dimension of calculus,'
hymned *Film Comment*.

Keanu was contrasted with him unfavourably by several
reviewers: a typical comment in the *Village Voice* said, 'Where
Phoenix vanishes with reckless triumph into his role, Reeves
stands, or occasionally struts, uneasily beside his.' But if
Keanu seemed mannered and theatrical in many of his scenes,
that was in large part because he had to be. Unlike Phoenix,
he had large chunks of mock-antique dialogue and even
several long soliloquies to deliver. He had to wrap his tongue
around lines like, 'You wouldn't even look at a clock unless
hours were lines of coke, dials looked like the signs of gay
bars or Time itself was a fair hustler in black leather.' It was a
performance in another key, and more suited in some ways
to *Idaho*'s surreal poetic register.

Keanu's acting was beginning to move away from the gutsy
realism of early films like *Under the Influence* and *Permanent
Record* towards a more detached screen presence. He was, of
course, playing different kinds of characters from the ago-
nized, exuberant adolescents he specialized in at the start of
his career. And he was also being cast by directors who had
higher artistic ambitions and were working in a more stylized
vein: Amiel, Van Sant and, later, Coppola and Bertolucci. But
his performances, even in an action role like Johnny Utah,
were also increasingly marked by a more deadpan, withdrawn,
almost secretive quality – a route he was to travel much
further down in work like *Little Buddha* and *Johnny Mnemonic*. Sometimes, as in the former, he was spectacularly

successful; sometimes, as in the latter, he fell flat on his face. It was the price he paid for taking a different and more difficult tack from his peers. Meanwhile, however, a familiar figure was hovering.

6

BOGUS JOURNEYS

It had seemed inevitable that there would be a sequel to *Bill and Ted's Excellent Adventure*, but setting it up had been tricky. The rights had lapsed with the demise of the original production company, DEG, and had to be renegotiated. More delicately, Keanu and his co-star Alex Winter were four years older and unlikely to want to return to playing a pair of juvenile (in both senses) under-achievers. The producer, Scott Kroopf, wooed them with the idea that the appeal of the characters did not spring from their youth. Bill and Ted were, he argued, a classic comedy duo, like Abbott and Costello, Bing Crosby and Bob Hope or Laurel and Hardy, and could continue to hang out together 'until they're senior citizens'.

Alex Winter, at least, bought the line. 'We were dying to make a better movie,' he claimed. 'We even kicked around the idea of doing a third one, something you could do with those characters being old, just milking their pathetic aspect and looking at what they would do in a world that beats the hell out of them' (indeed the second film, which featured Bill and Ted as slackers half-heartedly holding down McJobs in a fast food outlet and, later, as ageing, bewhiskered rockers, did exactly that). Keanu sounded slightly less enthusiastic, joking

that the main difference was that now they were old enough
to drink beer. When Gus Van Sant asked him what new
dimensions he had found to the character, he shook his hair,
Ted-like, and confided, 'Basically Ted is a lot dumber this
time.'

Part of the deal was that the two would be more actively
involved in developing the script. 'Keanu and I, the two
writers and the producer sat down and worked out a story
we thought we would really want to see,' Winter said. 'We
had a lot of story conferences. I had more control, more
power to deal with it.' The concept they came up with
involved sending Bill and Ted to Hell and Heaven – where-
upon the backers promptly took fright at the thought of
offending Middle America and asked for an alternative
scenario which would have Bill and Ted travelling into
famous works of literature and rounding up their protagonists
in order to pass their English exam.

This seemed to the writers and producers a boring near-
clone of the first film (and hardly consistent with an older
Bill and Ted, who had long since left high school). They
turned to the actors for support. 'Keanu and Alex were
terribly helpful to us; they were really like collaborators,'
Kroopf said. 'Actors hold tremendous sway in sequels and
when we were losing the argument a little bit we all went up
to Lenox, Massachusetts, where Keanu was performing in *The
Tempest*, and hashed out all the ideas.' The studio was
convinced and the original proposal prevailed, although the
title was changed from *Bill and Ted Go To Hell* to *Bill and
Ted's Bogus Journey* to avoid problems with television
advertising.

Stephen Herek, who had made the first *B&T*, was unavailable and the producers decided to go for a young first-timer who would be cheap and would have the energy to cope with what would be a punishing shooting schedule. After considering over fifty candidates, their eye fell upon a twenty-seven-year-old British film-maker named Peter Hewitt. Hewitt had recently left the National Film and Television School, winning a BAFTA (British Academy Award) for his graduation film, *The Candy Show*. Kroopf liked this short; it reminded him of a Terry Gilliam film and, even more persuasively, looked handsome on a tiny budget.

'It definitely brought a different perspective to the film,' Winter remembered. 'Pete's a British director with a British sensibility and the films that are in his lexicon are different from the films in Steve Herek's lexicon. He was influenced a lot by Michael Powell and it's very present in the movie. There's a European stamp on it and, I'd say, a decidedly British stamp on it as well. I was apprehensive about it at the start because the characters are so American, but Peter did a good job.'

Hewitt, for his part, enjoyed the rapport between the two actors. 'Often Keanu and Alex would sit around and just be Bill and Ted as other things, like as Holmes and Watson for instance,' he said. 'Sometimes it was X-rated Bill and Ted, too, which, again, was pretty funny. They both had a very firm grasp on it and were very professional.' But he also had the distinct feeling that Keanu would rather be somewhere else, very far away. 'While we were filming he would seem at times to be fine and having a good time, and then get very moody and broody. I'd be talking to him and he was smiling and really into it, and then there would almost be a click: you could see it in his eyes that he'd gone. I thought, "He's suddenly realized that we're talking about a Bill and Ted movie here." He didn't allow himself to get completely involved.'

Scott Kroopf disagreed with that perception. 'To some degree the people who represent him were reluctant for him to do it because they felt it was perpetuating an image they were trying to break. It was Keanu who wanted to make the second one because of the idea of working with Alex again and the general ambition of the movie, which was more of a challenge on an acting level. There was no money issue to speak of at all. The issue was, "Is this good for my career?" And ultimately I guess he and his managers felt that it was.'

But the timing had not panned out well for Keanu. He had signed up for three films which had wound up being made virtually back to back: *Point Break* had begun shooting at the beginning of July 1990, after which he had flown directly to *My Own Private Idaho* in September. Both had taken a heavy physical toll upon the actor. Now, before he had had a moment to catch his breath, Ted beckoned. 'I think he was pushing himself, or was being pushed too hard,' said Hewitt. 'We were supposed to start filming some time in September and it kept getting put back because of his schedule. He didn't have much of a break, certainly not enough for him.

'He was shooting pick-ups for *Private Idaho* in December, and then we started filming around 7 January. There were still residues of his characters from both those films running round in his head. There he was, trying to be a hustling FBI agent turned Valley surfer. He's very likeable, incredibly beautiful – you can just stare at him for hours – and charming. But it wasn't a particularly good experience. We got together after the film and I told him he was a pain in the arse.' Like John Mackenzie before him, Hewitt thought Keanu had been completely unaware of the problems he was causing. 'It came as a real surprise to him; he had no idea.'

Everyone was under pressure. Despite the late start the studio wanted *Bill and Ted's Bogus Journey* to be ready for the beginning of the lucrative summer season. It would, therefore, have to proceed at a fast lick, with the editing and special effects being worked on as the film was being shot. The script, too, had not been polished as brightly as it should. 'There was a very difficult, convoluted ending which we were always struggling with and was never quite right, but I went ahead and shot it anyway,' Hewitt said. 'Then, three weeks after the end of principal photography in March, we had a preview screening and it just didn't work. So we – me, the writers and the producers – had this summit to come up with another one, which we shot at the beginning of June, while I was finalling all the other reels. The premiere was 11 July. It was crazy.'

The film's complicated, indeed somewhat confusing, story involved a villainous conspiracy 'to totally kill' Bill and Ted by replacing them with two evil robot replicas. Sent to Hell, they encountered William Sadler as the sequel's best new character: Death, an ineffectual black-hooded individual modelled on the rather grimmer reaper in Ingmar Bergman's *The Seventh Seal*. After thrashing him at Battleships, Cluedo and Twister (the traditional game of chess was naturally a tad beyond the intellectual powers of Bill and Ted), they went to

Heaven accompanied by Death, now their new best friend, where they constructed two good robot doubles to fight the evil ones and return to Earth to restore the status quo.

The budget was about twice as large as it had been on the first, shoestring *Bill and Ted*, although part of this was swallowed up by the race to meet the deadline. 'They just chucked money at us to get it finished on time,' said Hewitt. But the money was also up there on the screen, in the elaborate designs and numerous optical and prosthetic special effects: Winter, to his great satisfaction, got to play Bill's grotesque ancient granny under seven hours of make-up. Hewitt (who appeared briefly in a supermarket scene, as a smoker to whom Death mutters, 'See you *real* soon') had the idea of uniting the numerous sets by a circular motif. The Michael Powell presence was evident in Heaven, inspired by Powell's *A Matter of Life and Death*, with its angels in military uniforms and (although they are barely visible) statues of that film's director and its star, David Niven, in the massive stairway.

Winter and Reeves had a ball as Evil Bill and Evil Ted, trashing their apartment, running down kittens in a stolen Porsche, slavering over the real Bill and Ted's princesses ('I gotta full-on robot chubby,' gasped Ted); it indicated what the two would be like if they weren't so lovably (and improbably) innocuous. Their images had evolved in a manner of speaking. Bill had acquired a perky back-to-front baseball cap; Ted's original pudding-basin tonsure had sprouted into a 360-degree curtain that covered his face like Cousin Itt's in *The Addams Family*. 'It's shorter in the back but longer in the front than the first film,' Kroopf said. 'So he went for kind of a sheepdog thing, which I have to say we took an incredible amount of grief from the studio for. They kept saying, "You can't see Keanu's eyes, you can't see his face, he's so cute, shouldn't we let everyone see him?" We said, "No, this is the new Ted Hair and we can't do it because it will blow his characterization."'

Aided by the Hair, Keanu had done a skilful job of concealing the strain he was under. But both performances seemed more exaggerated, self-conscious and knowing. The faintly disreputable, seat-of-the-pants quality of *Bill and Ted's Excellent Adventure* was a large part of its freshness and charm. While the new film was witty, stylishly directed and its reprobates were as irrepressible as ever ('How's it hangin', Death?' they would chirp. 'Catch ya later, God.'), they often seemed dwarfed and eclipsed by the huge sets.

'It was a very bold and interesting move to have them die, and go to Hell and Heaven, and you have to spend a bit of money on those kind of places,' said Hewitt. 'At the time it seemed like the right thing to do, but there's certainly a case in retrospect for thinking it would have been better to put Bill and Ted in a siege or a haunted house, to downscale it rather than blow it up into this huge thing.'

The film was reasonably well reviewed but, inevitably, failed to meet the backers' inflated expectations. 'It actually did pretty well, but it didn't do as well as everyone had hoped,' Hewitt said. 'It was expected to be a huge blockbuster, which it wasn't. So I think it left everyone feeling that it had somehow sort of failed.' But there was also *Point Break*, released in America the previous week, which had been panned by critics but was commercially buoyant. And, opening in September, there was *My Own Private Idaho*, which was already building up a head of steam as a *succès d'estime* and a cult movie.

Keanu had also somehow managed to squeeze in an appearance in the video for Paula Abdul's *Rush Rush*, in which, as an unconvincing James Dean figure, he re-enacted classic moments from *Rebel Without a Cause*. The back-breaking workload of the past few months was beginning to pay off: he was suddenly a celebrity. According to one newspaper, there was now an official word for his fans: 'Keanu-nunus'. Fortunately it didn't seem to catch on.

Perhaps, taken singly, the three parts would have had a lesser impact. Together, Ted, Johnny Utah and Scott Favor all made a striking showing. 'I have', wrote the critic Roger Ebert, 'seen Keanu Reeves in vastly different roles ... and am a little astonished by the range of these performances.' Janet Maslin of the *New York Times* was also impressed. 'Mr Reeves ... displays considerable discipline and range,' she wrote of *Point Break*. 'He moves easily between the buttoned-down demeanour that suits a police procedural story and the loose-jointed manner of his comic roles.'

Interviews were another matter. That July, on the heaviest, most intense promotional tour of his career so far, reporters consistently remarked on Keanu's scruffy, even grubby appearance, stained suede jacket, several days' growth of beard, uncombed hair, jeans matted with dirt and black fingernails. One writer commented that he looked 'more like one of the street beggars who loiter outside the hotel than a hot new star of the Nineties'. He began one group interview by belching into journalists' microphones, then imitating a fart. On stage with the cast of *My Own Private Idaho* at the New York Film Festival that autumn, he struck observers as not entirely sober, and at one moment spat on the floor.

Keanu was exhausted. And he was not altogether happy with *Bill and Ted's Bogus Journey*, the film he was supposed to be promoting. He had already been disgusted with the glut of crass merchandising which had been rushed out to cash in on the movies, pronouncing one toy 'garbage' which had nothing to do with the spirit of Bill and Ted. Later he described the sequel itself as a 'really bad experience. The film wasn't supported by the people who made it, the money people. Alex Winter and I fondly called it *Bill and Ted's Omitted Journey* because they cut out so much of the script.'

Hewitt reckoned that, while the film was generously financed, there was a cynicism towards it on the part of the 'money people' which the cast and crew found dispiriting. And turning an off-the-wall surprise hit into a formula franchise had become a bit of a chore. 'I suppose it wasn't supported in that they were trying to sell us the whole time. The joke on the set was, "If it's Tuesday it must be Paramount." One day the producer would turn up and say, "Looks like we're going to be at Paramount." The next day it was, "We may be bought by Fox." In the end they thought this was their big summer hit, so they kept hold of it. It was a business thing, whereas on the first *Bill and Ted* Keanu and Alex probably just ran around and had a ball and the film then became this inadvertent success.'

Alex Winter disagreed. 'Keanu doesn't like promoting films, ever,' he said. 'That's always his attitude. In fact we promoted the shit out of that movie. We sat in a hotel room and did seventy-five interviews back to back in two days.' While dutifully going through the motions of talking up his movie, Keanu was becoming impatient; on one occasion he ironically mocked the process of self-publicity, pretending to flag down an interview as though hailing a cab: 'Is there anyone I can talk to today? From *US* or *People* perhaps. Any animal periodicals I can do? Oh! I had an operation. Perhaps I can be in a medical guide, *Actors on Operations*.'

One reporter from the *Los Angeles Times*, after plying him fruitlessly with questions for forty-five minutes, was astonished to see the actor vanish onto the tiny balcony of his hotel suite, where he could be glimpsed through the white curtain windmilling his arms and swearing vociferously at himself to the puzzlement of passing pedestrians on the Beverly Hills boulevard below. Then he returned, rewound the tape and continued as if nothing had happened, saying by way of explanation, 'I'm a basket case, man. Look at me, man. I'm a basket case.' This was to become an increasingly frequent Reeves interview experience.

But everyone found him basically benign, in short a 'nice dude'. The same journalist was disarmed when Keanu confided that he was going to take home the complimentary sandwiches provided by the hotel, offering to share them. His anxiety became the key to his charm, a refreshing change from the smooth professional platitudes of other rising young Brat-packers. 'I don't want to be superfamous, man,' he said at this time, with apparent sincerity. 'That would be awful.'

That October Keanu hurtled directly into yet another major role, in Francis Ford Coppola's version of the Dracula myth.

He would be playing Jonathan Harker, the young estate agent who travels to Transylvania to close a property deal with Gary Oldman's sinister, mysterious Count. The other leading cast members were Anthony Hopkins as Van Helsing and Winona Ryder as Harker's fiancée.

It was Ryder who had initiated the project. She had had an uneasy relationship with Coppola ever since withdrawing at the last minute from *The Godfather Part III*, leaving the director without a leading lady. The two organized a reconciliatory meeting and, as Ryder was leaving, she gave Coppola a screenplay she thought might be interesting: *Dracula: The Untold Story*, adapted by James V. Hart – the writer of *Hook* – directly from Bram Stoker's 1897 novel.

Three days later Coppola called back in a non-committal way to say he liked the material and thought it might make a successful movie. Then he went off to Japan on a promotional tour for *The Godfather Part III* and thought no more of it until he received a phone call informing him that Columbia Pictures had decided to greenlight the film and was awaiting his return to direct it. Conceived as a low-budget piece for cable television, the production now had a $40 million price tag on it.

Coppola made no secret of the fact that he took on the assignment not as a labour of love but as a means of relaunching himself and his company, American Zoetrope, on an even keel. Ever since his experimental musical *One From The Heart* had bombed stupendously in 1982, Coppola had been lurching from one financial crisis to another (indeed he was to declare bankruptcy for the second time in three years in June 1992, only months before *Dracula* was due to open in America). This was a chance to secure the immediate future of American Zoetrope, and also to re-establish the director, a notorious over-spender in the eyes of the studios, as able to bring a bankable movie in on time and within budget.

Even so, Coppola, true to form, planned to approach the story on a highly unconventional tack. There would be copious special effects, but conceived in the naive manner of the early cinema (which was being invented even as Bram Stoker was writing his story) rather than using state of the art computer technology: small snippets were eventually shot with a hand-cranked Pathé camera made in 1905. The director wanted a stylized, shadowy, dreamlike film with minimal sets – and for a while even considered dispensing with these altogether in favour of slide projections. The emphasis, and the bulk of the budget, would be devoted instead to the costumes, for which he hired the Japanese conceptual artist Eiko Ishioka.

Above all, the movie was to be performance-driven; the director did not want its emotional impact smothered by the design and special effects. To this end, he convened the cast to his estate in California's Napa Valley, where they were required to participate in Victorian activities like hot air ballooning and to work their way through a thick rehearsal script which incorporated elements of Tai Chi, dance, improvisation sessions and other theatre games. 'We are looking for very *deep* emotional relationships and resonances in these characters,' Coppola noted in his journal. 'Make Gary, Winona and Keanu make very personal connections with these themes.'

Bram Stoker's Dracula, as the film was now known, was filmed entirely on Columbia's sound stages and reports soon began percolating through of rivers of blood in more senses than one. Things began badly when Coppola (who had been overruled by the studio over his plan to eliminate the sets) fired his star designer, Dante Ferretti, and hired a young art director to start from scratch just six weeks before shooting. Oldman and Ryder, the film's passionate lovers, did not get on. Nor did Oldman and Coppola, who on one occasion shut down the set because he thought his star was showing off. He also disapproved of Oldman's drinking (on one occasion the actor was picked up for drink driving, for which he received a reported six-month driving ban and eighty-nine hours of house arrest). Oldman had his own reasons to be miserable: he was experiencing serious allergic reactions to his heavy latex make-up.

One reason why Frank Price, the former chairman of Columbia, had approved the picture was that he liked the idea of '*Dracula* with young appeal'. But Coppola, for all his love of experiment, was at heart a traditionalist from the old Hollywood school, and his impressions of some of his cast, which also included Bill Campbell and Cary Elwes, was that the new generation of American actors was spoiled and temperamental. Keanu was going through a bad time too; the physical excesses of *My Own Private Idaho* were taking their toll. By some accounts he was close to collapse. Nonetheless, in the glossy book published to accompany *Dracula*, he gushed in approved Hollywood PR style, 'I've had some of the best days of my life on this film'.

The troubles rumbled on into post-production. Coppola's

journal described a rollercoaster of elation and despair. 'That was really one of the worst previews I had ever had,' he wrote after an early screening on 17 April 1992. By 15 May, he thought, 'It looks, for now, that *Dracula* will be a good film,' but on 17 July the skies had darkened: 'This is a time of desperation, I guess ... I have made a movie that looks like it's going to bomb both critically and at the box-office.' Five days later he added, 'We are on the cusp of disaster and of sublimity.'

On 2 September, after another hostile preview, he was trying to find a glimmer of hope in the total blackness. 'They [the audience] disliked it so much that it just might be a potentially great film.' But, interviewed three weeks before the American premiere, he was on a high again: 'There is no way this film is not going to make a fortune the first week it comes out.' Even so, by the time *Dracula* was finally ready, after reshoots in August and September, it had been recut thirty-seven times, had become far less radical than Coppola had hoped for (he later declared himself only '60 per cent' satisfied with the end product) and had picked up the nickname *Bonfire of the Vampires*, a reference to the previous year's spectacular megaflop, Brian De Palma's *Bonfire of the Vanities*.

But *Dracula* emerged blinking into the daylight (on Thanksgiving Weekend: Friday the Thirteenth of November) to packed houses and record business. 'It's one of the biggest fall openings in history,' said the member of a company which monitored box-office grosses. Nor was that first week-end a flash in the pan; the film continued to draw audiences for months afterwards, becoming *the* major box-office surprise of the year. Indeed, when it arrived in Britain in January 1993, Columbia – in an extraordinary step – pruned back its advertising budget by 25 per cent, realizing that there was no need for a hard sell. The gossip and publicity, combined with a media blitz of think pieces on vampires, Aids metaphors and most other things under the moon, had piqued the public's interest.

Though billed as the fourth lead, Keanu kept a low profile during the publicity junkets, which focused on Coppola and the three other stars. His collaboration with one of the world's premier directors, on a film explicitly intended to showcase the talents of its actors, had proved a severe disappointment; by his own later admission, his performance ranked among the worst of his career.

Part of it was the fake English accent, which, when imperfectly assumed by American actors, seems to have the effect of knotting their tongues. Partly it was the stuffy clerk he was playing – 'a very conservative man, a family man', in Keanu's description – hardly a character that the actor would be likely to find congenial. It was, in fact, an odd, almost perverse casting decision: Oldman, who was the first to admit he was not conventionally good-looking, was meant to be the seductive, sexually irresistible lover. Keanu, the babe magnet, played the dull cuckold whom Ryder shunned in favour of the vampire.

Indeed, he appeared to particularly unflattering effect alongside Oldman's baroque, even slightly hammy Dracula. In one typical exchange near the beginning, Oldman, sporting an extravagant pompadour wig and rolling Romanian accent, rhapsodized, 'I do so long to go through the crowded streets of your mighty land, to be in the midst of the whirl and the rush of humanity. To share its life, its changes, its death.' To which poor Keanu was required to reply primly, 'There! You, Count, are the owner of Carfax Abbey, Purfleet. Congratulations.' There was not a lot an actor could do with lines like that. To compound his problems, the character of Harker occupied a curious position in the story, starting out as the notional hero but then disappearing for a long stretch (at early previews audiences thought he had died) and ceding centre stage to the charismatic Count.

'The other actors' performances were so operatic, and I didn't hold up my end of the bargain,' Keanu said later. 'My performance was too introverted and closed-in and safe. I wish someone could have put strings to my arms and my face and made me go somewhere because I couldn't go anywhere. Since *Dracula* came out I've always felt that I could have played it much more aggressive ... I didn't act very well. I'll leave it at that.'

There was one good scene, in which he was ravished by three lascivious female vampires, who emerged like malevolent Venuses from the swirl of sheets on his bed. Then one, noticing his erection, sank her fangs into his genitals. It was a classic Keanu moment: much of the actor's allure sprang from his passive sexual persona – the way that, in his films, he was often the object of desire rather than the aggressive seducer. This little interlude summed that up to perfection (it was filmed, incidentally, by the second unit: Coppola, somewhat unfortunately for a story which took female desire as one of its main themes, had always been uncomfortable directing his actresses in erotic scenes).

Keanu had coasted through *Bill and Ted's Bogus Journey* on Ted's manic energy; here all the life seemed to be leeched from him. He had played buttoned-down characters before – in *Point Break*, for instance – with a good deal more charm, humour and energy. Here, waxen-faced and dead-eyed as if sleep-walking through the role or reading his lines off cue cards, he was spookier than the vampires. The reviews – which were kinder to the film itself than had been anticipated – did not spare him. 'Horribly miscast' (*New York Post*); 'a major stroke of miscasting' (*Philadelphia Inquirer*); 'pale and lifeless, he looks like a ghoul too, even though he's nominally the hero' (*New York*); 'so wanly out of it he seems to have had his blood drained already' (*Village Voice*).

It was possibly time for Keanu to cast his net outside Hollywood. Apart from his mid-Atlantic Jonathan Harker and the small role in *Dangerous Liaisons*, he had not had much truck with the European art cinema: he still tended to be seen as the ingenuous all-American youth. In 1990 he was asked why he had not yet made a film with someone like Antonioni. 'Oh yeah,' he replied mockingly. 'I'll just send them a tape of me going "Whoa! Bodacious!" Sure.' But he was definitely interested in working again in Europe.

One unexpected approach came from the French film-maker Jean-Paul Rappeneau, who had just scored a major international hit with his adaptation of *Cyrano de Bergerac*. His next project was Jean Giono's *The Horseman on the Roof*, a high-romantic historical novel about the unconsummated love between a young Italian and a French noblewoman in Provence in the 1830s. The male lead was impetuous, passionate and armed with a kind of fearlessness that made him immune from the cholera plague then cutting a swathe through France.

Rappeneau was having problems finding a French actor for this role, and his casting director suggested Keanu Reeves. The director was not familiar with his work but that evening he went to look at *My Own Private Idaho* and thought, 'yes, maybe'. He did not want to meet the actor at such an early stage, but called the States tentatively to check on Keanu's availability. 'We weren't expecting a reply at all,' he recalled. 'But the answer came back, "He'll be in Paris on Monday."'

He was taken aback by the speedy response. But throughout his career Keanu, unlike some of his peers, had shown little interest in developing his own material. He preferred to sit back and wait for offers – to which he would react quickly and with an open mind. At the moment he did not have too much lined up on the horizon and it was time to tout more actively for work. And besides, he had been wanting for some time to chill out in Paris and here was the ideal opportunity.

'He walked through the restaurant towards us, a strand of brown hair falling over his face, and it's true he made a strong impression on me. He wasn't only a beautiful young man; there was a child in him which you could still see,' Rappeneau said of their meeting. Keanu had not only managed to dig out an English translation of what was, outside France, an obscure novel, but had polished it off over the last couple of days. 'He said, "Well, I'm ready!" He was rather touching, a little like a mad dog.'

Rappeneau was taken by this keenness. But he was also worried about the language problem. Keanu had assured him

he would learn French for the role, but the director was sure
he would need to be dubbed. And he couldn't reconcile
himself to the idea of making an English-language movie
about an Italian man in nineteenth-century Provence: 'the
film would have lost its soul, I think'. Still, he kept Keanu in
suspense for a long time because his search for a French-
speaking actor was not going at all well. 'Three years went by.
We wrote to each other; he even sent me some faxes from
Kathmandu while he was filming *Little Buddha*.' But finally
Rappeneau made up his mind to cast a young Frenchman,
Olivier Martinez, and the opportunity to storm Europe was
gone.

Keanu now took a (by his standards) long sabbatical to
flush the previous year out of his system. It was not until the
spring of 1992 that he signed up for a small acting job – not
quite a European art movie, but a silly project that might be
fun to do – with his old friend Alex Winter. Unlike Reeves,
Winter had not parlayed Bill and Ted's brief blaze of fame
into a celebrity career. His first love was directing and he had
used the success of the films to talk MTV into signing him to
write, direct and act in a comedy series called *The Idiot Box*.

He had also been working on a film project, *Hideous
Mutant Freakz*, a savage, special-effects-heavy comedy about
a mad impresario who used a toxic fertilizer to mutate unwary
visitors into exhibits in his travelling freak show. Winter had,
for all his protestations of enthusiasm, also been a mite jaded
by life on the *Bill and Ted* bandwagon, and was, he said,
intrigued by the parallels between Hollywood and the
eighteenth-century travelling show, between being in show
business and being a freak.

Twentieth Century-Fox agreed to finance the picture, and, slightly to Winter's surprise, he found his name still possessed enough marquee value for the studio to insist he return temporarily to acting to play the lead, Ricky Coogan, an arrogant young actor who became the showman's ugliest specimen. In fact, Coogan could almost be a malevolent send-up of Bill: in the story he had become famous for playing a character whose catchphrase was 'Boo, dude!'

At the same time, Winter would have been only too happy not to have taken the role. 'Directing is so time-consuming,' he said. 'Acting under four and a half hours of make-up every day on top of it was extremely gruelling and painful. I'd rather have played a sideline character and had more fun.' His part was certainly the most arduous from that point of view. Randy Quaid accepted the other main role, as the sinister showman, but it did not require elaborate pros-thetics. Winter was able to recruit some celebrities for cameo appearances: Brooke Shields as a gushing talk show hostess, Mr T as a befrocked 'bearded lady', William Sadler, the Death Dude from *Bill and Ted's Bogus Journey*, as the oily chairman of a multinational corporation dumping toxic waste in the Third World – and Keanu as Ortiz the Dog Boy, leader of the freaks.

'Keanu's not in all that many scenes,' Winter pointed out, and indeed the Dog Boy scampered off after a squirrel mid-way through the film, and only resurfaced briefly towards the end. 'But he did have to go through an extraordinary ordeal, make-up wise, hours and hours, five hours. The make-up team didn't want to make a mask for him, they wanted to lay the hair on individually, so that it would really form-fit his face. And he was such a trouper: he would just come in and sit patiently and did a great job.'

Unrecognizable under a gleaming set of canines and thick coat of facial hair, Ortiz was what Winter described as 'this rabid, libidinous type who's all male sexuality'; Keanu said he based him on a slightly mind-boggling combination of 'Che Guevara, Fidel Castro and Tom Jones'. He was capable of scratching his head with his foot (which we see him doing) and also his balls (which we don't). 'Maybe people don't know who it is, but I wouldn't have wanted anyone else to play it,' Winter said, 'because it's just the kind of character he can do really well – a hyper-theatrical, Shakespearean rogue.'

The Dog Boy was hardly a *tour de force* of screen acting, but his make-up, as often with masks, seemed to liberate Keanu, allowing him to loosen up and lose the stiffness which had blighted his performance in *Dracula*; it was a very athletic part, and he looked as if he had fun doing it. His appearance was uncredited on the print of *Freaked* (as the film was eventually called), although he was featured on the video sleeve. Winter shrugged off suggestions that the role could be damaging for him: 'Nah, he does all kinds of crazy stuff.'

In any case, the film barely received enough exposure to dent Keanu's image. The extensive and elaborate special effects work took a year, by which time a new broom had arrived at Twentieth Century-Fox. Peter Chernin, who had succeeded Joe Roth as Head of Production, declared himself against dark movies like David Cronenberg's *The Naked Lunch* – which Roth had picked up for distribution – and *Freaked*. In October 1993, Winter's film was finally given the smallest of releases in a couple of New York and Los Angeles cinemas, without any advertising or even a press screening ('to find it you practically had to be psychic', wrote one reviewer) before proceeding straight to video. In the American print, cuts were made to Keanu's already brief role, including a scene in which he compered a grotesque game show, although it survived intact in the UK version.

The declared inspiration behind the film was *Freaks*, Tod Browning's classic 1932 movie about a circus midget who fell in love with a trapeze artist. But the tone of *Freaked* was quite different, owing less to Browning's compassionate vision than to the brash, cruel, scatological comedy of Tex Avery and Robert Crumb. The story took potshots at ruthless Western capitalism, but also mocked the politically correct brigade ('physical beauty is merely a socially enforced myth,' intones one character, before projectile vomiting at the sight of Winter in full freak regalia). The humour was fast, chaotic, surreal and puerile, but occasionally found its mark, and this, combined with the impressive prosthetics, secured *Freaked* a small following among body-horror fans.

It had, however, not been a vintage year for Keanu. His poor showing in *Dracula* was not in itself enough seriously to damage his career, but it certainly chipped at his credibility: the scornful references to his lack of acting ability began to gather force around this time. He had also made some choices which were, perhaps, commercially imprudent, turning down the role in the hit basketball comedy *White Men Can't Jump* which eventually went to Woody Harrelson and established him as a major star. Keanu had reached a low point – but he was to reinvent himself spectacularly over the next two years.

7

THE MIDDLE WAY

In 1992 Keanu finally got his wish to do a European art movie. Kenneth Branagh's film of Shakespeare's *Much Ado About Nothing* was based in the green hills of Tuscany, in the beautiful fourteenth-century Villa Vignamaggio where once, long ago, Leonardo da Vinci had been commissioned to paint *La Gioconda*. It would be shot in August, the height of summer, and one of the cast's missions was to acquire deep tans to give the film a sunkissed, Latin feel. It was a relatively painless baptism into the rigours of low-budget, non-Hollywood film-making.

On past form, the obvious casting for Keanu would be Claudio, the impetuous young count hoodwinked into thinking his virginal bride had betrayed him with another man. But Branagh wanted to keep a substantial age difference between the two couples who fall in love in the story. Benedick and Beatrice were to be played by himself and Emma Thompson, then both in their early thirties. His eventual choices for the younger pair, Robert Sean Leonard and Kate Beckinsale, over ten years their juniors, would be a better contrast than Keanu, who was nudging twenty-eight.

Besides, when Branagh was first approached by Reeves

(who made the initial contact), he had the distinct impression that the actor was not in the market for yet another juvenile lead. 'He had nothing specific in mind, but he knew *Much Ado* was on the cards and we met up when he was passing through London,' Branagh said. 'He never spoke about it, but it would be hard to have been unaware of the way he'd been bracketed, chiefly because of the *Bill and Ted* movies. Which I had always admired because it seemed to me they required a degree of real comic skill. But the perceived wisdom was that he had fallen into them and was a male bimbo type.

'He didn't seem bothered by it; I didn't sense an angry guy resisting this, just someone who wanted to play every variety of character and realized that, looking as he does and having a certain innocence as well – which some people confuse with a lack of intelligence – he would have to work hard to jiggle their imaginations a bit. It was clear that it would interest him much more to play something villainous than to play the more conventional romantic juve.'

Branagh was also a little surprised at the extent to which Keanu had done his homework on the play, which he had seen several times on stage (there was no modern film version). 'That was an impressive thing; there was no sense of "I am a Hollywood star coming to do you a favour because my casting might be important to the completion of the money" – sometimes you get that. It was a sort of passionate enthusiasm. He was quoting lines from the play to me over lunch, but without advertising his swottiness. He was very bright about it: not only the images and the structure of the language, which he did talk about with some technical knowledge, but also the general way in which the play spoke to him. He responded to it with some degree of poetic imagination.'

And so it was that Keanu ended up as the malevolent Don John, the character who seemed to hate everyone as a result of a mysterious feud with his half-brother (played in the film by Denzel Washington) and who engineered Claudio's near-tragic misunderstanding. It was his first Shakespearean role since his Trinculo in the Shakespeare and Company *Tempest*, and one that would be a good deal more in the public eye.

Branagh had planted American actors in several key parts, amid a mainly British cast, partly to smooth the film's path across the Atlantic; by some accounts he had come under strong pressure from his backers, the Samuel Goldwyn Company, to do so. Goldwyn Jr himself later joked about how it was so difficult to attract audiences to the test previews that the film was billed as a 'romantic comedy with Keanu Reeves', with nary a mention of Shakespeare. But the director also thought – as had Stephen Frears before him when casting *Dangerous Liaisons* – that the Americans would bring a breezy modernity to the play and 'blow the cobwebs off any potentially smug English Shakespearean acting from people like me'. It was decided that they would not strain for British accents, so at least Keanu would not be exposed to the ridicule he had suffered for his fake-English Jonathan Harker in *Dracula*. Another advantage for him was that Don John was the strong silent type (his first words were, 'I thank you. I am not of many words, but I thank you'). And much of the play was, unusually for Shakespeare, written in prose rather than verse.

Which was not to say that the part was a breeze. Keanu's

Shakespearean work was a regular target for criticism: a number of reviewers had fingered the *Henry IV* scenes as a weak point in *My Own Private Idaho* (and the attacks would be resumed with double vigour when he later tackled Hamlet). 'I made a couple of trips to America between that meeting and when we started shooting,' Branagh said. 'We had several sessions of weird vocal exercises. I encouraged Keanu to do some singing, which is very helpful for anybody who has suddenly got to sustain their breath during long sentences expressed with many words, and he practised some speeches while doing press-ups. He was up for all of that. His incredible keenness reminded me of an army cadet.'

There were other problems with Don John: he was, in his own words, a 'plain-dealing villain' without the psychological shadings of the great Shakespearean mischief-makers like Iago, for whom this was a pale prototype. 'I'm an unresolved character,' said the actor. 'I come in as a malcontent. I leave as a malcontent.' Indeed he disappeared from the action altogether about two-thirds in, only resurfacing fleetingly near the end. But Keanu applied himself to squeezing as much juice as he could from the slightly meagre role.

'It's a strange relationship in that play between these two brothers, it's not made terribly explicit as to why they hate each other,' Branagh conceded. On the first day of rehearsal, the entire cast gathered round the table and we started talking about sibling rivalry. One actor in the company had developed a terrible relationship with his brother over some will that had gone wrong and was challenged. 'Once the rehearsal was finished Keanu went straight to him and said, "Right, tell me all about this guy." His instinct for scavenging for what was underneath the role was very strong; he didn't just want to be a cape-swirling machiavel. It's not the biggest part in the world, but it was important that it was addressed in the proper way and he went at it from every direction.'

It had also not escaped Branagh's attention that Keanu would look mighty fetching in the leather trousers which the director had in mind for the younger male characters. 'Pretty tight,' he admitted later with disarming frankness. 'I'd pay money to see Keanu Reeves in leather trousers and I think a lot of other people would as well.' Moreover, Keanu was to play his first big scene, in which he hatched the plot against Claudio, stripped to the waist and being massaged with oil by one of his servants. But Branagh denied that the idea was to showcase Keanu-as-sex-god; after all, there was already plenty of nudity in the film before Don John turned up, in the early scenes where the villagers shower and prepare for the soldiers' arrival. 'We wanted the sensual circus of pleasure you have when guys who have been away at war come back and have this brief window in which to indulge their romantic instincts,' he said.

Besides, Branagh argued, Keanu's massage scene could be justified as helping to establish the character's narcissistic, overbearing manner. 'We wanted him to have a kind of languid pleasure in his own body, and in being served: he has two henchmen. Not being in his brother's position, he enjoys what power he has.' And anyway, why not avail himself of one of his actor's great assets? 'He has a gorgeous bod. It was hard to wander around Tuscany with him and not see the head-turning effect.'

Needless to say, when *Much Ado* competed at the Cannes

Film Festival in May 1993, the media fastened less upon the niceties of his character's motivation than upon the gorgeous bod. 'Do you prefer sex to Shakespeare?' was among the scholarly questions directed at Keanu at the press conference after the screening, and he gave the only possible answer. 'Yes,' he said, without a glimmer of hesitation.

By all accounts a high old time was had by all on location: there were wild and unsubstantiated rumours of on-set affairs, including one between Emma Thompson and Keanu, who was actually smitten with Kate Beckinsale though with little success. But his spirits seemed undampened. 'It amazed me that during the shoot he was very, very jocular and he mixed in, although his disposition might have been to be rather monkish about it,' Branagh said – Don John was, after all, the quintessential party pooper. 'He certainly embraced the fact that we did it a slightly different way, which was to be serious-minded but also to try and enjoy it and have a bit of a laugh at ourselves as we went.' Keanu himself was as enthusiastic about the shoot, if slightly less eloquent. '*Much Ado About Nothing* was like *Les Enfants du Paradis*,' he said. 'We had a place to eat, a place to sleep and a place to play as humans. We got to frolic in our joys and passions and everyone's humour was brought out with open hearts.'

As so often, the fun did not always spill over from cast to viewers, and some were exasperated by the film's unrelenting jollity. The decision, too, to relocate the action from Sicily, where the play was set, to the much lusher, more verdant hillscapes of Tuscany was thought to soften the story's dark undertones. Don John was a welcome antidote to all the manic bonhomie, and Keanu, swarthy and brooding in his trim black beard and, yes, skintight black leather trousers, was fine, though without the more subtle and ambivalent cruelty of Scott Favor in *My Own Private Idaho*, his only other major bad-guy role so far.

If, as some critics complained, he just scowled a lot, that was mainly what Don John was called upon to do. Any hostility British reviewers might have felt towards the American actors was largely deflected on to Michael Keaton's performance as Dogberry, the play's comic relief. And Branagh was successful in his mission to popularize *Much Ado* in that his film was a substantial box-office hit, grossing some $48 million worldwide.

Just before Thanksgiving Keanu flew to New York where Gus Van Sant was shooting the final scenes of *Even Cowgirls Get The Blues*, an adaptation of Tom Robbins' novel. Robbins had got the idea for his book from two sources. One was his interest in cowgirls. The other was *The Naked Ape*, Desmond Morris's influential work of pop anthropology, which put forward the theory that we are what we are because we use tools, which, in turn, is because we have opposable thumbs. The thumb is the symbol and cause of our human nature. Which is by way of explaining how Robbins came to make the heroine of his novel, Sissy Hankshaw, a cowgirl with outsize appendages.

If that sounded strange, it was only the half of it. Thanks to her thumbs' magical power, Sissy's adventures on the road included a spell in New York with various decadent Warholian trendies, an affair with an oriental mystic known as The Chink and an interlude at the Rubber Rose, a ranch-cum-health-spa run by a posse of militant lesbian-feminist cowgirls led by the feisty Bonanza Jellybean, with whom Sissy fell in love. Yet more subplots included Sissy's being hired as a model for the Yoni-Yum range of feminine hygiene sprays and the cowgirls' plot to abduct a flock of rare whooping cranes by drugging them with peyote.

Written in 1976, *Even Cowgirls Get The Blues* was originally published in serial form in a magazine called *High Times* and became something of a countercultural classic. Gus Van Sant read it then, and was drawn to it as one of the few modern, 'hip' novels with a female protagonist (there was also a curious personal connection: as a junior producer at a Manhattan advertising agency in the early Eighties he had worked on the account for o.b. sanitary tampons). At that point the rights belonged to the actress Shelley Duvall, who had written a screenplay with a view to starring in it herself (and would have made an intriguingly gawky Sissy Hankshaw).

By the early Nineties, Van Sant had acquired the rights and was wrestling with the screenplay: with its freewheeling structure, long, declamatory speeches and plethora of odd and eccentric characters, the novel did not lend itself easily to dramatization. Around this time, Keanu expressed an interest. 'We were talking at a party – it could have been a year before we filmed it, but he knew about the project,' Van Sant remembered. 'He'd already read the book. And he really wanted to play Julian. He demonstrated it – by jumping up on a table! And I thought, well, OK, he'd be great. That character was a problem in casting and he was one person that could be a second-generation Indian.'

Julian was, it was true, a full-blooded Mohawk Indian –

but a gentrified, Ivy League-educated, conservative-minded Indian living in Manhattan and well out of touch with his roots. In the novel he was a substantial character: Sissy married him and for a while became a housewife until she ran away, feeling trapped by domesticity. But Van Sant had always been more interested in unconventional, alternative communities than in straight nuclear couples. As he worried away at the script, shedding, he said, many of the characters and 'a lot of the more esoteric, whimsical scenes', the emphasis shifted to the Rubber Rose ranch and Sissy's lesbian affair with Jellybean. By the time filming began, after a series of false starts, near Portland in September 1992, New York and Julian had faded into the background.

Van Sant's reputation had been growing steadily on the back of *Drugstore Cowboy* and, especially, *My Own Private Idaho*. *Cowgirls* was to have marked his move to a major studio – TriStar – but when that fell through, New Line, flushed with the relative success of its involvement in *Idaho*, picked up the project and gave him a generous $8.5 million, by far the most money he had yet had to play with. He also attracted a colourful and eclectic cast. As Sissy, Uma Thurman was, once again, Keanu's love interest, if in a rather different context from *Dangerous Liaisons*; Bonanza Jellybean was played by River Phoenix's sister, Rain. Further down the list nestled such names as John Hurt, Buck Henry, Angie Dickinson, Crispin Glover, Lorraine Braccio, Ken Kesey, Udo Kier, William Burroughs and Roseanne Arnold. But others, like Elizabeth Taylor, Peter O'Toole, Faye Dunaway, Lily Tomlin and Madonna, all announced in early press reports as appearing in the film, had dropped by the wayside.

Although it had all the makings of a cult movie, like many a self-conscious cult before it *Cowgirls* flopped dismally when it saw the light of day. World premiered at the Venice Festival in September 1993, it got an emphatic thumbs down (as all the punning headlines could not resist putting it), and fared no better with North American critics shortly afterwards at the Toronto Festival.

New Line had just acquired a new boss: the cable television mogul Ted Turner, who had bought the company that August. This, combined with the adverse press reaction, convinced them to pull the film abruptly from the American release that November, even though a full-scale publicity and marketing campaign was already in place, including a tie-in album by k. d. lang and Ben Mink, who had written the soundtrack. The press release said, in typically bland PR-speak, that Van Sant was being given the chance to 'get some distance from the project' and make another pass at it.

It was May 1994 before *Even Cowgirls Get The Blues* finally hit American cinemas, by then about ten minutes shorter. It was liked no better. Even publications which might have been assumed to be sympathetic towards the material, like the *Village Voice*, found it 'basically an increasingly dull series of riffs against an intermittently busy background'. Most of the cuts nibbled away at the character of The Chink and his pseudo-mystical maunderings, although Keanu's appearance, already brief to begin with, had suffered too.

His prominent billing in the opening credits as one of the stars of the movie bore no relation to his role in the final film, effectively no more than a cameo. In his first scene, absurdly resplendent in long sideburns, a floppy bow tie, tartan tuxedo and gold cummerbund, he met Sissy on a date in a New York hotel but was so excited by the sight of her that he succumbed to an asthma attack, falling asleep after a paroxysm of coughing and wheezing. Later, after she had been ravished by some of Julian's friends at his apartment, they exchanged a few words before she hit the road again. And that – apart from a facetious sequence in which Sissy, masturbating in a field, had a vision of his face shimmering down at her from the sky – was the extent of his role. Two additional scenes in the published screenplay, a discussion of Sissy between Julian and the transvestite countess who had introduced the couple, and a farcical love-making interlude, had not made the final cut.

Keanu had no need to worry: he had not been excised from a masterpiece. There were many reasons why the film did not work. Partly, as Van Sant himself tacitly acknowledged, it was that Sissy remained something of a cipher. 'You are experiencing things along with her, but they're not necessarily told from her perspective,' he said. '*Mala Noche, Drugstore Cowboy* and *My Own Private Idaho* are definitely films that are told through the characters' eyes. Less so with Sissy. She's an object that you're watching as opposed to someone you're watching the world through.'

Partly, it was the novel's long speeches, a number of which Van Sant had transferred wholesale on to the screen. 'I saw he was trying to be too faithful to the book,' said Robbins himself, who took an interest in the project and who narrated the movie. 'I said from the beginning, "Gus, it's your baby, take it." I kept telling him, "It would be a mistake to make a Tom Robbins movie, you should make a Gus Van Sant movie and just use my material as a springboard." He didn't really take that advice . . . I think he made the mistake of taking too much dialogue from the book.'

Most of all, though, the problem was the story's dated, Seventies-style lesbian-separatist feminism; the film (set, like the novel, in 1971) was either, as its few fans maintained, ahead of its time, or else several decades too late. Its free love ethos struck a hollow note in the era of Aids, as did the drug-happy hedonism, only underlined by the dedication to River Phoenix who had died of these excesses the previous autumn.

That same year Keanu played another ethnic-minority character, a part which also, to its director, had seemed impossible to cast: perhaps nobody other than he could have played it. There, however, the resemblances between *Even Cowgirls Get The Blues* and Bernardo Bertolucci's *Little Buddha* definitely ended. Bertolucci had made his name in the Sixties and Seventies with enigmatic, cerebral art movies like *The Spider's Stratagem* and *The Conformist*, but had now changed tack and was attempting to cast his net wider with a series of exotic extravaganzas like *The Last Emperor*. The new film, the fruit of a long fascination with Buddhism, would also have a generous budget ($35 million). And it was to be his most accessible movie yet, a story even a child would understand.

There would be two strands: one, set in the present day, focused on a small American boy from a middle-class family who was thought to be the reincarnation of a respected lama. The other strand would travel back 2,500 years to the early life of Siddhartha, the young prince who became the Buddha. Kept locked up, Last Emperor like, by his father inside the luxurious cloisters of his court, he slipped away early one morning to search for spiritual enlightenment. And, after travelling through a dark night of the soul, he discovered the Middle Way: a life of moderation between licentiousness and asceticism.

The big question was: who would play Siddhartha? Bertolucci had gone to India to trawl through shoals of actors, from theatre groups and even amateur dramatics societies. 'We looked for at least three or four months, which is practically the whole pre-production period,' he recalled. He had eventually offered the part to an Indian actor, Rahul Roy, who turned it down because of prior commitments. He was getting desperate when he saw Keanu tackling tricky, stylized material in *My Own Private Idaho* and read about his mixed bloodline. 'The whole visual code of the Indian sections was inspired by the iconography that you see in India in any tobacconist's: Shiva, Krishna, the gods and goddesses. These images are between East and West; they're not completely Indian, they're a kind of popular vision of angels. And I thought that Keanu, because of his Canadian-Hawaiian origins, had that.'

They met in Manhattan. 'It was so strange to meet Siddhartha in a hotel on Central Park South,' said Bertolucci, amused by the idea of finding his dream, after so many travels, so relatively close to home. 'He obviously wanted the part because he arrived dressed in a way I've never seen him dressed since. He was wearing a suit and tie. I guess he thought I was an old European academician. He was shy and not too articulate, and he blushed a bit and occasionally burst into nervous laughter. He was adorable and I was very taken.

I knew people would find this an outrageous choice. How can Keanu, the idol of American teenagers, be Buddha? I tried to put such things out of my mind.

'As soon as we met I was struck by his extreme openness. I didn't know if his inner life was complicated or not but his face, his eyes and his movements revealed the most perfect innocence. Imagine a young man who has never left home, who does not know the meaning of the words "old age", "sickness" or "death". Siddhartha was as innocent as that and Keanu convinced me he could be that person.' He would also be, coincidentally, the same age (twenty-nine) as Siddhartha had been as he began his quest at the moment when the film was released.

Keanu knew nothing about the history of Buddhism, but was fascinated by Bertolucci's story-telling skills, and his passion. At that point the director was still toying with the possibility of using an Indian actor, but when Reeves went off to Tuscany to shoot *Much Ado About Nothing* he took with him some books about the Buddha, just in case. The two talked again twice in Rome and finally he got the call to say he had the part. 'I shouted with joy,' he remembered.

Bertolucci did not state the obvious: unlike the Indian contenders for the role, Keanu would be a substantial box-office attraction in America. That, for him, was an unexpected bonus; he had never considered any other young Hollywood actor. It had occurred, though, to the producer, Jeremy Thomas. 'It was a terribly difficult and long decision. The immediate reaction is, you cast Keanu because he's Keanu. After all, you want as many people to see the film as possible,' Thomas said. There was a potential downside: resistance in

India both to the general idea of a film about the Buddha as well as to Keanu in particular. 'I remember that when I was going through Bangkok on the way to the location, the air stewards and people in the streets asked me what I had come to do,' the actor said. 'I told them, *Little Buddha*. "Really, and what role are you playing?" "Prince Siddhartha." Each time their mouths dropped open. I read their surprise in their eyes.'

On site, the title was changed temporarily to *Little Lama* so as not to offend strict Buddhists. Even so, some threw stones and there were a few demonstrations. But these were isolated incidents. 'There was a group of people who didn't agree with the idea of a film being made in Nepal about Siddhartha,' Thomas explained. 'There's still a big controversy about whether Siddhartha lived in Nepal or India, so we had some problems. But that didn't involve the casting of Keanu. We never had any local problems with that.' Indeed Thomas, an old hand at shooting in difficult places, had taken the precaution of going to the top and securing the blessing of the Dalai Lama before production began. Whenever anyone wrote objecting to the project, he simply whisked his ace out from up his sleeve and mailed them back a copy of the Dalai Lama's letter saying that there was nothing wrong with a Western director and a Western actor making a film about the Buddha if there was illumination in their hearts.

Little Buddha was shot in Seattle and the remote Himalayan kingdoms of Bhutan and Nepal. Bhaktapour (Bhutan), four-teen kilometres east of Kathmandu, on the roof of the Himalayas, was a beautiful and spectacular area virtually closed to the West. The northern border with Tibet was sealed off too. Conditions were primitive: no cars, no running water, little electricity, only one tiny airstrip. The entire Bhutanese phone directory was only six pages long, and listed the king's official apartment numbers. Television had once existed briefly there but had been abolished ten years ago for cultural reasons.

It enabled Keanu to find a welcome anonymity. 'The place we were staying in was a timber guest house perhaps a mile from the main location across these paddy fields,' recalled Chris Auty, a member of Thomas's production team. 'After work we'd get into the crew bus that took us back from the location. And halfway up the hill there would be Keanu in his Buddhist robes and his big clumpy Timberland boots with the laces half undone, talking to the local children and with a dog or two in tow, because he liked to have the walk there in the evening light. Incredible, really, in a world where people expect to have their motorized trailer home.'

Nepal, by contrast, was Westernized and chaotic and Keanu was besieged by young girls seeking his autograph: they had seen him on video in *Point Break*. Here, there was no escaping his celebrity. 'He took their breath away,' remembered Bertolucci of local reactions to his star. 'We had a little poll in Nepal to find out who was the most beautiful person on the set.' No prizes for guessing the winner. But, the director added, 'there was one problem: he was a bit too thin. One of the qualities of beauty in the East is to be fat because it means you're rich. But because he had to prepare himself to be the ascetic Siddhartha he was already losing weight. So that was the only thing they maybe didn't find completely accurate.'

Rejecting Bertolucci's suggestion to find a body double for scenes in which a dramatically reduced Siddhartha emerged from a six-year fast, Keanu launched himself on a crash diet of oranges and water. 'I fasted throughout the duration of the shoot, which made it hard to keep my energy up, but I loved how I felt – I called it the white zone. I wasn't sleeping much and my mind was very active – I felt like I was sticking my finger into an electric socket. I dreamed about bread and cheese and had fantasies of pouring wine on my head while I rolled naked in the dirt. The appetites I quelled – not vanquished but quelled – returned with a vengeance when I quit fasting. My desire for chocolate was ferocious.'

Trickier than his physical appearance was Siddhartha's way of speaking. 'About thirty hours before I was due to utter my first words, Bernardo said, "I think Siddhartha should have some kind of accent." The accent that I've developed, it's kinda Indian–English–American,' Keanu said. The end result was fairly convincing without sounding like Peter Sellers. He also learned about meditation and studied with the film's technical adviser, Dzongsar Khyentse Rinpoche. A little while before shooting began he had gone on a first visit to India where he saw a cremation, on the banks of the Ganges. As the body burned, children and monkeys played and life generally bustled on around it. He felt something of the interconnectedness of birth and death and was greatly impressed by this mixture of celebration and suffering.

Keanu was drawn to many aspects of Buddhism, especially its disregard for impermanent material possessions. His itinerant childhood had left him with little interest in these and indeed later, at the very moment when *Speed* made him financially able to buy a spectacular villa, he voluntarily became homeless, basing himself in a series of hotels and taking pride in living out of a suitcase. He discoursed enthusiastically in interviews about the ideas behind the film and there were the inevitable tabloid reports that he had become a Buddhist. But he resisted the temptation that many a Hollywood New Ager had yielded to before him, and drew back from embracing it as a religion. 'I realized that, in order to continue being an actor, I couldn't do that. But there's certainly the attraction to go over the hill and become a yogi. I mean, the higher lamas like Khyentse Rinpoche . . . He's venerable. You'd go to the town and the leader of the army prostrated to this man,' said Keanu adding (momentarily slipping back into Ted mode), 'and I'm going, "Hey, man, how's it going?"'

Just as Ben Kingsley had been attacked twelve years earlier for playing Gandhi and had emerged triumphant, so did Keanu. In the early scenes he was a magnificent beast – and almost unrecognizable – with his fabulous costumes, long black curls and kohl-rimmed eyes; he had read a Buddhist poem comparing Siddhartha to a lion and tried to give his movements a sinuous, leonine elegance and power. 'When I come out of the gates, I look like Cleopatra,' he later said of the sequence in which he processed in state through the streets of his kingdom. A joke, but also true: he had the fabulous, unworldly glamour of an old-time Hollywood star. He wore six different wigs in the course of the picture and went through some startling physical transformations.

The scene in which Siddhartha became a hermit gave a spooky glimpse of a ravaged Keanu, gaunt and bearded with matted hair. At the end, beatific and enlightened, he radiated a blissed-out peace, despite conditions that would try the patience of . . . well, a Buddha. 'We had real trouble with that sequence,' Auty said. 'It was difficult to light and there were constant problems with getting the monkeys to appear in the tree. It was bloody uncomfortable for Keanu. He was sitting in the lotus position which is very difficult when you have long shins. What was incredible was his patience. We must have been under that tree for at least a week, but he managed to keep that stillness take after take after take.'

Nobody was nominating him for an Oscar (although his performance was, as so often with Keanu, a good deal more difficult to pull off than he made it seem). But, while he could have looked a complete fool, critics who had come to scoff at the Valley Boy as an Eastern mystic packed away their Ted jokes and went away reluctantly impressed. 'It was a dangerous role for him, and he pulled it off with grace. In a state of grace,' said Thomas. *Time* magazine wrote of Keanu's 'improbable persuasiveness' and *Variety* thought he made for 'a surprisingly watchable and dashing Siddhartha'.

The film itself drew a mixed response. Some took its simplicity for simple-mindedness, or found its imagery borderline kitsch: in fact the design deliberately drew not only on popular Indian art, but also on the stylized orientalism of Alexander Korda and Powell and Pressburger's films. If anything, the contemporary storyline looked dull and insipid compared to the sumptuous imagery of Keanu's scenes – a thinness amplified by Bertolucci's decision to shoot the American segments drenched in a harsh blue light and on 35 mm, as opposed to the 65 mm used for the ancient sequences. These had a noticeably richer colour and superior definition, as though the legend were more real than reality.

Little Buddha was released first in Italy and Germany, after which Bertolucci decided to re-edit it – which was to say, cut it, by about eighteen minutes – for America; he later said he preferred the shorter version. There was a minor irony in the way it was marketed there. It arrived in May 1994 after a campaign highlighting the film's mystery and the arthouse cachet of Bertolucci: newspaper ads carried an image of the small blond American boy surrounded by robed Indian Buddhists and the copyline, 'From the creator of *The Last Emperor* comes a magical journey to a place where the past and present meet.' But when *Little Buddha* opened quietly, and when Keanu's next film *Speed* broke spectacularly that June, Miramax, the distributor, quickly changed its tune. A new series of ads pictured Keanu bare-torsoed, braided hair cascading over his shoulders, with the slogan, 'Keanu Reeves, the summer's most explosive star in the season's most dazzling spectacle!'

Keanu regarded himself as, above all, an actor, and liked to submerge himself in his roles: it was this humility in his approach to Siddhartha which had enabled him to carry off the character with dignity and conviction. After *Speed*, however, he had moved on definitively to high-profile celebrity. And *Little Buddha*, a film about a holy man who preached the subordination of the ego, and who passed his life in obscurity, was being sold on the sex appeal of Keanu as a Hollywood superstar.

8

IN THE FAST LANE

The next year was a watershed for Keanu, professionally and personally: it brought him success greater than he had known before, but also anxiety and sadness. It began when a thriller called *Speed* came his way, about a bus boobytrapped to explode if its speed dropped below 50 mph. The script, by Graham Yost, a writer with no previous movie credits (his resumé included the television series *Hey Dude* and articles for the *Encyclopaedia Britannica*), had been languishing at Paramount, which eventually shelved it. It was picked up by Tom Jacobson at Twentieth Century-Fox and now had another unknown quantity attached: Jan De Bont, a Dutch-born cinematographer.

De Bont had begun his career in Holland with the director Paul Verhoeven, whom he followed to Hollywood to shoot *Basic Instinct*. There, he accumulated a great deal of experience on successful adventure movies like *The Jewel of the Nile*, *Lethal Weapon 3*, *The Hunt for Red October* and *Die Hard*, and had begun to supervise the shooting of action scenes in some of them, for instance the blowing up of the building at the beginning of *Lethal Weapon 3*. But he wanted his own movie. He had already tried to set up one project, *Drop Zone*, but was caught in a classic vicious circle: the studio demanded a star name, but no agent in Hollywood wanted to entrust his major clients to a new director (the film was eventually made by John Badham with Wesley Snipes). Now he was trying his luck again with *Speed*.

Keanu hesitated briefly, like the others before him, but for different reasons: his heart was with more idiosyncratic movies and he was dabbling with the idea of appearing in a friend's film as (in his own description) 'Apollo, Dionysus and Bacchus'. He would also be the first actor to sign on for *Speed*. Another possible worry was that De Bont might be a competent hack who understood the mechanics of the action movie without bringing to it the creative spark which would make it come alive.

However the project looked commercial and it was three years since Keanu had carried a major box-office hit. Taking on an action movie was becoming a popular power gambit for actors keen to bump up their asking price and attract better roles: hence Bruce Willis' presence in the *Die Hard* pictures or Ray Liotta's in *No Escape*. 'I would love to get the roles that Harrison Ford gets,' Liotta said, of his reasons for taking on that film. 'Or Nick Nolte. De Niro. Pacino. But to get to that level you have to be in movies that are hits, and a lot of the time that has to do with violence and action.'

Such was the pragmatic thinking behind Keanu's decision to do what was known around town, slightly scornfully, as the 'bus film'. Less rationally, he was drawn to the title, with its ambiguous, druggy connotations. And when they met, De Bont was able to convince him that he was genuinely excited by the project. His work seemed stylish to Keanu (who later eulogized the director as a 'beautiful warrior master'). He liked the constantly moving camera, the vibrant colours and small touches such as his way of framing actors in low-angle shots (a mannerism that would also be in evidence in *Speed*). De Bont preferred to operate the camera personally, staying behind the viewfinder even when working as a Director of Photography – a practice outlawed in principle by the unions in Hollywood. It was this which helped give his films a distinctive visual signature.

De Bont was taking as big a gamble in casting Keanu – who hardly had a track record as this kind of character – as a young SWAT agent who boarded the runaway vehicle and saved the day. But he had checked out his performance in *Point Break*, the closest approximation in his career to an action role, and liked what he saw. Besides, he had already worked with old hands like Mel Gibson and Bruce Willis and wanted a fresh face. Keanu, he thought, combined a physical presence with a quality that none of the more obvious choices could match. The gentleness which other directors had already seen in him could be made to work in his favour, even in this unlikely film.

'What makes him stand out is that he dares to let emotions show,' De Bont said. 'He has a vulnerable quality – if you had a daughter you'd let him take her out. A little old fashioned, chivalrous. We've had enough cartoon-type action heroes.' The success later that year of Meryl Streep in the whitewater rafting drama *The River Wild* suggested that film-goers, particularly women, were bored with macho superheroes and ready to buy another kind of protagonist. Keanu appealed to a different, but adjacent gap in the market: the only other action star to make a serious attempt to position himself as a sexy, sensitive, romantic type, Jean-Claude Van Damme, had singularly failed to cross over to a female audience.

Keanu's age – he would be twenty-nine that year – was another factor: it was time for him to quit once and for all playing mixed-up, rebellious kids. At the same time his relative youth still gave him a real edge over more established action heroes, most of whom were beginning to look a mite long in the tooth: Arnold Schwarzenegger (47), Mel Gibson (38), Sylvester Stallone (48), Bruce Willis (39), Harrison Ford (51) and Steven Seagal (44). Action pictures with plausibly young protagonists were thin on the ground. And he was a snip compared to Schwarzenegger and Gibson: his asking price was then in the region of $1.2 million. 'Keanu was not at that time a big star,' De Bont recalled. 'Not in the United States. He was well-known but he had never done a movie that really made it big, apart from *Bill and Ted*, which was considered a freak success.'

The next action hero was regarded at first as a joke: *Speed* was informally and unflatteringly known as *Die Hard Four and a Half*. De Bont, however, defended his choice. 'Keanu's heard too many times that he's not taken seriously,' he said. 'But he's worked with Bertolucci, with Coppola. Acting for him is a very serious thing.' Meanwhile the actor was busily applying himself with due seriousness to his new image. The hair, as ever, was crucial: Keanu wanted it short, and De Bont, keen that he not look too boyish, agreed. The studio was horrified when he returned from the barber's shaven-headed. But by the time shooting began two weeks later the hair had grown to a dramatic and elegant buzzcut.

He also took gymnastics classes to improve his balance and agility, and did weights training for his body tone. By the end, he had gained 30 lb of muscle, though without ever approaching mega-macho proportions. 'I wanted him to get big,' the director said. 'But I didn't want him to be one of those action heroes with giant muscles.' And he slightly alarmed De Bont on the set by performing some of his own stunts.

It was eight weeks into filming when River Phoenix died from a drugs overdose after collapsing on the pavement in front of the Viper Room, a nightclub in West Hollywood co-owned by Johnny Depp. The coroner's report found in his body a cocktail of morphine (thought to have been heroin when it entered his blood), cocaine, Valium, traces of marijuana and cold medication. He was twenty-three. Keanu was shocked and stricken. 'He became very quiet,' said De Bont, 'and it took him quite a while to work it out by himself and calm down. It scared the hell out of him.' The director did not postpone the shoot – that would be prohibitively expensive and besides it seemed best to keep his star busy – but he did reorganize the schedule around the actor. 'He said it was a good idea to keep working but he did need a lot of time to himself. He wandered about a lot.'

As the media descended to canvass tributes, Keanu declined to comment. He 'prefers to be quiet', said his publicist in response to enquiries. 'He's a kind of quiet person, anyway, and this is his way of dealing with it.' Hollywood was closing ranks against Phoenix. While in some quarters his fast living had lent him a mythic aura, causing all the James Dean

comparisons to be wheeled out again, to others he looked
more like a junkie who had it coming. But Keanu's silence at
the time was not an act of rejection: he had been genuinely
and deeply upset by his friend's death. 'I think of it as an
accident. I can't make sense of it,' he said while promoting
Speed the following summer. He did, however, eventually
become irked and insulted by the constant probing, and by
journalists' assumptions that he would make a show of grief
for them upon demand. 'I still have people asking about River
in an interview when they have three minutes,' he said two
years later. 'It's like, "Tell me how you feel." And I'm
astounded because they want to have a moment of seeing
whether a person's affected or not. It's the form which is so
completely disrespectful and inconsiderate.'

Keanu also remarked that, in all his years on movie sets, he
had never seen any signs of drug abuse. 'None. Really,' he
insisted. 'That's why Bernardo [Bertolucci] hired me. Because
of my innocence.' It was a claim which was, to say the least,
surprising given the reports which had filtered through from
My Own Private Idaho and John Mackenzie's memories of *Act
of Vengeance*. Clive Donner had the impression that soft drugs
were being used, around the same time, during the production
of *Babes in Toyland*, in which Keanu had co-starred with the
former wild child Drew Barrymore. 'I know that there was a
lot of smoking off the set,' he recalled. 'I said, "Don't ever
come to work and do it." And they didn't. As long as they
showed up and worked I didn't care and didn't want to
know.' Erwin Stoff, his manager, eventually commented on
the matter: 'Keanu was as wild as anybody. Like the rest of
us, he experimented,' he said, but emphasized that by the

time he came on to *Speed* he was clean. 'He loves acting. And you don't do the kind of work he has done unless you put the past behind you.'

That assertion was supported by another source, a childhood friend of Keanu's from Jesse Ketchum who visited him for a few days in 1994 and who told his former teacher, Donald Mason, that 'there were a lot of people hanging around Keanu that were sort of sponging off of him in one way or another. Some of them were into drugs and stuff like that, but Keanu apparently was pretty clean.'

The last word on the subject, however, is an ambiguous remark made by the actor two years later: 'Heroin goes in and out of fashion. It is numbing. And when you stop feeling, you can't feel other people's pain. I wouldn't suggest it for a politician or clergy, but it is an environment that has created some great music and art.'

When *Speed* was completed, it turned out that Keanu did not have much chance to display his newly toned pectorals: for a change, he did not get to take his shirt off once. Nor did he dispatch regiments of baddies; the final body count was in single figures – indeed, when the bus finally collided with a plane, both of them were empty. The number of vehicles crashed, however, ran into the hundreds. De Bont concealed the lack of corpses with a clever sleight of hand, constantly setting the audience on edge for carnage which never happened. Minor characters were dispatched in early scenes, making viewers assume that they were to be the first of many; a mother and her pram appeared in the path of the bus, only for the pram to be revealed as full of empty cans.

One reason why action pictures were increasingly falling

foul of the anti-violence lobby, in Britain and America, was
the comic strip factor. In many of them the bloodshed,
besides being plentiful, was also ironic, camp, self-mocking;
the hero would blow away the villains with a smirk and a
quip. But the wisecracks that had spattered the original script
of *Speed* had been eliminated, partly at Reeves' insistence.
One remained (Keanu's comment, 'He lost his head,' after
the bad guy, played by Dennis Hopper, was decapitated), and
it stuck out like a sore thumb: cynicism did not become him.
'I wanted to give my character of Jack Traven some sort of
Everyman quality,' he said. 'I wanted him to be good,
altruistic, imaginative, experienced in special weapons and
tactics. I was more interested in those qualities than in just
being another artificial hero.'

He fired a gun just once, and then not to kill; on the
contrary, he shot his partner, played by Jeff Daniels, in the
leg to save his life. 'Jan didn't want gratuitous violence in the
film and it doesn't fetishize gore,' he said. 'It plays instead on
very real human anxieties – the fear of elevators, buses and
public places. It's a film about suspense, movement and
physical speed.'

Much of *Speed*'s appeal, especially to women, also stemmed
from the fact that Keanu did not run the show. He was often
dependent on Sandra Bullock, playing a passenger who had
to take control of the bus when the driver was disabled. In
that sense *Speed*, for all that it was a slick, fast-moving
adventure movie, fitted in perfectly with Keanu's gentle,
brooding image. He was the first passive action hero.

His character was also refreshingly uncomplicated. The
loner haunted by his past and his difficult relations with

women, like Mel Gibson in the *Lethal Weapon* films or Bruce Willis in the *Die Hard* cycle, had become an action cliché. Early drafts of *Speed* had included perfunctory attempts to suggest some kind of troubled history for Jack Traven, but these had been ironed out and he now existed purely in the present tense. Even the romance with Bullock was a brisk, no-nonsense affair. The couple got together in the course of the bus ride, but had no intimate bedroom or dramatic scenes together. Similarly the movie wasted no time on providing Hopper with silly motives. 'What'd we do, bomb the guy's country or something?' asked Bullock at one point. 'No, it's just a guy who wants some money,' Keanu replied. For De Bont such matters were supremely unimportant. 'People always say you have to know the character's background, you have to understand his psychology,' he said. 'The audience doesn't need all that bullshit. We learn everything we need to know about the characters from how they *react* to things.'

There was one main reason why the film-makers were able to deviate from the genre blueprint in a number of small, but cumulatively significant ways: nobody expected *Speed* to be a blockbuster. 'They [Fox] thought it was going to be a tiny little B-movie they could fit in somewhere in the schedule,' De Bont remembered. Its budget was originally pegged at $20 million according to the director, who convinced the studio that this would be technically impossible and got it raised to $26 million: still a modest sum compared to the amounts lavished on comparable movies. *True Lies*, Fox's other big summer action picture, was racking up a bill of around $120 million (Arnold Schwarzenegger's fee alone was said to account for $10 million).

The upside of this was that De Bont had an unusually free hand. 'They left me kind of alone, which is always a good thing because then you can be the most creative,' he said. And after he had edited the film together, Fox executives were amazed by what they saw. Money which they had at first refused the director to complete some of the special effects in the final sequence suddenly became available and the release date, originally at the fag end of the summer, was rushed forward to a prime slot at the beginning of the holiday season.

Then, just as *Speed* was rolling out across America, Keanu's father was arrested at the airport in Hilo, Hawaii, for possession of large quantities of cocaine and heroin. It was heavy-duty dealing. Police claimed he was in contact with a Mexican gang responsible for smuggling black tar heroin on to the island. His accomplice, Hermilo Castillo, put up $100,000 bail after being arrested with Reeves then fled the country. Samuel pleaded no contest to reduced charges of promoting a dangerous drug in the second degree, and told the judge in his defence that he had hurt nobody in his dealings and that drugs should be legalized. But his request for probation was turned down after the prosecution had submitted that his involvement with narcotics had been expanding and, on 21 June 1994, he was sentenced to ten years in Halawa State Prison, just north of Pearl Harbor.

Samuel had never been there for his son and daughter when they were small and now he had re-emerged into the spotlight at exactly the moment when he was least wanted. Keanu's long-repressed anger burst to the surface. 'Who the hell needs this?' he erupted according to his cousin Leslie

Reeves, who added, 'He does not love his father. He has nothing but contempt for him. He hates him.' Reeves senior expressed contrition a few weeks later from his prison cell, saying, 'I'm not very proud of myself as a father, but I am proud of him. I hope we can be reconciled one day, so I can explain why he didn't have a father as a young boy. I hope he doesn't think I'm some evil drug lord.' But as things stood a resumption of friendly relations was scarcely on the cards.

Keanu had said of Samuel, 'A lot of who I am is a reaction against his actions.' His extraordinarily disciplined dedication to his work, as well as his rise to wealth and his apparent lack of interest in spending it, were a very public rejection of the way the self-indulgent Samuel had squandered his own inheritance and his life. A further impulse had come when Keanu himself was arrested the previous year, on 5 May 1993, albeit on the rather less serious charge of driving under the influence. It was said that when the actor saw the mug shot taken by the police on that occasion, he was startled by his resemblance to Samuel and resolved to clean up his act.

There were deeper scars too, and that childhood sense of abandonment seemed to have translated itself into a striking inability to form lasting relationships, particularly with women. Meanwhile, forced to face up to the despised figure from his past, he dispensed with Samuel, in a stupendous act of denial, by pretending to ignore him. Asked about the conviction only months afterwards, Keanu, to his interviewer's astonishment, flatly disavowed all knowledge of it.

Dismayed, the studio warned its new star to stay clear. But it need not have worried. Exit polls on *Speed*'s opening night revealed that 97 per cent of both men and women loved it.

And so did the critics. *Variety* found Keanu 'surprisingly forceful and commanding in the sort of role he's never tackled before'. It was the very lack of pretensions which appealed: the *New Yorker* wrote, '*Speed* is bare of emotional development. Its characters are no more than sketches. It addresses no social concerns. It is morally inert. It's the movie of the year.' Bernardo Bertolucci was another, slightly unlikely fan. 'There's a fantastic line about Henry James – I think it was T. S. Eliot who said it: "His sublime mind was never violated by an idea," meaning that James was beyond ideas. And *Speed* is the perfect superficiality of pure action. It's never violated by the dirt of psychology,' Bertolucci said.

It entered the charts in first place and went on to become the holiday season's most unexpected hit, eventually taking well over $330 million worldwide. *True Lies* did reasonably well, too, but a substantial slice of its earnings would be creamed off by Schwarzenegger and others who had points – profit participation – in the movie. *Speed* offered a much better return on the original investment. And it had paid its stars a flat fee.

Keanu was slightly fazed by the media's efforts to tout him as an action hero. 'To me, it's not a hero piece. The protagonist isn't the prow.' His desire not to be typecast was natural. Still, it was the first time, after a career playing in ensemble casts and double acts, that he had carried a major movie on his own shoulders. It also marked his graduation from Valley Dude to adult, albeit slightly offbeat, leading man.

Even so, Ted had not been laid to rest and still returned to haunt him. 'On *Little Buddha* and I guess on *Speed* they're all saying, "Doesn't it seem like a lifetime ago since you did *Bill and Ted?*"' Keanu remarked wryly. 'And all I can say is "No! It seems like only yesterday because everybody keeps reminding me."' But interviewers were struck by how he had smartened up his act compared to his scruffy, sullen showing on the promotional tour of summer 1991. Now he was likely to appear in a designer suit, even if, as often as not, the effect would be finished off with a pair of elderly and battered biker boots. And his answers were (by Keanu standards) articulate.

The Los Angeles building Keanu had been renting an apartment in had been sold just as he was leaving town to do *Johnny Mnemonic* and he moved out to the Chateau Marmont, the hotel on Sunset Boulevard famous as a celebrity haunt and notorious as the place where John Belushi had died. Apart from his two motorbikes, bass guitar, hockey stick, and a mountain of clothes, he took nothing with him. 'I don't need a house,' he said. What, then, did he do with all his newfound money? 'It affords one a certain amount of freedom and travel and I can buy older Bordeaux. I can afford my two Nortons, which is akin to sending a child to a middle-expensive university in the US.' And that was it, apart from a few treasured possessions (like the sword he later acquired when playing Hamlet) which he kept in storage at Kim's house.

The writer Robert Mark Kamen remembered going to dinner with Keanu one evening. He brought along some friends who, to Kamen's slight surprise (this was Los Angeles), were 'so . . . *not* in the movie business. There wasn't any real grounding to them; they were still trying to find what they wanted to do. It was just like normal people. We came outside and one of the guys had a bike that didn't work. Keanu got down on his hands and knees and the two of them started fiddling around with it in a parking lot in East LA at 11 o'clock at night. It wasn't movie star stuff.'

Keanu's friends from his Toronto days were unsurprised to see that fame seemed not to have changed him. Some thought that he was getting a little old to be acting the bohemian. 'When it comes down to it, I don't think he's a very responsible person,' said Alan Powell. 'You can say, "This guy, he's living out of suitcases, it's really cool, he doesn't have a mortgage, he doesn't have a family, he can do whatever the hell he wants. It's great!" But turn it around, the guy's over thirty. This is the point in his life where he's gotta start focusing.' Or perhaps there was a touch of envy in such responses. Shael Risman remembered, of Keanu's outlook: 'He'd say, "You live on a day-to-day basis, you do the best you can, and you have fun." It would be a cliché if he didn't still live like that today. I don't; I don't know anyone of our age who does. He hasn't changed, hasn't adapted to the LA lifestyle at all even though he's a multi-millionaire. And people don't accept that.'

One thing was certain: although he made vague noises to the press about wanting a wife and children, being footloose and fancy free had become integral to the spell Keanu cast on his admirers. 'He's got something at the back of the eyes that says, "No, I won't be committing here,"' said Kenneth Branagh. 'He'll always be on the bus heading off. And I think there is something tremendously attractive to men and women about that combination of the utterly desirable and the definitely unattainable.'

The sudden runaway success of Speed had wrongfooted the studio. Fox had hoped to secure Keanu for Speed 2, but had made the error of signing him for the first film without locking him into a sequel. His salary would need to be renegotiated, and the star, besides having a raft of other prior commitments, had a whole set of new conditions including script approval. In any case, dollars were not the main thing on his mind. Asked what was the worst advice he'd ever been given about his career, he said, 'Take the money and run. People still say it to me, either directly or in metaphors.'

A rival studio, Warner Brothers, was already making moves to poach him with $5.5 million for a winter film, any film. And $7 million was on the table for him to star in *Without Remorse*, an adaptation of Tom Clancy's bestseller, as John Kelly, a younger version of the Navy SEAL played by Willem Dafoe in *Clear and Present Danger*. The production company, Savoy Pictures, hoped to launch a new movie franchise centred on the Kelly character. Keanu declined these offers, and a number of others including a tempting part opposite Robert De Niro and Al Pacino in *Heat*, a crime drama directed by Michael Mann. He had already lined up his next starring role: in a small Canadian stage production of *Hamlet* in Winnipeg (pop. 652,000) for a standard Equity fee of less than $2,000 a week.

The idea had originated with Steven Schipper, the Artistic Director of the Manitoba Theatre Centre, who had auditioned Keanu as a sixteen-year-old kid for a juvenile role in a Sam Shepard play at the Toronto Free Theatre. On that occasion Reeves had been unlucky (too tall, supposedly), but now Schipper was eager to offer him anything he would care to play. He called the director Lewis Baumander, who had nursed the actor through his first public Shakespearean excursion, *Romeo and Juliet*, in 1985 and had remained in occasional contact with him. Asked whether there was a play that might tempt Keanu to darkest Winnipeg, Baumander recalled that recently, during one of their phone chats, the conversation had turned to *Hamlet*.

Not for the first time in his career, Keanu found his new scheme the subject of some suspicion, not to say derision. He had spoken repeatedly of his love for Shakespeare and was well known for the bursts of impromptu iambic pentameter which he used to help himself relax on the film set and at the hockey rink. But ... *Hamlet*? This was, after all, one of the most taxing roles in the classical repertoire. And, since leaving Toronto, his stage experience had been non-existent, apart from his brief appearance as Trinculo in *The Tempest* in 1989.

Keanu was succinct about his reasons: 'The play's the thing, man,' he said. Choosing such a spectacularly non-Hollywood project was also an act of rebellion against his sudden rise to supercelebrity: a way of announcing to the world that here was a serious actor, not a frivolous star. He would be thirty-one, a good age for a first Hamlet, a Hamlet which would emphasize the character's youth. And the show would be tucked away in a remote provincial centre. 'As it turned out,' Baumander recalled, 'the world came to him.'

No one was doubting Keanu's enthusiasm. Kenneth Branagh, who had already tested his Shakespearean mettle, albeit in a small role, in *Much Ado About Nothing*, talked to him – or rather listened to him talking – about the play while Reeves was still deciding whether to do it. 'He came to see the *Hamlet* that I did for the Royal Shakespeare Company in the winter of 1992–1993 and sent over the most fantastic, ancient bottle of red wine. When he came round to the dressing room he then told me exactly where it was from and why it was good and we made the decision – rather brave, I thought – to open it there and then.

'He gave me this hour and a half lecture on the production: where it went wrong and where it went right, and the proper way to do *Hamlet*. He had so many questions and criticisms – very passionately held views. At that stage he was still havering but the Winnipeg connection was there and he was on fire with it. He was a great person to have round because after doing that play you're so knackered that it's a bit of a pain to do the talking yourself. And I certainly encouraged him to do it.'

Richard Hurst, Keanu's line coach, was astonished at how thoroughly the actor had pored over the play before he came to Winnipeg. 'He arrived having learned it from beginning to end, every single solitary word that Hamlet has to speak and most of the other characters' words as well. It amazed me how easily he could pull out quotes from other characters in the play to reference back to his own. His knowledge was encyclopaedic, not only of *Hamlet* but also of other Shake-speare plays and of the revenge tragedies which were the bases for *Hamlet*.'

Keanu looked up Baumander in February 1994 while he was in Toronto working on *Johnny Mnemonic*. It was a solemn occasion. 'We met, each of us clutching his Arden Shake-speare and First Folio, had a shy, embarrassed hug, then sat down and started talking,' Baumander recalled. They spent another week in Winnipeg at the beginning of May, finding their bearings on the stage where the production would eventually play, and in late October, when Keanu's next film, *A Walk in the Clouds*, had wrapped, Baumander went to Los Angeles to work intensively, mainly on the long soliloquies.

He found him not much changed since doing *Romeo and Juliet*, when Reeves would call the director in the middle of the night: once again the role had taken over his life, and not always during working hours. 'Sometimes Lewis would find himself at three o'clock in the afternoon in a movie house with Keanu beside him watching a film because Keanu didn't feel like working,' Hurst said. 'And then at two o'clock in the morning they would be into an in-depth analysis of some part of the play. It was relatively erratic.' Finally, four weeks of full-cast rehearsals began in Winnipeg in December. Such a long gestation period was slightly unusual but by no means extraordinary, Baumander said. Another actor he knew had wanted at least eighteen months to prepare himself for this demanding role.

Several decisions emerged from these meetings. The director knew that the play would be seen, for better or worse, as a vehicle for Keanu, and resolved to build the show around his star. The production would begin with a striking tableau of the prince centre stage, mourning at the tomb of his father. And this Hamlet would be a man of action, immobilized by conscience, but not neurotic: a clean-cut hero not so dissimilar, in an odd way, to Jack Traven in *Speed*. 'I've always hated those passive, morose Hamlets, those whiners,' Baumander said. 'I've always seen Hamlet as a young man of great courage who wouldn't be beguiled or forced into anything. In these times we're very impulsive; we don't think enough about the consequences of our acts.'

This emphasis would play to Keanu's strengths as a physical actor and, perhaps, disguise any difficulties he might have with the more meditative, wordy scenes. But he had seen the character a little differently. 'I guess the first thing that drew me to Hamlet was the angst,' he said. 'The journey he goes through to search his own soul is fascinating.' According to Richard Hurst, 'his take on *Hamlet* was that it was a departure from what was known as the revenge tragedy. There was an awful lot of philosophy which reveals what the man is going through from a mental and emotional point of view. This was something that Keanu found very attractive about the play. However, with the cuts made for this production, he felt it had been turned back into a revenge tragedy and that there weren't as many insights into the character as Shakespeare had originally intended. That was slightly frustrating for him.'

The *Winnipeg Free Press* reported his eventual coming to town on 8 December under the headline 'Keanu Krazy', and launched a telephone hotline to register sightings, only to abandon it days later when it emerged that all he did was shuttle between his hotel and the theatre, with the occasional restaurant meal. And anyway, the locals seemed to respect his privacy. A mini-riot did, however, nearly erupt at a shopping mall when Keanu left his charge card in a store and was paged by the manager (wisely, he sent a friend to retrieve it).

The entire run – 20,000 seats – had long since been sold out (even though it involved taking out a subscription to the theatre's entire winter season) and scalpers were said to be offering $36 seats for upward of $750. For the less well heeled, $20 bought a black T-shirt emblazoned with Keanu's Dane on the front and Polonius's admonition on the back: 'To thine own self be true.' And to his fans' delighted surprise, the Reeves signature was available gratis upon demand.

'It was incredibly cold, at times down to minus 25 degrees Celsius,' Hurst said. 'But each night after the show there were two or three hundred people standing out by the stage door for thirty-five, forty minutes while he took off his make-up, waiting for him to come out and sign autographs. Which he would do, sometimes until one or two o'clock in the morning; he wouldn't stop until they were all done. Sometimes I'd be with him, we'd planned to go out or something, but when he saw the people pressed against the door, he'd look back at me and say, "I can't go, Rich." And he'd take off his gloves and his hat and start signing at the guard's table. I asked him about that at one point and he said, "I'd feel guilty if I didn't."'

The international media were also on the scene and Baumander found himself constantly fielding phone calls from American tabloid television shows like *Hard Copy* and *Current Affair*. In an attempt to curb the feeding frenzy, Erwin Stoff turned down all interview requests except for a handful of ten-minute slots with local papers and placed a ban on video recordings of the production; even the Canadian network television station CBC was not allowed to use a clip of him in action. There were to be no press tickets and no photocalls. In the programme notes, Keanu's biography was buried between those of other members of the cast.

Meanwhile rehearsals continued. Over the years his acting had become calibrated to the film medium – and even there hostile critics thought his performances minimal to the point of non-existence. Now he had to readjust to the demands of the theatre. 'The difference between stage craft and film craft is pretty vast — having to fill a frame is really different from having to fill a stage,' Hurst said. 'We had a number of discussions about how to let the audience into what the character is experiencing, not just through what a film audience could see happening in his eyes. How to let the emotions out physically a lot more. He found that difficult because he was so used to having the camera come to him.'

For Baumander, the challenge was in getting the actor to pace his performance: 'There's a level of honesty that he wants to play. Doing a scene five times in a row he wouldn't hold back — he wanted to go full out every time. I suspected he had to learn to hold something in reserve.'

Keanu was also anxious about remembering his 1,530 lines and had nightmares about drying up on stage: he had already done so twice at dress rehearsals before audiences of high-school students. He was alone in town, without a major star's usual protective entourage, and the impression was that the Hollywood spin doctors would rather the whole thing were not happening; they would, it was said, not fly out to see him until they were assured he was not a disaster. Some wondered whether the actor would lose his nerve. To these doubters, Baumander riposted, 'One of the things people are not banking on is Keanu's integrity. He made a promise and he'll honour that promise.' Reeves, for his part, asked only to be judged on his own merits. 'Deal justly with me,' he said, quoting a line from the play.

Meanwhile Keanu's fellow actors were relieved that the production was not turning into a Hollywood star's ego trip. 'He's very serious,' said Donald Carrier (who played Horatio).

For Stephen Russell (Claudius), 'It was apparent that this was not going to be ... a romp in the park.' Recalled Wayne Nicklas (Marcellus): 'Everyone was nervous except Keanu. He was the bravest, always leading the way.' The twenty-odd cast members celebrated a convivial Christmas and New Year together, united, perhaps, by a shared sense of the forthcoming ordeal. 'We ended up being so protective of him, because we could see the turmoil and the upheaval he was putting himself through,' Hurst said. 'These are people who have been in the business for a lot of years and are somewhat jaded. We were wary of him to begin with but then we saw his devotion and his utter focus on what he was doing. It was just a lovefest.'

In the end, the reviews were not that bad. There was something in Keanu – his solitary, self-contained, enigmatic quality – which fitted him, better than the sceptics had expected, for the role. There were two unalloyed raves, in (predictably) the local paper, the *Winnipeg Free Press*, and (less so) in the *Sunday Times*, whose critic Roger Lewis penned a florid panegyric ('with his face inclined towards me, and so intent you would swear he could listen to the wolves barking amid the ice and frozen rivers, he was very beautiful') which ranked Keanu among the best three Hamlets he had ever seen.

Critics were generally impressed by his grace and energy in the fights, by his adroitness with the comic elements of the character and by his intriguing stage presence. But Keanu was let down, they also said, by his lack of classical technique. 'There's a real problem with a number of Hamlet's speeches,' wrote the *Vancouver Sun*. 'The impression is of a relatively inexperienced classical actor for whom being able to recite all those lines, including the long, philosophical soliloquies, is accomplishment enough,' said the *Toronto Star*. The *Guardian* was tarter, comparing him to the lead actor in a school play.

A big factor was stage fright. Keanu later compared himself to a deer caught in truck lights ('one of the most horrific nights of my life, oh my gosh!'), but said that, on two nights, he felt he *was* Hamlet. And he believed the show had the great merit of simplicity. 'I'll say one thing about our production – and I don't *care* what you think about my Hamlet – you could hear it, it made sense, it wasn't abstract, it wasn't convoluted or sensationalistic.' Baumander (whose work on this, his own first *Hamlet*, also came in for harsh words) admitted that the opening night 'wasn't his best performance. But when I left town at the end of the first week, he was up to cruising speed. And when I came back on closing night I was astonished by his growth and confidence.'

Hurst, who played several bit parts in the production, watched Keanu nightly from his vantage point stage left throughout the run. 'He was absolutely spectacular in the fight sequences and the physical connection with his mother and Ophelia and when he's antic, and so on,' he said. 'I think he was slightly trepidatious about the three major soliloquies. But they all grew to such a point that some nights there were moments of such marvellous brilliance it would bring tears to my eyes.'

However Keanu's performance varied widely from night to night. He played Hamlet without a net, which made it thrilling, but also sometimes nail-biting for his co-actors. 'He discovered that, having made choices and done them the same way each night, he was getting bored,' Hurst remembered. 'I said to him, "That's the challenge of theatre acting, to make it interesting for yourself every night." It struck me as odd that he didn't remember this, that on stage you don't have the luxury of spoiling the take each time you don't like what you're doing.

'When that happened the rest of the cast would go "uh-oh", because he would try anything he could on stage with other people to make it come back. As a result everyone was on their mettle, never knowing what to expect from Keanu. But it was always something incredibly interesting, a choice that no one would have anticipated. And we all had to adjust to the moment. It was never dull, that's for sure.'

Above all, it was clear that, absurd as it might seem at this late stage in his career, Keanu's Hamlet was haunted by the ghost, not of his father but of Ted Theodore Logan III. The press referred to the production with slightly depressing regularity as 'Keanu's Excellent Adventure'. A ripple of laughter ran through the audience on opening night whenever Hamlet was required to pronounce the innocent adjective, greeting Rosencrantz and Guildenstern as 'my excellent good friends' or referring to 'this most excellent canopy – the air'.

The Canadian weekly *Maclean's* contrived to weave no fewer than three of the star's popular film roles into its review: 'Perhaps it was just opening night nerves, but Reeves raced through some lines at such a clip that the sense was almost unintelligible. He whipped through the soliloquies, the signature tunes of Hamlet, as if they were air guitar solos. Locked into Shakespeare's iambic pentameter, he surfed from one consonant to the next, faster and faster. He rode the play as if it were wired to blow up below a certain speed.' The *Guardian* headlined its pan, 'Excellent – not!'

Baumander was incensed by the glib wisecracks: 'These are the remarks of a media with the mental capabilities of a Ted. I was disgusted by the cheapness of it.' Still, Keanu would not have been the first victim of this syndrome: Mel Gibson had to suffer through many a Mad Max joke when he played Hamlet on film in 1990. And, like Gibson (whose reviews were unexpectedly positive), he won respect for his courage in tackling the role in the full glare of public scrutiny. 'One can't fault Reeves for his ambition and guts,' wrote *Vanity Fair*. 'For actors such as Reeves and Mel Gibson, *Hamlet* may have been a reach, but it reflects well upon them that they tried.'

9

THE COOLEST HEAD IN TOWN

The success of *Speed* had made Keanu a superstar, with all
the unwelcome attention which this entailed. For a while
Samuel Reeves' conviction for drugs trafficking had kept
gossip columnists happy but now something new was needed.
Keith Mayerson's *Keanu Sightings*, a seven-year annotated
chronicle of occasions when the actor had been spotted in
public by the artist's friends, might have offered rich
pickings. But Mayerson left it deliberately vague as to whether
the individual incidents were fact, gossip, fantasy or urban
myth. 'The stories may or may not be true,' he explained.
'They may be as benign as Keanu saying of a girl, "Ooo her
jeans are *so* flared," or they may be really bad, like somebody
shot up with him or he arrived on a set completely out of it
in the same clothes he was wearing the night before. In one,
Keanu was making love to a girl in the same room as her flat-
mate.

'There's a sighting of him dining in a Tribeca restaurant
with the drummer of the Red Hot Chilli Peppers. They got
into a food fight with the neighbouring table and then they
both took off all their clothes, danced a little jig on top of the
table, ran off into a cab and sped into the night. Another was

of him in a bar called the Gaslight in Los Angeles where his band used to play. He lined up all sorts of different whisky drinks in front of him, got wildly drunk and made out really sloppily with girls. You can't really prove them and a lot of the gay ones, in particular, are very mythic. I think people make them up.'

Even if only one of these stories were true, one might have expected to see rather more of Keanu splashed across the *National Enquirer* than has been the case. But, Mayerson said, the sightings began at a time when the actor was too obscure to attract the mass media: indeed, that was the point of the project. Keanu's allure was as an underground hero, unknown to the mainstream, and the artist's interest had waned as the actor's star had risen.

Now, however, the tabloids were labouring mightily to produce stories on him. In October 1994, a month after the British release of *Speed*, a report appeared in the *Daily Star* under the banner headline 'Sleaze Trips of Hollywood Hell-raiser'. Keanu had been sighted at 'a second-hand clothes shop that flogs punk togs in the heart of sleazy Soho'. There he sought out an old drinking buddy and headed for a basement music club 'set among seedy sex shops and strip joints' for an impromptu, 48-hour jamming and boozing session. But despite the paper's ingenious attempts to embellish its tale, the 'sleaze trips', as reported, were startlingly tame.

Sex was another matter. Keanu seemed to have no love life and the media were eager to invent one for him. In July 1994, some popular papers ran stories of him splashing with Sharon Stone in a hotel swimming pool one night. 'Their

Smooching with his fellow-actor Carl Marotte in a publicity shot for *Wolfboy*: the photographer David Hlynsky sprayed the pair with water for a 'sweaty glow' and remembered Keanu as 'nervous but professional'. Staged in Toronto in 1984, the play secured him an enthusiastic gay following.

Under five hours of make-up for a small role in *Freaked* (above left) a surreal comedy directed by Alex Winter: his character, Ortiz the Dog Boy, was, he said, a mix of 'Che Guevara, Fidel Castro and Tom Jones'; a portrait by the LAPD, which pulled the actor over in May 1993 for driving under the influence (above right); being ravished by three female vampires in *Bram Stoker's Dracula* in a pose which typified Keanu's passive sexual persona (below).

Looking, Keanu said, 'like Cleopatra' as Prince Siddhartha in Bernardo Bertolucci's *Little Buddha*, a film which put the actor through some startling physical transformations; and as the prince turned mystic in the same film, after a crash diet of oranges and water.

Shakespearean adventures: to Tuscany in August to play Don John, one of Keanu's rare villains, in Kenneth Branagh's *Much Ado About Nothing*.

Playing bass with
Dogstar, his 'folk thrash'
band, on the summer
1995 tour; riding one of
his motorbikes, a hobby
which has left Keanu
with numerous knocks
including a long scar
snaking down his
abdomen.

Women in his life: with Karina, his younger sister, and (below) with Sofia, the daughter of Francis Ford Coppola

Women in his films: with Sandra Bullock in *Speed*
and with Aitana Sanchez-Gijon in the period love
story *A Walk in the Clouds*: romance has been
as sparse in Keanu's films as it appears to have
been in his life.

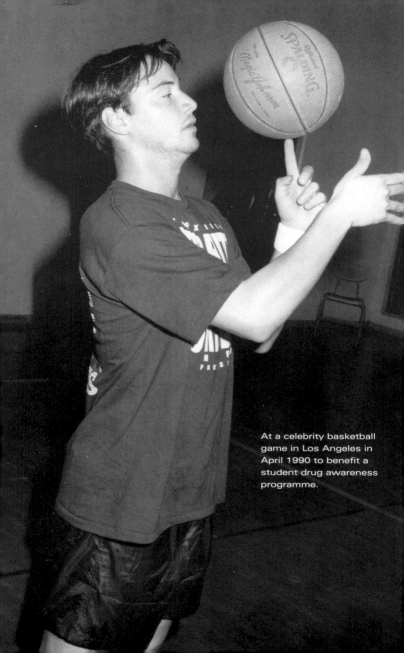

At a celebrity basketball game in Los Angeles in April 1990 to benefit a student drug awareness programme.

passionate love play almost turned the pool into a sauna,' the *Daily Mirror* drooled. Within weeks they were to change their tune.

Reports began to appear that autumn that Keanu had been seen at parties with David Geffen, the billionaire record producer. Geffen was of interest to entertainment columnists for several reasons. He was about to form, along with Steven Spielberg and Jeffrey Katzenberg, a new studio, DreamWorks, thus becoming one of the most formidable new powerbrokers in the film business. Geffen had another distinction: since coming out in 1992, he was one of the few openly gay senior executives in Hollywood. Soon it was being claimed (by the *Daily Mirror* again) that Geffen had spent some $15,000 on clothes for Keanu at Barneys, an upscale men's clothing store on Wilshire Boulevard in Los Angeles. According to one account, they were 'giggling like schoolboys' as they tried on mounds of expensive shirts. In another, Keanu charged up thousands of dollars' worth of clothing to Geffen's credit card.

It was, Keanu said, while he was in Winnipeg working on Hamlet that he first heard he had allegedly entered into a secret marriage with Geffen on a Mexican beach. In an alternative version, the ceremony, conducted by a rabbi, was held in the grounds of a Hollywood restaurant in the presence of Elizabeth Taylor, Cindy Crawford, Claudia Schiffer and Steven Spielberg. The magazine which recorded the happy event also described in detail the outfits worn by everyone present and noted that a hired band of twelve musicians entertained the party until 2 a.m.

The rumour – which had been circulating for a while on

the Hollywood grapevine – had first broken into print in European papers, but quickly crossed the Atlantic, hitting the American press in late December, first as a blind item in *Hollywood Reporter.* 'Sources close to Geffen have sworn it's true,' the *Boston Globe* claimed. As a story it was seductive, combining as it did, in the words of one commentator, a potent cocktail of 'hidden desire, New Age ceremony and conspicuous consumption'. This columnist also observed that it was 'the kind of package that fits our notion of the Dream Factory – a sex 'n' shopping blend of perversity and excess.'

It was easy to see why Keanu attracted speculation. Back in 1984, at the beginning of his career, the stage production of *Wolfboy* in Toronto had established him as a local homosexual icon; later, the New Lavender Panthers, a group of Canadian punks, had named a dance after him called the Keanu Stomp and based on his loping walk in *The Prince of Pennsylvania.* He had been a cult figure in the gay community for years, at least since *River's Edge. Interview* magazine asked him bluntly in 1990, 'Are you gay, or what? Come on, make it official.' Keanu said he was not but added coquettishly, after a long pause, 'but ya never know'.

On paper his childhood profile – an absent father and a family of strong women – seemed to fit the picture. And, more specifically, he was (like Geffen at the time) not visibly involved in a serious relationship. He had kept clear of the actresses he had worked with, in an attempt to avoid 'the Hollywood gossip-mongers', even though, as he said, 'if you don't have relationships with the women you work with then people say you're gay. You're damned if you do and damned if you don't ... I know actors that have become involved with actresses, women, on the set and it makes it harder, much harder.'

Since arriving in Hollywood he had dated a few women, including Sofia Coppola, Francis Ford Coppola's daughter, and an actress-model named Autumn Mackintosh, but had only had one long-term lover, 'an on-again-off-again thing a few years ago that lasted about a year', according to his sister Kim. These liaisons took place well away from the public eye; they were rarely recorded in photographs and never in interviews. He was not seen squiring supermodels or starlets around night clubs and movie premieres. This was more than just another case of an actor, overwhelmed by the unwanted side-effects of his sudden celebrity, secreting his love life. There seemed to *be* no love life. Colleagues on his movies speculated in vain about his sexuality; 'monkish' was a word often used to describe him. Keanu had now become a public fantasy, and was committing what was, for an object of desire, a cardinal sin: he seemed unburdened with sexual or emotional entanglements.

There was, on the other hand, not much in the way of hard evidence to support the marriage rumour. One observer, the Los Angeles columnist Steven Gaines, believed the Barneys story may have begun as a case of mistaken identity, since Geffen had a close friend who resembled Keanu (others remarked that Reeves' grunge style was anyway hardly that of a man who shopped at one of the most exclusive clothing stores in Beverly Hills). Witnesses to the marriage ceremony itself proved shy about coming forward; nor did photographs begin to circulate.

None of his friends, or indeed the numerous Keanuwatchers in the gay community, thought the story plausible (although some claimed a friendly connection between him and Geffen, who had, they alleged, taken the actor under his wing at a difficult time in his life and career). 'On our summer camping trip in 1978 he was certainly very much turned on by women,' said his childhood friend Shawn Aberle, while others remembered him at acting school with a steady stream of girlfriends. Alan Powell dismissed the idea succinctly. 'When I knew him? Not a chance.'

The idea was also discounted by professional colleagues, even and especially those who had worked with Keanu on gay-themed material, like John Palmer, who directed *Wolfboy*, and Gus Van Sant, who made *My Own Private Idaho* and is himself openly gay. 'He seems pretty heterosexual to me; it's kind of like calling Clinton gay,' Van Sant said. 'Doesn't quite fit. The older I get, the more experienced I get with the media, the more I realize that everything is a complete fabrication. I think Keanu probably would come out and say he was gay if that were true; he doesn't really care. But he's not. It's like the Richard Gere story. Why were the gerbil rumours running around? It probably somehow stems from what the public wants to believe. Anyone can start a rumour. And if it's a good one, if it has a ring to it, it goes all over the place.'

Both parties maintained silence on the subject until the end of March when Geffen was moved to comment, albeit discreetly, towards the end of a long report on DreamWorks in the business section of *Time* magazine, 'I hear that I'm supposed to be married to Keanu Reeves, a person I've never met or laid eyes on,' he said. 'I hear all kinds of idiotic things.

But people believe them and there's nothing you can do about it.' Eventually, that summer, Keanu followed suit and gave an interview broaching the subject. His choice of publication, however, was more provocative: the gay monthly *Out*.

To dispel doubts, the magazine was prominently flagged as 'The Straight Issue' on its cover. Keanu said he had never met Geffen and, asked about attitudes towards homosexuals in Hollywood, even went so far as to claim, somewhat mind-bogglingly, that he had never come across homophobia and had no gay friends in the acting community. Tim Allis, the *Out* interviewer, was convinced that the marriage was a canard. 'Keanu has been the target of one of these unbeliev-able, oversized rumours that even made it to Kansas,' he said later. 'He comes across as a straight guy with a very open mind.'

Talking shortly afterwards to the journalist Michael Shnayerson (who also had the same impression), Keanu was even blunter. 'The fact is, I've never had a male sexual experience in my life,' he said. 'But what am I supposed to do, talk about every woman I've slept with?' To Shnayerson's disappointment his prize quote was cut out when the inter-view was published in *Vanity Fair*, which left the issue slightly cloudy.

It may have been that the magazine's editors wanted to preserve what was, after all, Keanu's trump card: his ambigu-ity. Indeed, another school of thought held that his vague sexuality was a calculated ploy. 'He's really smart,' said John Palmer. 'I think what he says about himself is probably for marketing, to interest everybody.' David Hlynsky, who photographed Reeves in a clinch with his fellow-actor for *Wolfboy*, remarked, 'He understands what mystery is and leaves a bunch of stuff out so that people have to lean forward.'

The gossip persisted. According to the *Toronto Star* in May, sources in Winnipeg claimed Geffen was a regular visitor during the run of *Hamlet*. Another story had it that Keanu had been dating a male dancer in the Royal Winnipeg Ballet in the same period, to which he indignantly riposted, 'Only ignorant people assume all those ballet dudes are gay. They're as athletic as Michael Jordan and I respect their work. Just because I enjoy watching them on stage doesn't mean I want to date them.'

For a self-professed goof, Keanu's handling of the affair was a brilliant piece of media management. He had, he said, only addressed the rumour at the urging of his advisers, who felt that it was 'freaking people out'; there was, surely, nothing wrong with being gay, so why should he need to deny it? Above all, he projected an air of insouciance, joking to his manager that maybe he should return the clothes to Barneys and seeming to interviewers amused by the whole business and even filled with 'childlike pleasure' at it.

He did not suddenly acquire a girlfriend, much less enter a 'lavender marriage' as certain of his peers were suspected of doing, to establish an alibi; it was a year before the tabloids made a half-hearted attempt to link his name with Amanda De Cadenet (Geffen was not even mentioned in those stories: showbusiness reporters have short memories). His laid-back reaction enabled him to hold on to his female admirers while at the same time not alienating gay fans who, if anything, warmed to him further.

Keanu's next project after *Speed* was another action movie, but an action movie with pretensions: *Johnny Mnemonic*, an adaptation of an early short story by William Gibson. Thanks to the enormous impact of his 1984 novel *Neuromancer*, Gibson had become the unofficial godfather of cyberpunk – that contemporary cocktail of high-tech science fiction and gloomy pulp thriller – and the object of keen interest in Hollywood. *Blade Runner* and *Total Recall*, both based on the work of the late Philip K. Dick, had created a minor vogue for *tech noir*, and Gibson's writing looked like it also had big-ticket potential. Soon producers were snapping up the rights to his backlist and the writer himself was contracted three times to turn his stories into film scripts. But nothing came to fruition.

'This has taken longer than it did for me to get a BA in English,' said Gibson shortly after *Johnny Mnemonic* finally went before the cameras. 'My previous experiences in Hollywood were so frustrating – I wound up with screenplays that I actually didn't *want* to be produced after they'd gone through the development process and been massaged into cream cheese. I'd told people I wasn't going to do it any more and then Robert came in and talked me into it. I liked his determination. I thought of him as like Ahab and the white whale.'

'Robert' was Robert Longo, a pony-tailed New York artist who had staged his first solo show in 1981, the same year that 'Johnny Mnemonic' was first published in *Omni* magazine. Over the next few years he had built up a reputation for large-scale performance art works and had made rock videos for Talking Heads and New Order among others (Longo had himself played in various punk bands). He had also dabbled in film-making with an episode of *Tales From The Crypt* for cable television and *Arena Brains*, an half-hour short starring Ray Liotta.

Then his backers, Elektra Records, thought they might fund something more ambitious. Cynics suggested Longo was keen to segue into cinema because the high rollers who had fuelled the art market throughout the Eighties were fading from the scene. And several critics thought that Longo himself had lost his way as an artist – Roberta Smith of the *New York Times* dubbed him 'Robert Long-Ago'. His major retrospective at LACMA (Los Angeles County Museum of Art) in 1989 got terrible reviews. For whatever reason, Longo contacted Gibson, optioned the rights to *Johnny Mnemonic* and wrote a draft script.

That was in 1989. After Elektra abandoned the project, the two started touring the studios with *Johnny*, which they still intended to make as a low-budget semi-experimental movie. 'We were going around saying, "Would you give us $2 million to make a black-and-white art film?"' Gibson remembered. 'And they'd say, "No. The door." It's when you say, "Would you give us $30 or $40 million?" They don't say, "Here you are," but they do kind of go, "Hmmmm ..."' The film was eventually picked up by Carolco, which planned to make it for around $7 million, then, when the company ran into financial difficulties, passed into the hands of Peter Hoffman, who had been a tax attorney at Carolco and was now setting up as an independent producer. His idea was to fund *Johnny* by pre-selling it to as many foreign territories as he could.

The fly in the ointment was Longo. He had been no

THE COOLEST HEAD IN TOWN

problem while the budget was small, but it had been steadily nudging upwards and there was nothing in the artist's background to suggest he could handle a film of that order. But he and Gibson had formed a kind of mutual admiration society and power bloc, and he was still firmly attached to the project. 'Because Robert and I were both outsiders and really very weird by Hollywood standards we were able to invent our working relationship, which was wildly unorthodox and was initially, I think, quite alarming to the producers,' the writer said of these manoeuvrings. 'One of them was reputed to have used the term "the conspiracy of the talent", which I thought would make a great T-shirt. That's a typical Hollywood way of looking at it: "Let's get the talent out of the loop, then it will all be much simpler."'

And so at the 1993 Cannes Film Festival a carefully coached Longo was grilled by a roomful of potential buyers and conducted himself plausibly enough to secure $15 million in presales from nineteen countries. Their interests were reflected in a cast which Gibson described as 'big-time eclectic' and Longo said was 'specifically structured around the idea of presenting a very bizarre and unusual movie' but which, viewed in another light, looked more like an arrangement of convenience.

There was Val Kilmer, a medium-level (and not too expensive) star as Johnny and the rapper Ice-T to pull in a hip, black audience. Germany chipped in with Udo Kier and Barbara Sukowa (who was also Longo's wife). There was Dolph Lundgren to please the Swedes and the star's substantial video following, and Takeshi ('Beat') Kitano, the cult actor-writer-talk show host, to attract the Japanese distributor, who also required a special edition of the film for local release featuring extra footage of Kitano. The nuts and bolts of mounting what was now a large-scale movie outside the Hollywood studio system meant that *Johnny Mnemonic*, which had started life as an extraordinary experiment, was looking suspiciously like a compromised and stateless co-production.

The budget was in the region of $26 million by the time the film, based in Toronto and Montreal, was ready to roll in the autumn of 1993. Then disaster: Kilmer dropped out because of 'creative and financial differences', as his representative phrased it with the customary vagueness. The actor said later that he had been unhappy with the script and had only agreed to do it subject to agreed changes which, as the start date approached, had still not materialized. *Johnny* nearly collapsed: Kilmer had been a cornerstone of the distribution deals behind it.

Hoffman was livid and for a while made noises about suing. '[Val] acted very badly,' he said. 'It's going to harm him more in the long run. You know something? It was the luckiest thing that ever happened to us because we got Keanu.' Keanu's arrival was another odd story. He had not been advised of the project by his agency, CAA (which also represented Kilmer and perhaps had some inkling of trouble), and was passed the script, he said, by 'a friend of a friend'; according to one account it was hurled unsolicited into his front yard. In the middle of filming *Speed*, he was intrigued by the prospect of working with Gibson and Longo, and took a quick break to meet them. 'He asked me just what the character of Johnny was all about,' Gibson said. 'I told him I was never really sure. Keanu said, "Cool," gave me a couple of ideas and roared off on his motorcycle.'

THE COOLEST HEAD IN TOWN

From Hoffman's point of view, Keanu was the perfect replacement. The yet-to-be-released *Speed* had not confirmed that he could carry an action movie. But it had also not yet sent his price shooting through the roof: he got a reported $2 million for *Johnny Mnemonic*, as opposed to the $7 million he could have commanded a few months later. And, as a Canadian national, he (along with Gibson, an American based in Canada) meant that the film could take advantage of north-of-the-border tax shelters.

Of the other actors of Keanu's generation, Kilmer was the one whose career had criss-crossed most often with his own. Reeves had, he said, auditioned several times for the role of Jim Morrison in Oliver Stone's *The Doors*, which eventually went to Kilmer (Stone himself has no recollection of this). Kilmer also took over the part in *Heat* which Keanu had passed on in order to do Hamlet. Neither actor emerged as the clear winner from these minor skirmishes. They merely proved yet again what a crap shoot choosing films could be for an earlythirtysomething actor in Hollywood where there is no longer a studio system to nurture talent and provide it with a steady stream of suitable vehicles. Kilmer was much praised for *The Doors*, but the general silliness of Stone's hagiography prevented it from turning him into a major star. And while *Heat* was successful, Kilmer's role was small and overshadowed by the looming presence of Al Pacino and Robert De Niro. Conversely, though, Keanu did just as badly out of the *Johnny Mnemonic* swap.

He was to play an information courier capable of transporting electronic data via implants in his brain. The story began when he accepted a shipment – the cure to an epidemic nervous disorder – far too big for his storage capacity. Unless he downloaded the data quickly, his head would explode. Meanwhile various bad guys were on his tail to intercept his mission. By now Gibson had worked out a new rap to explain the character. 'In the beginning he's a slick, superficial asshole,' he said. 'And as he bumps into more and more terrible immovable objects, the surface starts to crack, and underneath is this vulnerable human being.'

But the fact remained that Kilmer's instincts had been right: Johnny was still unsympathetic and underwritten. He had no interest in, or access to the ideas he was transporting, and had erased all his own childhood memories to create more space in his brain (when the memories were retrieved, they turned out to be desperately banal). There was nothing to give him substance. In beefing up the role, Keanu concentrated on his physical contours, gradually losing weight with perfect control in the course of the picture. And he certainly looked cool, with his sharply tailored haircut and shiny, geometric suit.

'He's very self-centred. Very angular,' the actor said. 'I got to work with a lot of shapes and emotions of shapes (*sic*).' Elsewhere, he explained, just as unenlighteningly, 'I was doing a whole thing of, like, mother equals round. Anger equals straight. I saw the heart as a round notion. The journey of this character starts out very angular and straight. By breaking him down, compassion is born. And he gains responsibility and compassion and a warming. Then he's open for an embrace.'

His emphasis on the look of the character seemed to reflect Longo's origins in visual art. The director, for his part, was citing his own, suitably impressive, sources of inspiration: Chris Marker's *La Jetée*, Jean-Luc Godard's *Alphaville*, Orson Welles' *Touch of Evil* and Terry Gilliam's *Brazil*. In more confident moments he bragged, 'At times this film feels like *Blade Runner* directed by Fellini.'

All of which was viewed with a jaundiced eye by the old hands on Longo's crew. Several times, after he issued an instruction, a member whistled 'If I Only Had A Brain' from *The Wizard of Oz*. Another technician said that he had been told by the producer Don Carmody (a veteran whose credits included the *Porky's* comedies and who had been brought in as a condition of refinancing *Johnny Mnemonic* when Kilmer walked) to ignore Longo and listen only to him. 'Robert is a star in the art world,' Gibson recalled, 'and it wasn't easy for him when someone would tell him in front of the whole film crew that he didn't know what the hell he was doing. But he's one stubborn, determined guy, and he pulled through.'

Despite these problems, as the backers watched *Speed*'s grosses and Keanu's stock rising (and Gibson's new novel, *Virtual Light*, sitting on the bestseller list), it seemed to them that they were on to a surefire winner. All the preparations for a massive multi-media franchise – soundtrack, merchandising, video games – kicked into gear and TriStar, the US distributor, was so excited it moved the release date back from February to 26 May: Memorial Weekend, one of the film-going peaks of the American year.

But when *Johnny Mnemonic* emerged nobody had a good word to say for it. Few could resist punning on the title, cruelly redubbing it *Johnny Moronic*, or *Johnny Forgettable*, while Keanu drew a stream of venom: 'robotic delivery',

'dazed, pallid, amazingly uninflected', 'the world's most unre-
sponsive romantic lead', 'monotonic', 'gruff, hostile and
selfish, all in one dimension', 'terrific – except when he opens
his mouth', 'even if Reeves could act, his character as written
would be flatter than a floppy disk'. Most of them agreed that
the Jesus-freak bounty hunter played by Lundgren was the
film's best character – Keanu had to be *really* bad if the
Swede, whose performances were normally solid pine, looked
good beside him.

Asked what would distinguish *Johnny Mnemonic* from, say,
The Terminator, Gibson had said, 'Our film has soul. Our
film has heart, I can't think of a better way to put it. This is a
very down and dirty kitchen sink future and yet there's a kind
of underlying humanity to it.' And yet that was precisely what
was missing from the final film. Keanu later claimed that it
had been spoiled by the distributor's tampering. 'It's not the
vision that William Gibson and Robert Longo and I had,' he
said. 'It's been recut. TriStar, they wanted to make an action
picture out of it. It's a very different movie. But it's their gig.
They paid for it.'

There was no doubt about how it was being sold: the
American publicity campaign featured the copyline 'meet the
ultimate hard drive' over a menacing low-angle shot of Keanu
brandishing a huge gun, even though in the film he only held
it briefly and fired it once, missing his target. By a final irony,
when it opened in America a week after *Die Hard With A
Vengeance*, the third film in the Bruce Willis franchise, it was
soundly thrashed by this unassuming example of the action
genre. *Johnny Mnemonic* ended up grossing a pitiful $19
million in the domestic market (it fared little better inter-

nationally). The British distributor reinvented the film as a smart futuristic mystery: the new poster featured Keanu's mask-like face over a sort of palimpsest of electronic data, while the slogan had morphed into 'the hottest data on earth – in the coolest head in town'. The concept came closer to the makers' intentions although it scarcely improved *Johnny Mnemonic's* fortunes at the UK box office. *Speed* had evidently not made Keanu into a cast-iron attraction. Or perhaps his fans did not like the idea of him as a hard drive. No matter: he already had his next role lined up.

A Walk in the Clouds had started life in 1942 as an Italian love story called *Four Steps in the Clouds*. The remake rights had been acquired in 1987 by David and Jerry Zucker (the brothers responsible for *Airplane!* and the *Naked Gun* movies) and their partner, Gil Netter. The trio tried unsuccessfully for some time to attach a film-maker to the project until finally, in 1992, Netter saw and was much taken by *Like Water for Chocolate*, a magical-realist romance from Mexico. The director, Alfonso Arau, was hired.

Arau had started his career as a stand-up comic and actor (his American credits included *The Wild Bunch*, *Romancing the Stone* and *Three Amigos!*). His first love was directing but, such were the problems of raising finance in his homeland, he had made only seven films, mainly popular satirical comedies, in twenty-five years. 'I would shoot from Monday to Friday,' he said, 'and then Saturday and Sunday I would have to get some extra money for the next week's shooting.'

That all changed in 1992 when Arau filmed *Like Water for Chocolate*, based on a bestselling novel by Laura Esquivel, his then wife. The film was also successful, in fact it became the highest-grossing foreign-language picture in history. With it, Arau was suddenly bankable enough to realize his long-cherished dream: to make a big-budget Hollywood movie. On *A Walk in the Clouds*, he would have around $20 million to play with.

His first move was to turn the Italians of the original film into Mexican-Americans. His cast, culled from Spain, Italy, Mexico and various other Latin American countries, included Aitana Sanchez-Gijon, a Spanish actress unknown in the United States, as the female lead; the distinguished Italian actor Giancarlo Giannini as her stern father and Anthony Quinn as the indulgent, *bon vivant* head of the dynasty.

Keanu was to play a young GI returning from the trenches in 1945 who befriended the daughter of a Mexican-American wine-growing family (in a new and not wholly convincing spin on his all-purpose ethnicity, he would be the 'gringo' constantly contrasted with the story's Hispanic characters). Discovering her to be unmarried, pregnant and terrified of her father's reaction, he gallantly agreed to pose as her husband for a single night, then to abscond taking with him the blame for her condition. But once he arrived at her home in California's Napa Valley, he fell under the spell of the countryside's other-worldly beauty, Sanchez-Gijon's exuberant family and the young woman herself.

This was for Keanu a strategically important film; indeed his managers had advised him in strong terms to do it. It was high time for him to step up to the plate and take on a romantic lead; it would be his first love story since becoming a major star – in fact his only substantial romantic role since

Jon Amiel's *Aunt Julia and the Scriptwriter* in 1989. It was also the chance to reposition himself in the wake of the Geffen business.

The cast embarked on an intensive three-week period of rehearsal and improvisations before shooting began. Keanu's character was meant to be haunted by his harrowing experiences during the war. 'We designed exercises that reveal and, in some ways, use your fears,' he recalled. 'I met with this man, a Marine, who fought in the Pacific. And he said, "Well, I didn't take my socks off for three months. I was always hot and wet. There was fungus and dysentery and disease and hunger." And I was trying to lay those feelings on myself.' In another exercise he imagined turning to a fellow-soldier on the battlefield and seeing that his jaw had been shot away.

Gary Cooper was his inspiration for the romantic scenes. But the rehearsals intended to create a sexual tension with his screen lover were trickier and Sanchez-Gijon found her co-star a little shy. Arau, too, thought him too buttoned up. 'I said, "Keanu, you are going to have to interpret as a grown man, as opposed to an adolescent,"' recalled the director, adding, on another occasion, 'He was stressed and insecure about it. When I'd ask him to say a romantic phrase differently, I could sense he was worried he'd be criticized.'

It was obvious from Keanu's early films that he had plenty of clinches and bedroom scenes under his belt, as it were. But his image had been changing and the romantic moments in his movies becoming sparser, he was out of practice with them, and at the same time under heavier pressure to perform than ever before. Now, on *A Walk in the Clouds*, one rumour (which the actor crossly denied) even claimed his snogging

technique was so poor that Arau told him to study videos of
Richard Gere and Kevin Costner, of all people, to improve it;
Gary Cooper was, apparently, old hat. (There was one good
reason why Keanu might have been below par in the kissing
department: his lip had been split open during a friendly
hockey game the night before one of his love scenes, leaving
him with six stitches on the inside and outside of his mouth:
soon afterwards he was barred from playing contact sports
while filming to prevent such injuries.)

Principal photography began on 27 July 1994: it was to
have been 28 July, but the official start date was hurriedly
brought forward on the advice of Arau's personal astrologer.
The director was convinced that this seer was to thank for his
present good fortune ever since she had advised his wife –
who had never tried her hand at a novel before – to write
Like Water for Chocolate and then urged Arau to film it. The
new venture would also be a great success, she said, favoured
by the happy alignment of the planets.

Arau, as befitted a true practitioner of magical realism,
turned out to be a child of the New Age. He would rise daily
at 4.30 a.m. to meditate and wore a crystal round his neck to
enhance his energy. Various gurus appeared on the set: an
acting coach who taught Keanu to make sounds before
shooting a scene to put himself 'into a certain emotional
place', and the astrologer, who held his hand and prescribed
him Bach flower remedies to drink daily. The actor was
doubtful about their effectiveness but conceded that he might
have felt worse without them.

Some of the cast were moved by the good karma. Quinn
applauded Arau's 'mystic message of opening the doors of

the mind, of love, affection, and reason', while Giannini spoke admiringly of his 'incredible fantasies'. Keanu was more equivocal. 'Mr Arau is a man of great pragmatism with a belief in, and a wanting to create, magic,' he said, adding with a shade of irony, 'maybe he knows how to talk to angels.'

There was one bright spot. Keanu had retained his youthful interest in wine and was now able to afford rather better vintages than when he was working for the Pastissima franchise in Toronto in the early Eighties. He had taken advantage of *Much Ado About Nothing*, shot in the heart of Chianti country, to inspect at length the local vineyards. 'He was very pleased to be in Tuscany,' Kenneth Branagh recalled. 'He's a genuine buff; he's not a huge drinker but he certainly likes his wine. And he's very generous with it; in the past he's given Em [Emma Thompson] and I some lovely bottles. I think he regards it as one of life's great pleasures.' Now Keanu had another chance to indulge his passion and swapped notes with Robert Mark Kamen, the screenwriter of *A Walk in the Clouds*, who himself owned a vineyard in Sonoma County in Northern California near the film's locations.

The movie was being readied for release on 14 April 1995, but the reactions at early preview screenings persuaded Fox to postpone it. Kamen recalled, 'When we saw it with an audience for the first time, the studio knew it had something that would take careful selling. It's not your standard Hollywood fare; it might have been forty years ago but it isn't now. And they really needed some time to position it in the marketplace.' America was about to be assailed by a wave of sexually explicit movies, including *Strippers* and *Showgirls*, Paul Verhoeven's much hyped film about lap dancers, which had a restrictive NC-17 rating in America but was nonetheless opening on no fewer than 1,300 screens. How, the studio wondered, would audiences react to a film with a couple of chaste screen kisses and a hero implacably opposed to adultery?

When *A Walk in the Clouds* eventually opened on 11 August, the reviews veered wildly from 'lovely' (the *Chicago Tribune*) and 'terrific' (*Newsday*) to 'contrived and not just a little silly' (the *Los Angeles Times*) and even 'phenomenally atrocious' (the *Washington Post*). Several critics found the syrupy, highly filtered and colour-saturated images as empty and superficial as a wine commercial.

Arau had expressed his desire to depict Hispanics in a more sympathetic and realistic light than was still the norm in Hollywood, and so his choice of scriptwriter was slightly surprising. Kamen was certainly familiar with the wine-growing business, but had neither any major romantic films to his credit (he had scripted *Lethal Weapon 3* and the *Karate Kid* cycle) nor a Latin background. As a crash course, the director invited him on a ten-day trip to his country, taking in the pyramids at Teotihuacan and – predictably, given Arau's fascination with cooking – the cream of the restaurants in Mexico City; his production designers got similar treatment. Kamen declared himself 'completely swept away by the otherworldliness of these places and the texture and richness of their culture'. And Arau's film ended up as an idealized vision of middle-class Mexican-American culture.

One visitor to the set, eyeing the way the family's luxuriously appointed hacienda was groaning with fine farm food and designer-rustic accessories, described it as a Martha

Stewart wet dream, referring to America's high priestess of domestic chic. Lavish dinners were accompanied by silver candlesticks and the strains of Vivaldi. One pseudo-mystical scene featured an 'Aztec ritual' involving a conch shell.

Critics were also sharply divided over Keanu. Some felt that his personal star presence was sufficient to carry the role. 'This is his most engaging performance yet,' judged the *Boston Globe*. 'While his character is anything but complex, he finds and projects a decency that fills him out a bit and adds to his appeal.' For the *San Francisco Chronicle*, the film signalled his emergence as a 'mature, charismatic movie star ... Reeves' face is the movie's locus of kindness and decency – and he stands up to scrutiny. There's not just sweetness there but depth.'

The *New York Times*, by contrast, found 'Keanu Reeves in one of his off roles, sleepwalking dutifully but seeming to share the audience's bewilderment over how he wound up in this awkward, slow-moving story.' *USA Today* compared him to 'a flat root beer'. Any hopes the producers might have had that the film could be hitched to a real-life romance were doomed to failure. 'That's a private question,' the actor retorted when quizzed on his love life. His date for *Walk*'s LA premiere was his mother.

There were several reasons why Keanu did not appear to his best advantage. For one thing, the troubled, shell-shocked soldier he played was humourless and stolid compared to the flamboyant Latin types around him. And his highly interior acting style was, anyway, in a different, lower key than that of booming, larger-than-life players like Quinn; these two performers' scenes together set each man off to his worst advantage, making the one look hammy and the other wooden. None of the cast came well out of the picture: Arau's over-fondness for emotional reaction shots required them to deliver a constant series of teary close-ups and sentimental smiles, while some of the lines ('You're waiting for a ride?' 'No! A miracle!') defied all attempts to make them credible.

Keanu himself believed that the film had been edited in a way which impaired his performance: even before it opened, he had already, in the obligatory round of promotional interviews, declared himself disappointed with the final cut because scenes showing his character's weaker side had been lost. 'Now he's Superman,' he sighed. 'I think sometimes in films they don't want actors to take real risks that might complicate the image they are hoping will sell a few more tickets. I like to show my insecurities, but I find more often than not they cut them. A hero who brings real life to the screen, well, maybe they're not sure they want such a person.'

Arau, for his part, declared that it was always his intention to make a simple, deliberately old-fashioned movie. 'Listen, I was an actor. We actors *always* criticize the director for missing scenes. But we did a classic melodrama that doesn't run too deep. What Keanu had in his mind was never in my plan.' And he seemed vindicated, at least in commercial terms. *A Walk in the Clouds* did solid, if not blockbusting business in America, remaining in the chart for many weeks that autumn, while sexually explicit films like *Showgirls* and *The Scarlet Letter* (the literary classic, transformed into a 'seventeenth-century sex sizzler') bombed resoundingly.

10

THE LEAP FROM THE BRIDGE

Keanu had not shone in his last two movies, and scornful comments were becoming commonplace. The generous and respectful notices he had earned regularly at the beginning of his career were long forgotten and, while his contemporaries – River Phoenix, Tom Cruise, Robert Downey Jr, Brad Pitt, Woody Harrelson, Edward Norton – were notching up their Oscar nominations, official peer-group recognition continued to elude him. For many he was now a pretty boy star who did not deserve serious consideration.

His admirers claimed that the poor reviews of those films, and of *Hamlet*, were no more than another instance of mean-spirited critics keen to knock him off his new perch on the Hollywood A-list. Some argued that he was being reviled for failing – or refusing – to fit into the established mould of American Method acting which had shaped most of his peers. 'I don't talk about his work as acting, I talk about it in terms of performance,' said the artist-lecturer Stephen Prina of his college course on Reeves' films. 'There's a difference. Performance means that you adopt many different methods or tropes; you don't become the character. Good acting seems to imply that there's one way to do it; you get all the technique down but it always produces the same kind of effect, the same kind of naturalistic acting style.'

For the British director Clive Donner, who had followed Keanu's films since working with him at the beginning of his career on *Babes in Toyland*, it was Keanu's unusual itinerant childhood which set him apart from the rest of the Hollywood Bratpack. 'The same values underlie a huge amount of the young talent that's come through in American acting,' he said. 'They all bring the same baggage – television, movies on television – and this in a sense defines them. Some are obviously more talented than others, but what makes them tick comes basically from an American – the American – cultural consciousness. An enormous number of people who make it to the top in Hollywood have had some other thing to kickstart them. And what it is with Keanu is that curious cosmopolitan family background – curious in the rich sense. It has produced something that is slightly different and has, I think, more depth; it gives him an edge over your traditional classic American character.'

On the other hand 'different' does not always necessarily mean 'better' and the fact remained that *A Walk in the Clouds*, despite a couple of good reviews and reasonable box-office, made its way onto a fair sprinkling of Year's Worst lists at the end of 1995, while *Johnny Mnemonic* had been an outright critical and commercial flop. Keanu's work was stiff in both films, comparing unfavourably to the fresh and lively characterizations he delivered effortlessly at the beginning of his career. It was as if, for all the acting coaching, reaidng and honing of technique he had become momentarily transfixed in the spotlight of his own star power.

Keanu was not one for coasting through a role on autopilot: as his colleagues on *Hamlet* had observed, when he fell, he fell spectacularly. 'He's a very honest actor and when he can't get his hands around a role he fails,' said Alex Winter, his old friend and fellow dude. The writer Christopher Hampton recalled such an occasion during the shooting of *Dangerous Liaisons*. 'His first appearance in the film comes at the end of a very long tracking shot all round the opera house which finishes with him looking down from the gods, moved by the music. It was a fantastically elaborate shot to set up and he couldn't do it at all.

'Eventually we spoke to him about it and he said, "I can't understand this music." We suggested he go off and listen to something on his Walkman which he could get into, so that he wouldn't be unduly put off by the Gluck. I think he's very truthful. He may not have a large expressive range but, in a sense, that's a positive anecdote. My impression is that he doesn't fake things.'

Jon Amiel, who had drawn a performance of some warmth and charm from Keanu in *Aung Julia and the Scriptwriter* five years ago, thought the problem might be the lack of guidance from intimidated or lazy directors which actors increasingly encounter as they rise to the top of their profession. 'What seemed to me very clear in the choices that Keanu has made was that here was somebody with great ability who was looking to learn,' he said. 'He needed a lot of help, by which I don't mean to say that he's a bad actor or that he needed more than other actors do. He's someone who looks for and responds to close work with the director.

'Unfortunately, I don't think he got that in either *Johnny*

Mnemonic or *A Walk in the Clouds*. I'm afraid that one of the things that happens to actors is the higher up the salary scale they climb, often, the less directors tend to involve themselves in what they're doing on camera: it's bizarre but a lot of film directors don't like actors that much or don't know what to do with them. And I don't think that helps Keanu at all. He has tremendous natural talent but he's not bullet-proof on the screen and if he's not fully inside a moment, inside a line, inside his character, he can appear very gauche.'

Keanu himself did not seem overly anxious about these setbacks. When it was put to him that he had 'moved into the driver's seat in Hollywood' post-*Speed*, he simply joked. 'No, man, not after *Johnny Mnemonic*, they took me out. I was just getting in the car and they said, "Excuse me sir, can we see your ID?"' And in the summer of 1995 he made a left turn and took off on tour with his band, Dogstar.

This was nothing new. Rock music had played an integral part in his childhood. And he had long been an enthusiastic, if not especially accomplished guitarist. 'We played bass together,' said Winter, recalling the filming of *Bill and Ted's Excellent Adventure*. 'We would just sit together and jam for about nine hours a day.' The movie itself called for the pair to play together in a fictional band, Wyld Stallyns, the joke being that the group was terrible.

That aspect of the film did not require much acting. Scott Kroopf, the producer, had the misfortune of occupying the apartment above Keanu's during the shoot. 'He and Alex would jam on bass almost constantly. It was like listening to someone learning how to play. I found it ultimately relaxing but at first . . . Believe me, he's really gotten a *lot* better.' On *Bill and*

Ted's Bogus Journey, Reeves and Winter were joined on drums by Peter Hewitt, the director, who was equally umimpressed. 'He was lousy, we were all lousy, we would just make a lot of noise and thrash around,' he said. But Keanu persisted.

Dogstar proper had been born in 1991 in a Los Angeles supermarket, where Keanu ran into Bob Mailhouse, an actor who had once been a regular on the television soap opera *Days of Our Lives*. The two discovered a shared love of hockey and music – Mailhouse was a drummer – and began playing together for fun. Soon afterwards Gregg Miller, another actor, came on board as guitarist and vocalist and they became Dogstar: the name, meaning Sirius, the brightest star in the sky, had been picked by Mailahouse out of Henry Miller's *Sexus*. Finally in 1994 the group acquired another guitarist, Bret Domrose, a veteran of a San Francisco punk band called The Nuns. Dogstar's style, which Keanu described as 'Folk thrash', was influenced by garage bands like The Pixies and included a cover of The Jam's 'The Modern World'.

Dogstar played a few odd gigs that year, in small bars like the Belly Up tavern in San Diego, and at a heavy metal concert in Milwaukee whose hardcore audience failed to warm to its folk thrash covers of Grateful Dead classics. Rock critics, too, were less than bowled over: one wrote in 1993 (before Domrose's arrival), Dogstar 'is not a good band. It's not a bad band. It's three friends making a noise... Their original [songs] sound something like Flipper meets ... an industrial accident.' Another reviewer compared Keanu in equally unflattering terms to 'a confused puppy: a little dazed, sort of cute and eager to please', and remained unimpressed by his strummings on a white bass guitar.

Keanu did not take his night job too seriously. 'It's just some fun and some free beer with friends,' he said. 'I still can't play what I want to hear. I'm not good enough yet. I'm still just learning, but I'm working on it.' But the gigs sold sufficiently well for Dogstar to essay a twenty-city american tour in the summer of 1995, preceded by six concerts in Japan. The band prudently confined itself to small and funky independent venues, and was rewarded with sell-out bookings. The set consisted of about fifteen or sixteen songs, mainly originals, although it also included cover versions of Neil Young's 'Rockin' In The Free World' and Fugazi's 'Merchandise'. At this stage Dogstar had not secured a record contract.

On stage Keanu did his best to keep a low profile, avoiding eye contact with his fans and favouring his customary grunge look: check shirt, steel-capped black boots, black jeans and black knit cap pulled down low over his eyes. He contributed one number, an Elvis Costello-like tune called 'Isabel' which he had written himself and sang 'worse than badly', according to one reviewer. As for his playing, another wrote that he 'managed to thump out acceptable basslines', even if he did effectively use only one string. Above all, he seemed painfully self-conscious and ill-at-ease, his body language as robotic as Johnny Mnemonic's. He could hardly be blamed, since his predominantly teenage, female fans would not allow him to move or speak, let alone sing, without responding with a chorus of shrieks and a shower of underwear (other band members had the impression of playing to a sea of left ears.) They were definitely agreed: Dogstar was a whole lot better than the Wyld Stallyns.

The critics were cooler (though by no means scathing), describing the Dogstar sound variously as 'passable' or 'credible', neither better nor worse than any number of other West Coast garage bands. Some sniped at the tour as a vanity project that would never have happened without the pulling power of its bassist. Others, more sympathetic, remarked that Keanu would not be the first film star to moonlight as a rocker (others include Johnny Depp, Lou Diamond Phillips and River Phoenix) and asked: why begrudge him this modest pleasure? 'Anybody who has ever played music with someone else knows the reason K.R. was up on stage,' wrote the *New York Post*. 'Because making music with and for friends is not only addictively fun, it's an ancient part of what makes us human.'

By the end of September Dogstar – now minus Miller, who had left the group over 'artistic differences' – had graduated to a higher league, opening a Bon Jovi concert in Los Angeles. And, marvellous to relate, the reviews were relatively kind. The *Los Angeles Times* compared them favourably to the slick and over-packaged superficiality of the headline act, suggesting 'it is more interesting watching a band struggling to find its voice than one that has settled for a borrowed one.' The following month the trio also supported David Bowie at the Hollywood Palladium and, in November, took off with Bon Jovi on a ten-day tour of Australia and New Zealand.

Most importantly, they were having a ball. Some nights, high on the excitement of performing, they would make tracks to a hockey ground after a gig and play into the early hours of the morning. They planned to send themselves up gently by shooting a 'mockumentary' of the tour modelled on

Rob Reiner's classic comedy about a no-talent band, *This Is Spinal Tap*. The film would present Dogstar as the 'embodiment of Bill and Ted' and would feature a number of running jokes about their fans' miraculous ability to outwit security guards and the regularity with which the group always lost its post-gig hocky games.

The tour was a welcome break from the acting treadmill which had been taking over Keanu's world. 'Between films, I can't understand why, I don't really have the feeling I exist,' he said in 1993. 'Perhaps it's due to the fact that, after all, I'm still a novice and it's normal that everything revolves around cinema.' To colleagues like Scott Kroopf, it looked like a sign that the actor was finally getting himself a life. 'He's got a ton of energy and sometimes when you have that much energy you can work yourself a little too hard,' Kroopf said. 'Last time I saw him he seemed to have gotten a little wiser about that and built in some time to kick back and have some fun. Doing the music is a whole different rhythm for him.'

Filmwise, Keanu was at a crossroads. The obvious route would be to cash in on *Speed*'s big payday and sign up for another lucrative action picture. But, true to form, he had been drawn instead to an odd script which had come his way; a dark comedy called *Feeling Minnesota* by an unknown filmmaker, Steven Baigelman. Baigelman, aged thirty-four and, like Keanu, an ex-Torontonian, had developed his script at a Sundance workshop; it would be his first project both as writer and as director. The story (and the title) was inspired by a verse from a song by the Seattle band Soundgarden. Baigelman was haunted by its indefinable melancholy. 'It evoked a feeling in me, a feeling of being stuck, a feeling of malaise,' he said. 'I sort of felt grey when I heard those two words.'

Keanu would play a petty criminal who fell for a woman marrying his brother to settle a gangland debt. The couple eloped to Las Vegas with bloody consequences. But, Baigelman underlined, there was a happy end – of sorts. 'Their escapades, as dark and extreme as they are, are, at least in my own perverse mind, also funny. I also find it very romantic but that may be perceived as perverse as well, because it's not straightahead "boy meets girl, boy loses girl, boy gets girl." It's more like "boy meets girl and has sex with her in the bathroom on the day she gets married to his brother" or it's "boy finds dead body of girl and buries her while he's still in love with her." That kind of thing.' At first Keanu found the tone harsh and puzzling (in one scene his character's ear was severely bitten by his brother in a fight). But on a second reading it seemed to fall into place. 'One of his last speeches in the film is that you've got to read between the lines,' Baigelman said. 'The second time round he was able to read between the lines of the script and see it as a very romantic story.'

The two met at the offices of Danny De Vito's Jersey Films – the company producing the picture – on the Sony lot and hit it off; the director was pleasantly surprised at how easily the pieces fell into place. 'We were talking to this actor and that actor in a preliminary situation, but there were so many agents and lawyers and this and that, and innuendo coming back our way. But with Keanu it was very straightforward. Once he'd decided that he liked the script he came in and had a meeting and two days later said he'd like to do it and never stepped away from the project.

'This was all before *Speed*. It came out some short time later and of course was a big smash. At that point his commitment to the film was moral, not contractual – in Hollywood it takes longer to make a deal than it does to make a movie, not because there was any hold-up on Keanu's part, but because lawyers need to collect their pay cheques at the end of the week and therefore spend most of their time making other people miserable. So he was certainly within his legal rights to bail.

'In my experience, limited as it is, people tend to fear the worst because oftentimes in Hollywood the worst happens: you think your film's about to go and suddenly the sky falls in. But there was never the fear of God put into me that maybe Keanu would bolt or some movie that could pay his full price would come along or with so many new offers maybe my film would have to wait in line behind one or two others. And I think the reason was that he is a person of his word. He was doing the movie because he wanted to play the part, because he wanted to work with Vincent D'Onofrio [who would play Keanu's brother], because he trusted me as a director. He's very honourable that way. It never seems to be about the money for him.' This was as well since, with a budget nudging $10 million, *Feeling Minnesota* was hardly likely to be offering Keanu a fee of *Speed* proportions: he would receive in the region of $200,000.

It seemed like a shrewd move. More and more actors in Hollywood were following a zig-zag course between commercial and independent projects. On their way up the ladder they might, like Keanu, take on a genre picture to boost their bargaining muscle. But afterwards just as many opted – like

Bruce Willis in *Pulp Fiction* or Wesley Snipes in *To Wong Foo Thanks For Everything! Julie Neumar* – to return to low-budget, performance-driven pieces as a long-term career investment. As an industry analyst in *Variety* pointed out, one failure in a small film could do far less damage to a star than an expensive flop like Sylvester Stallone's *Oscar* or Arnold Schwarzenegger's *The Last Action Hero*. Working for small change had become a badge of integrity.

Feeling Minnesota went into production in Minneapolis in mid-April 1995, wrapping in Las Vegas in early June. A romantic comedy, if of a strikingly unconventional kind, it required Keanu to draw on some of the characteristics which Baigelman had liked in his early work but which he had not seen for a while: the 'heroic outsider quality' of *River's Edge*, the 'goofiness and gawkiness' of the Bill and Ted movies and the tenderness of the campfire scene in *My Own Private Idaho*. 'My film gave him room to be strong and centred and passionate and sweet and hopeful,' the director said. 'Those were things I'd seen in bits and pieces throughout his different films that I wanted to bring together.

'In person he had many of those qualities all combined. He's sort of a paradox: he can be a brooder at times but there are other times when he is shamelessly hopeful. Recently he reminded me that I had every so often to send flowers to my wife: that was a very important thing for somebody who has been married for a while. So clearly there's this romantic side to him, although I wouldn't claim to know him very well. I'd like to know about the stuff he thinks about when he's by himself but he's very private. I don't get a strong impression of what his life is about.'

The film also required the actor to perform his first full-blown sex scene in quite a while, in the sequence where he met Diaz's character, and made furious love to her on her wedding day (as usual it was Keanu's leading lady who took the sexual initiative in seducing him). The director dismissed the predictable questions about Keanu's inexperience in this department. 'These are two really hot people who have some attraction for each other ... Keanu and Cameron looked like they were enjoying themselves,' he said. 'The most difficult part was keeping Keanu's thing inside the jock. If it fell out, he'd put it back in and go on. That was the only problem logistically.'

Above all, Baigelman intended *Feeling Minnesota* to be a sharp break from the high artifice of Keanu's last two movies. 'The film has a very real look; there's not a whole bunch of fancy stuff in it. I went for that kind of American Seventies look, as gritty and simple as I could get it. And I think what you see is a very naturalistic performance from Keanu; it was my intent and goal to get him there. I knew I didn't want a cold and once-removed kind of performance.'

In the event the film was received almost unanimously as a severe disappointment. *Variety* described it as unappealing and charmless, while the *Village Voice* reviewer found it 'so utterly and ineptly exploitative, so utterly and ineptly derivative, so utterly inept, period, that you have to consider why reputable actors signed on to it.' It was clear that like many other debut movies, *Feeling Minnesota* owed its existence to Quentin Tarantino, in both its lowlife setting and its mix of extreme violence and would-be comedy (even the ear-biting scene had its antecedents in Tarantino's *Reservoir Dogs* and, more distantly, David Lynch's *Blue Velvet*). Baigelman was by no means the first or last Tarantino wannabe to fail to pull off the sudden mood shifts and idiosyncratic humour of his mentor.

Few blamed Keanu for the film's failure. His performance was, as Baigelman had hoped, more relaxed and open than his other recent work. But he and Diaz were never allowed to become anything more than the least dislikeable of a large cast of unpleasant, foul-mouthed, aggressive characters. Indeed many critics wondered why he and the other actors had been attracted to the script so unworthy of their talents.

Keanu had also been considering an even smaller and quirkier project called *Voyeur: A Divine Comedy*, written and directed by another first-timer, a thirty-three-year-old British film-maker based in France named Rupert Wyatt. A loose modern adaptation of Dante's poem, the story concerned a writer who entered the underworld to research his new novel and met a series of characters representing the Seven Deadly Sins. It was budgeted in the region of $4 million. Through a mutual acquaintance Wyatt had asked Keanu to play 'Gluttony's Assistant', a cook in a Paris restaurant who succumbed in the course of the film to the sin of excess. Like his predecessors Wyatt found the actor undeterred by the thought of working with an untried talent. But when the production ran into extended financing difficulties Keanu eventually had to drop out of the project.

Malicious minds might have thought the role appropriate since he had been thoroughly indulging himself on the Dogstar tour, piling on the pounds, in the phrase of the tabloid cliché, and casually allowing his *Speed* muscles to run to flab; he had also been required to take up smoking for *Feeling Minnesota*. Now he had to shape up for *Chain Reaction* (originally titled *Dead Drop*), which should have gone into production in the autumn of 1995 but had been put back to January 1996, when filming began in Chicago.

It was to be directed by Andrew Davis, who had scored several substantial hits in this genre with *Under Siege* and *The Fugitive*. Keanu would earn $7 million plus a share of the box-office gross to star opposite Morgan Freeman, Fred Ward, Brian Cox and Rachel Weisz, as a young researcher who discovered the key to cheap, pollution-free energy but who then had to flee for his life when framed for a colleague's murder.

Applying himself to his new persona, Keanu spent time with a physics student at the University of Chicago's labs. Inevitably the press chortled at the thought of Keanu, science whizz. Quizzed about whether the actor had fully understood the mysteries of fusion by sonoluminescence, his adviser insisted, 'I think Keanu's intelligent,' to a disbelieving reporter. Elsewhere the *New York Post* created an 'I.Q. graph' to chronicle his improbable ease at getting cast as super-smart characters.

As usual the jibes were a little unfair. The script of *Chain Reaction* repeatedly insisted that Keanu's character was not a boffin but a humble machinist. He had flunked college after a failed experiment, was ingenuously impressed by Weisz's academic diplomas and had stumbled upon the magic formula by accident.

There was more substance in the observations that he moved 'with the speed and grace of someone in snowshoes' and was more than a tad jowly beneath the stubble. 'I wanted to look kind of heavy, have my hair long and greasy, grow a little bit of beard. Even the way I run, I tried to make it like someone who doesn't run much,' Keanu explained in his own defence: he was playing, as in *Feeling Minnesota*, a scruffy blue-collar character not a new edition of *Speed's* muscular, clean-cut Jack Traven. This was true enough, though the attention to detail was perhaps unnecessary in a movie where realism was not otherwise high on the agenda. And he may have been simply justifying his excess poundage.

The revuews – 'uninvolving'; 'relentlessly familiar' – were not good. The plot, which involved the interecine warfare between the FBI and the CIA, was confusing even to American critics. Another disappointment was the frosty chemistry between Keanu and Weisz, thanks mainly to the plodding, multi-authored script. The couple's most intimate scene as they holed up for the night in a deserted houser begins with Keanu asking his co-star if she would like sardines or sardines for dinner. 'Gosh, I think I'll have sardines' 'Good choice.' 'Is this how you seduce all the girls?' As witty, erotically charged sexual bandinage, this could have used some improvement.

Keanu took another brief detour into low budget film-making witha supporting role in *The Last Time I Committed Suicide*, a $2 million feature by a first-time writer-director named Stephen Kay. Set just after World War II, its slender story was based on the long letter written by Neal Cassady to his fellow beatnik Jack Kerouac, which eventually inspired the latter's classic Beat Generation novel, *On the Road*. Keanu played a slacker who became Cassady's friend.

Unveiled at the 1997 Sundance Festival, the movie won

guarded praise, but it was felt, the energy of its dialogue and visual style were let down by the rambling narrative. Keanu, wrote *Variety*, was 'OK, but far more comfortable in his early bard-of-the-pool-halol pose than he is in letting the pathos of a self-described "creepy and needy" figure come through.'

Further down the line *Speed 2* was on the cards for a while. But, after allowing his name to be linked to the sequel, which would have netted him a rumoured $11 million, Keanu withdrew in June on the eve of filming, pleading that the date clashed with plans for another Dogstar tour, although he later conceded that this was just an excuse.

Jan De Bont, the director of *Speed* and of its sequel, claimed he was not disappointed. In fact he hoped his new leading man (Jason Patric) would be able to bring the romance with co-star Sandra Bullock more into the foreground. 'I didn't fight that hard for Keanu,' he said. 'To me it's interesting to work with new people. Also, Keanu's a great actor: he has a very physical presence and charismatic looks. But spontaneity is not at the top of his abilities. It's very hard for him to express himself and to deal with direct emotions.

'When he's alone he's OK, but the moment he has other people around him he really freezes up. He doesn't enjoy the success of *Speed*. He came to the opening of *Twister* [De Bont's 1996 tornado blockbuster] and there were lots of photographers swarming around him. Some actors love it and that's what they do it for, and others freak out. He's one that freaks out. At the same time he likes to play music, where he's right up front. It's a very contradictory position.'

Keanu remained committed to the band, even renting warehouse space in Chicago so that they could rehearse during lulls in his schedule on *Chain Reaction*. Dogstar went on another five-week international tour in the summer of 1996, released a four-song EP in June, *Quattro Formaggi*, (named after a favourite pizza), produced by Ed Stasium at Zoo Records, and worked on an album, *Our Little Visionary*. But he was negotiating his new-found rock stardom with some difficulty. Journalists covering the British leg of Dogstar's 1996 tour noted his tendency to stand on stage a little aside and away from the spotlight, his insistence on being interviewed with the two other band members and, on some occasions, a reticence to the point of rudeness.

He had something to be grumpy about: Samuel Reeves had just been released from prison on parole, and proceeded to sell his story right and left. 'I love him and miss him greatly,' he told one magazine. 'I'm not interested in Keanu's money – never have been, never will be. But I'm proud of what he's achieved and I feel guilty because of the years I wasn't there for him.' His revelations were hardly embarrassing for his son: Keanu was, Samuel said, a bright, imaginative, well-behaved kid. But the unwanted return of this ghost from the past was undoubtedly disturbing.

De Bont believed that the decision to pass on *Speed 2* in favour of Dogstar stemmed from an emotional immaturity linked to the continuing lack of a father figure in Keanu's life. 'He's going through a difficult time right now. I'm not his dad – although he would like me to be – but I think he doesn't want to grow up: he wants to stay young. He's going through a growing process and if he finds something calmer in his personal life, it will change him a little bit. But it might take him a few years.'

Industry observers differed sharply over the wisdom of
making *Speed 2* without its key star. Some thought that, while
franchises with a strong pre-existing concept, such as the
Batman and Bond movies, could survive a radical cast change,
this was not the case with *Speed* which had depended on
Keanu's performance to make it a hit. Others argued that the
main draw of the first film had been its action sequences and,
besides, Bullock was by now established enough in her own
right to carry the sequel. 'There seems to be no consensus on
how *Speed 2* will do without Reeves,' concluded the *Los
Angeles Times*. One thing was certain, however: the film's
eventual success or failure would be a strong indicator of
Keanu's personal box-office clout.

Twentieth Century Fox, the studio behind the two *Speeds*,
A Walk in the Clouds and *Chain Reaction*, was hoping to keep
Keanu firmly tethered by offering him more action-oriented
scripts, like *Men of Honour*, a thriller about a journalist
targeted by the Mafia. And Warner Brothers was still wooing
him: he had reportedly been offered $9 million to star in a
big-budget sci-fi epic called *Soldier*. Both these came to
nought. But he was persuaded to take on a relatively commercial project for the same studio in the autumn of 1996.

Devil's Advocate, a supernatural thriller in the mould of
Rosemary's Baby, had almost gone before the cameras in 1992
as a vehicle for Brad Pitt with Joel Schumacher directing. The
film fell through when its other star, Al Pacino, dropped out
in order to make *Carlito's Way*. Now it was revived, with
Taylor Hackford at the helm.

Keanu was cast as an ambitious defence attorney, who
comes to New York from Florida and, after being inveigled

into helping free a guilty child molester, comes to believe that his boss might be the devil. One attraction of the project was the chance to work with Pacino, now back on board as the young lawyer's satanic mentor. Another was the Faustian story, which would allow Keanu to tackle a more ambiguous and complex character than he was usually asked to play.

'I become morally suspect,' he explained. 'I compromise and compromise. Gradually the evil entices and seduces me. I lose everything I love and believe in until there's a moment where you have to make a choice. Do you go all the way? Do you sell your soul for power and love of money?' Even so, he knew perfectly well that the film would involve all the conventional courtroom pyrotechnics: 'The problem is that [my character] is a bit of a Superman, a bit of a rock star in court.' And the early weeks of shooting were plagued by reports of friction, culminating in the dismissal of several key crew members.

As far as his future career went, Keanu did not look likely to be selling his soul either for big bucks or stardom. All his options were open. With one or two exceptions, like John Mackenzie and Peter Hewitt, Keanu's directors claimed he was an easy and enjoyable collaborator: Lawrence Kasdan was typical in saying, 'I'd work with him again in a second because we had a terrific time.'

But he had not formed anything resembling the creative long-term actor-director bond that Kasdan himself had developed with Kevin Kline, or Martin Scorsese with Robert De Niro. Indeed, with the exception of Gus Van Sant, he had never worked with any film-maker on more than one project.

It's hard to stick close to one's actors in the world we move in,' cautioned Jon Amiel. 'Those partnerships are actually quite rare. They're hard to form and I sense that Keanu's still really searching for some sort of screen identity. Until he finds that he's not going to find the director who would become his collaborative partner. My fear is that he'll make more dumb action movies because *Speed* has been his greatest success. My hope is that he continues to search, experiment and grow and that he will turn into one of Hollywood's most consistently interesting leading men.'

It is probable that an intimate professional relationship would be uncongenial to Keanu's loner streak. The order and pattern which this kind of regular teaming implied is at odds with a life which appeared to be wilfully without direction. In private he remained equally elusive. Unlike many Hollywood folk he kept aloof from politics: 'I guess I just deal with my own behaviour, my own life and friends there,' he said. 'I'm not involved, really, with any local community services but I've donated some money to some causes, which is the easiest thing to do.'

Most stars are loud in protesting that they hate the many incidental inconveniences of fame (protesting rather too much, one frequently feels), but Keanu was more justified than most in doing so since he availed himself of almost none of its material advantages. His personal possessions remained minimal. The downtime between movies would pass uneventfully, jamming with Dogstar, roaring around on one of his bikes (yet another accident in May 1996 left him with a broken ankle, although this one was the result not of reckless driving, but of swerving to avoid a car at a busy traffic junction), playing hockey, hanging out at coffee shops or spending an evening at Kim's Los Angeles home.

His sister had been fighting cancer for some years. Her illness had gone into remission, but Keanu spent time with her whenever he could and she was a frequent visitor to his film sets. He had also started taking ballroom dancing lessons – not, for once, in order to prepare for a role – just for the hell of it. He seemed interested in neither of the two most popular lifestyle choices traditionally open to film celebrities: settled domesticity in the Hollywood Hills, or a high-profile (and often rambunctious) nocturnal presence on the singles social circuit.

Asked about how he liked to relax, he recited a free-associational litany of modest pleasures: 'Lying in bed with my lover, riding my bike, sports, happy times with my friends, conversation, learning, the earth, dirt, a beautiful repast with friends and family, with wine and glorious food and happy tidings and energy and zest and lust for life. I like being in the desert, in nature, being in extraordinary spaces in nature, high in a tree or in the dirt, hanging out with my family, my sisters.'

Still loosely based at the Château Marmont with the rest of Dogstar, he remained of no fixed abode, and fans desiring to contact him were advised by his publicist, Robert Garlock, that he had no American fan club and no address to which letters could be sent. However an unofficial Keanu network existed in Britain, and there was a proliferation of websites on the Internet, mostly of a tongue-in-cheek mystical nature: Dudes of the Keanu Circle, Mirror Galaxy of Keanu Reeves, Planet Keanu, KeanuNet, The Society for Keanu Consciousness, and the like.

Like most stars Keanu was regularly asked why he had chosen his profession and his most vivid explanation was another rhetorical question: 'Did you ever want to jump off a bridge onto the back of a moving truck?' Acting gave him the same thrill as he found burning up the road on his motorbike, the thrill of risking his skin. His celebrity was, he always insisted, an unwanted by-product. He might be exposing himself to critical odium by taking those plunges into the blue, but he also earned the admiration of his peers. 'The way Keanu has run his career is very attractive to me,' said Lawrence Kasdan. 'He's interested in everything. He wants to be in *Much Ado* and he wants to be in *Johnny Mnemonic* and he wants to be in *Speed*. It's very unusual to have that seriousness about acting and that adventurousness about the parts. If you look at the young actors he's competing with, most of them don't take those chances. He has been interested in acting, not in stardom. An d, as often happens with actors like that, he has become a star.'

Therein lay the paradox of Keanu's position. To maintain that level of stardom he found himself under pressure to accept exactly the kinds of formula roles which offered little to attract him. 'Rob Lowe had quite a long run; so did Charlie Sheen, so did Rob Downey,' said Alex Winter of his friend's future prospects. 'What will happen to Keanu in ten years? He has just entered an echelon that those guys have left. I'm talking about how long one stays within a certain bracket. And I would say Keanu has as good a chance of falling out of it as any of them because that's the way Hollywood works. He will need to find a niche for himself that he can play better than anybody else. And he will need to have a string of hits. Otherwise he will be just another pretty face. So that's what he's up against for the first time in his career right now. It's a tough position for him to be in, only in that his longevity is questionable.'

Actors like to vanish into their roles. Stars might like to do so too, but their popularity springs from the niche marketing of a tested product. 'Perhaps in a way,' thought Clive Donner, 'even though Keanu has made all these unexpected movies, he's more in the tradition of the great Hollywood stars who are what they are: Greg Peck, Jimmy Stewart, Charlton Heston. He's obviously not as square as those gentlemen now seem. But he actually, with great seriousness, brings always what he has even though he does it in a different arena. I don't mean he's like Victor Mature who said, "You can have expression A or expression B". There is real acting there. But the great longevity of those people comes from the fact that audiences like to see what they've seen and enjoyed before.'

There was a striking consensus on what that something might be in Keanu's case: asked what had initially prompted them to cast him in their movies, directors pointed again and again to his innocence. Innocence is a peculiarly versatile, all-purpose virtue. It can qualify you equally well to play a valley boy, or a great oriental sage or a straight-arrow, all-American good guy. In a crucial sense its passive and intangible quality – bound up with the absence of experience, or of malice – lay at the heart of his spaced-out persona. 'It's really rare to find such a genuine level of out-of-it-ness,' said one former collaborator. 'The non-conventionalness of his attitude to the world is very disengaged, in a genial sort of way.'

Asked what he thought set him apart from other young

male actors, Keanu himself suggested that the point of comparison should perhaps be with *actresses*. 'I can't say that I *have* been totally different from other actors my age,' he said. 'I mean, I've always played the kind of male equivalent of the female ingénue. You know what I mean? I've always played innocents. That has been a recurring theme throughout my career. There's only been a few instances where I didn't play that role, *I Love You To Death* was one example. And *Speed*. Maybe *My Own Private Idaho*. My career throughline is innocence, in a variety of different genres.'

You might think that anyone who speaks of his innocence in such a way is displaying a knowingness which contradicts that very quality. But a gap always exists between what an actor *is* in life and what he projects on screen. There are just as many of Keanu's friends and professional associates who also detected in him an 'inner turmoil', in the words of Dennis Hopper (his co-star in *River's Edge* and *Speed*), a pain and anger. His meatiest roles, dramatically speaking; in *Under the Influence* and *River's Edge* at the beginning of his career; in *My Own Private Idaho* and in *Hamlet* more recently – tapped into those emotions. 'I'd say he's far better than most people realize,' said Alex Winter. 'And I would also say that, other than *River's Edge*, he's not really done anything that shows how complex a character he can play. I think he has yet to show people what he can do.' If all goes well, the best is yet to come.

Keanu's film and television work, with date of production FILMOGRAPHY

YOUNGBLOOD (1984)

Director: Peter Markle. Screenplay: Markle. Producers: Patrick Wells, Peter Bart / United Artists. Cast: Rob Lowe, Cynthia Gibb, Patrick Swayze, Ed Lauter, Fionnula Flanagan, KR.
Comedy-drama about a farm boy (Lowe) who joins a minor-league ice hockey team; Keanu plays the French-Canadian goalie.

FLYING a.k.a. DREAM TO BELIEVE (1984)

Director: Paul Lynch. Screenplay: John Sheppard. Producer: Anthony Kramreither / Brightstar Films. Cast: Olivia D'Abo, KR, Jessica Steen, Rita Tushingham, Samantha Langevin, Sean McCann, Renee Murphy, Samantha Logan.
Keanu plays the boyfriend of a young gymnast (D'Abo) fighting her way back from a leg injury.

YOUNG AGAIN (1985)

Director: Steven H. Stern. Screenplay: Barbara Hall. Producer: Stern / Walt Disney Productions. Cast: Lindsay Wagner, Robert Urich, KR, Jack Gilford, Jessica Steen.
Comedy about a middle-aged man (Urich) who is granted his wish to be seventeen again; Keanu plays him as a teenager.

UNDER THE INFLUENCE (1985)

Director: Thomas Carter. Screenplay: Joyce Rebeta-Burditt. Producer: Vanessa Greene / CBS. Cast: Andy Griffith, Paul Provenza, KR, Dana Andersen, Season Hubley.
Portrait of an alcoholic (Griffith) and his destructive effect on his family as his younger son (Keanu) starts to follow in his footsteps.

ACT OF VENGEANCE (1985)

Director: John Mackenzie. Screenplay: Scott Spencer. Producer: Jack Clements / Telepix Canada. Cast: Charles Bronson, Ellen Burstyn, Wilford Brimley, Hoyt Axton, Ellen Barkin, KR.
The true story of the United Mine Workers official Jock Yablonski and his fight against crooked labour leaders; Keanu plays a hired assassin.

RIVER'S EDGE (1986)

Director: Tim Hunter. Screenplay: Neal Jimenez. Producers: Sarah Pillsbury, Midge Sanford / Hemdale. Cast: Crispin Glover, KR, Ione Skye Leitch, Dennis Hopper, Joshua Miller, Daniel Roebuck.
When a youth murders his girlfriend, none of his friends dares tell the police until Keanu finally breaks the silence.

BROTHERHOOD OF JUSTICE (1986)

Director: Charles Braverman. Screenplay: Noah Jubelirer, Jeffrey Bloom. Producers: Judith R. James, Margot Winchester / Guber-Peters Entertainment. Cast: KR, Kiefer Sutherland, Lori Loughlin, Joe Spano, Billy Zane.
Keanu plays the leader of a high school vigilante gang who comes to have doubts about their activities.

BABES IN TOYLAND (1986)

Director: Clive Donner. Screenplay: Paul Zindel. Producers: Tony Ford, Neil T. Maffeo / Bavaria Film Studios. Cast: Drew Barrymore,

Pat Morita, Eileen Brennan, KR, Jill Schoelen, Richard Mulligan, Googy Gress.
A group of young people (including Barrymore and Keanu) are transported to a fairytale village where they must battle the evil Barnaby Barnacle.

THE NIGHT BEFORE (1986)

Director: Thom Eberhardt. Screenplay: Gregory Scherick, Eberhardt. Producer: Martin Hornstein / Kings Road. Cast: KR, Lori Loughlin, Trinidad Silva, Theresa Saldana, Susanne Snyder.
Keanu's prom date from hell ends in an evening of comic disasters on the wrong side of town.

BILL AND TED'S EXCELLENT ADVENTURE (1987)

Director: Stephen Herek. Screenplay: Chris Matheson, Ed Solomon. Producers: Scott Kroopf, Michael S. Murphey, Joel Soisson / Interscope Communications. Cast: KR, Alex Winter, George Carlin, Bernie Casey, Robert V. Barron, Rod Loomis, Jane Wiedlin, Tony Steadman, Terry Camilleri.
Two dopey Californian teenagers (Keanu and Winter) go time travelling to collect material for a school project.

MOVING DAY / TRYING TIMES (1987)

Director: Sandy Wilson. Screenplay: Bernard Slade. Producer: Jon S. Denny / Zorah Productions. Cast: Candice Bergen, Ted Stidder, Ketty Lester, Bruno Gerussi, KR.
In this final half-hour of a six-play television series, a family moves house amid growing chaos. Keanu plays the removal man's son, a would-be ballet dancer.

PERMANENT RECORD (1987)

Director: Marisa Silver. Screenplay: Jarre Fees, Alice Liddle, Larry Ketron. Producer: Frank Mancuso Jnr. / Frank Mancuso Jnr.

Productions for Paramount. Cast: Alan Boyce, KR, Michelle Meyrink, Lou Reed.
Keanu struggles to make sense of his best friend's suicide.

THE PRINCE OF PENNSYLVANIA (1987)

Director: Ron Nyswaner. Screenplay: Nyswaner. Producer: Joan Fishman / New Line. Cast: KR, Fred Ward, Bonnie Bedelia, Amy Madigan, Jeff Hayenga.
Keanu hatches a crackpot scheme to kidnap his own father (Ward).

DANGEROUS LIAISONS (1988)

Director: Stephen Frears. Screenplay: Christopher Hampton, based on the novel by Choderlos De Laclos. Producers: Norma Heyman, Hank Moonjean / Warner Brothers. Cast: John Malkovich, Glenn Close, Michelle Pfeiffer, Swoosie Kurtz, Uma Thurman, KR, Mildred Natwick, Peter Capaldi.
On the eve of the French Revolution, two decadent aristocrats manipulate the lives and loves of their peers; Keanu plays a young music teacher who becomes a pawn in their games.

LIFE UNDER WATER (1988)

Director: Jay Holman. Screenplay: Richard Greenberg, based on his own play. Producer: Holman / American Playhouse. Cast: KR, Sarah Jessica Parker, Haviland Morris, Joanna Gleason, Stephen McHattie.
A spoiled rich boy (Keanu) has a summer fling with a troubled young woman he meets on the beach, but shies away from emotional commitment.

PARENTHOOD (1989)

Director: Ron Howard. Screenplay: Lowell Ganz, Babaloo Mandel. Producer: Brian Grazer / Imagine. Cast: Steve Martin, Mary

Steenburgen, Dianne Wiest, Jason Robards, Rick Moranis, Tom Hulce, Martha Plimpton, KR, Leaf Phoenix.
Comedy about a large, mildly dysfunctional family; Keanu plays Plimpton's eccentric boyfriend.

I LOVE YOU TO DEATH (1989)

Director: Lawrence Kasdan. Screenplay: John Kostmayer. Producers: Jeffrey Lurie, Ron Moler / TriStar. Cast: Kevin Kline, Tracey Ullman, Joan Plowright, River Phoenix, William Hurt, KR, Miriam Margoyles.
A pair of incompetent hitmen (Keanu and Hurt) are hired by Ullman to kill her errant husband.

AUNT JULIA AND THE SCRIPTWRITER a.k.a. TUNE IN TOMORROW (1989)

Director: Jon Amiel. Screenplay: William Boyd, based on the novel by Mario Vargas Llosa. Producers: John Fiedler, Mark Tarlov / Polar Films. Cast: KR, Barbara Hershey, Peter Falk, Peter Gallagher, Elizabeth McGovern, Buck Henry.
In New Orleans, 1951, a young radio writer (Keanu) falls for his much older aunt (Hershey), while a colleague at the radio station (Falk) uses their relationship as the inspiration for a hit soap opera.

POINT BREAK (1990)

Director: Kathryn Bigelow. Screenplay: W. Peter Iliff. Producers: Peter Abrams, Robert L. Levy / Largo. Cast: Patrick Swayze, KR, Gary Busey, Lori Petty.
An FBI agent (Keanu) goes undercover to infiltrate a gang of bank robbers within the Southern Californian surfing community.

MY OWN PRIVATE IDAHO (1990)

Director: Gus Van Sant. Screenplay: Van Sant. Additional dialogue by William Shakespeare. Producer: Laurie Parker / New Line. Cast:

River Phoenix, KR, James Russo, William Richert, Michael Parker, Flea.
A rich kid slumming it on the streets of Seattle (Keanu) befriends then betrays a narcoleptic male hustler (Phoenix).

BILL AND TED'S BOGUS JOURNEY (1991)

Director: Peter Hewitt. Screenplay: Chris Matheson, Ed Solomon. Producer: Scott Kroopf / Interscope. Cast: KR, Alex Winter, George Carlin, William Sadler.
Bill and Ted travel to Heaven and Hell in order to prevent their evil robot alter egos from taking over the world.

BRAM STOKER'S DRACULA (1991)

Director: Francis Ford Coppola. Screenplay: James V. Hart, based on the novel by Bram Stoker. Producers: Coppola, Fred Fuchs, Charles Mulvehill / American Zoetrope. Cast: Gary Oldman, Winona Ryder, Anthony Hopkins, KR, Richard E. Grant.
Keanu plays a young English estate agent who is held prisoner at Dracula's castle while the vampire plots to seduce his fiancée.

FREAKED (1992)

Directors: Alex Winter, Tom Stern. Screenplay: Tim Burns, Winter, Stern. Producers: Mary J. Ufland, Howard Ufland / Pandora for Twentieth Century-Fox. Cast: Winter, Randy Quaid, Megan Ward, William Sadler, Mr T., Brooke Shields, KR.
While promoting toxic chemicals in the Third World, a jaded movie star (Winter) stumbles across a show of travelling freaks led by Ortiz the Dog Boy (Keanu).

MUCH ADO ABOUT NOTHING (1992)

Director: Kenneth Branagh. Screenplay: Branagh, adapted from the play by William Shakespeare. Producers: Stephen Evans, David Parfitt, Branagh / Renaissance. Cast: Branagh, Emma Thompson,

Denzel Washington, Richard Briers, Kate Beckinsale, Brian Blessed, Robert Sean Leonard, KR, Michael Keaton, Ben Elton.
Keanu plays the scheming Don John, who attempts to sabotage the match between Beckinsale and Leonard in Shakespeare's romantic comedy of errors.

EVEN COWGIRLS GET THE BLUES (1992)

Director: Gus Van Sant. Screenplay: Van Sant, based on the novel by Tom Robbins. Producer: Laurie Parker / Fourth Vision. Cast: Uma Thurman, Rain Phoenix, KR, Pat Morita, John Hurt, Lorraine Bracco, Angie Dickinson.
In America in the early Seventies, the travels of a hitch-hiker with giant thumbs (Thurman) lead her to a cowgirl ranch run by militant lesbians. Keanu plays the asthmatic Mohawk Indian with whom she has a brief date.

LITTLE BUDDHA (1992)

Director: Bernardo Bertolucci. Screenplay: Rudy Wurlitzer, Mark Peploe. Producer: Jeremy Thomas / Ciby 2000. Cast: KR, Ying Ruocheng, Chris Isaak, Bridget Fonda, Alex Wiesendanger.
A small American boy living in Seattle is chosen as the possible reincarnation of a respected lama. Keanu plays (in a flashback story) Prince Siddhartha, the young leader who became the Buddha 2,500 years ago.

SPEED (1993)

Director: Jan De Bont. Screenplay: Graham Yost. Producer: Mark Gordon / Twentieth Century-Fox. Cast: KR, Dennis Hopper, Sandra Bullock, Jeff Daniels.
A bus is wired to explode if its speed drops below 50 m.p.h. – unless a young SWAT agent (Keanu) can save it.

JOHNNY MNEMONIC (1994)

Director: Robert Longo. Screenplay: William Gibson, based on his own short story. Producer: Don Carmody / Alliance. Cast: KR,

Dina Meyer, Dolph Lundgren, Ice-T, Takeshi, Henry Rollins, Barbara Sukowa, Udo Kier.
In the twenty-first century, a courier (Keanu) transports electronic data via a microchip inside his head. But his latest consignment has overloaded his storage capacity.

A WALK IN THE CLOUDS (1994)

Director: Alfonso Arau. Screenplay: Robert Mark Kamen, Mark Miller, Harvey Weitzman. Producers: Gil Netter, David Zucker, Jerry Zucker / Twentieth Century-Fox. Cast: KR, Aitana Sanchez-Gijon, Anthony Quinn, Giancarlo Giannini.
A young GI returning from the Second World War (Keanu) agrees to pose as the husband of a beautiful but pregnant woman whom he meets on the bus and whose family owns a vineyard in the heart of Napa Valley.

FEELING MINNESOTA (1995)

Director: Steven Baigelman. Screenplay: Baigelman. Producers: Stacey Sher, Michael Shamberg, Danny DeVito / Jersey Films. Cast: KR, Cameron Diaz, Vincent D'Onofrio, Delroy Lindo, Courtney Love, Tuesday Weld, Dan Aykroyd.
Two brothers, both small-time hoods (Keanu and D'Onofrio), fall out violently over the love of a gangster's moll.

CHAIN REACTION (1996)

Director: Andrew Davis. Screenplay: Michael Bortman, J. F. Lawton, based on a story by Josh Friedman, Rick Seaman, Arne Schmidt. Producers: Schmidt, Davis / Twentieth Century-Fox. Cast: KR, Morgan Freeman, Fred Ward, Rachel Weisz, Brian Cox.
Two research scientists (Keanu and Weisz) who have discovered the key to cheap, pollution-free energy go on the run when they are framed for the murder of one of their colleagues.

THE LAST TIME I COMMITTED SUICIDE (1996)

Director: Stephen Kay. Screenplay: Kay. Producers: Louise Rosner, Ed Bates / Tapestry Films and Kushner-Locke. Cast: Thomas Jane, KR, Joe Doe, Tom Bower, Marg Helgenberger, Gretchen Mol, Claire Forlani, Adrien Brody.
Drama about the Beat Generation icons Jack Kerouac and Neal and Caroline Cassady based on a letter to Kerouac from Neal Cassady; Keanu plays Cassady's best friend Harry.

DEVIL'S ADVOCATE (1996)

Director: Taylor Hackford. Screenplay: Jonathan Lemkin, Tony Gilroy, based on the novel by Andrew Neiderman. Producers: Arnold Kopelson, Anne Kopelson, Arnon Milchan / Warner Bros and Regency Entertainment. Cast: KR, Al Pacino, Charlize Theron, Jeffrey Jones
Keanu plays a talented and ambitious defence attorney who suspects that the boss of the New York law firm he works for is the devil.

Theatre Work

WOLFBOY (1984)

Director: John Palmer. Playwright: Brad Fraser. Produced at the Theatre Passe Muraille, Toronto, April 1984. Cast: KR, Carl Marotte, Shirley Douglas, Beverley Cooper, Joanne Vannicola.
Keanu played a suicidal young man sent to a mental hospital, where he was seduced by a disturbed male prostitute who thought he was a wolf.

ROMEO AND JULIET (1985)

Director: Lewis Baumander. Playwright: William Shakespeare. Produced at the Leah Posluns Theatre School, Toronto, May/June 1985. Cast: The students of Leah Posluns.
Keanu played Mercutio, Romeo's brilliant and tragic best friend.

THE TEMPEST (1989)

Director: Tina Packer. Playwright: William Shakespeare. Produced at the Mount, Lenox, Massachusetts, July/September 1989. Cast: Andre Gregory, Marina Gregory, Midori Nakamura, Jonathan Epstein, Kenny Ransom, Robert Biggs, KR.
Keanu played Trinculo, one of Caliban's bibulous sidekicks.

HAMLET (1995)

Director: Lewis Baumander. Playwright: William Shakespeare. Produced at the Manitoba Theatre Center, Winnipeg, January/February 1995. Cast: KR, Stephen Russell, Robert Benson, Lisa Repo-Martell, Donald Carrier, Louisa Martin, Wayne Nicklas, Richard Hurst.
Keanu played the title role.

SOURCES

1   The Man in the Mickey Mouse Suit

Translation of Keanu from SJ interview with Liana Iaea-Honda, December 1995.

'Emilio and I sit around' *Movieline* September 1994.

Judith Church's Keanu poster from *Sunday Times* 2 April 1995.

'What's a keyring?' *Empire* December 1995.

Pinocchio The Big Fag reviewed in *Art Forum* April 1994.

Frisk by Dennis Cooper, Grove and Weidenfeld, 1991.

'I offered *Platoon* to Keanu' SJ interview with Oliver Stone, February 1996.

'Pre-*Speed* he was just customarily and ceremoniously written off' and following from SJ interview with Stephen Prina, October 1995.

'I hope the kids learn something worthwhile' *Dallas Morning News* 11 June 1994.

'I'm Mickey' *Vanity Fair* August 1995.

Keanu on his parents in Beirut from *Playboy* September 1988 and *Newsday* 18 September 1988.

Avoiding the draft from *Sunday Times Magazine* 17 April 1994.

'There were fights about Sam's drug-taking' *Mail on Sunday* 20 November 1994.

Keanu on his neighbourhood from *Interview* September 1990 and *Sugar* November 1994.

'It's not like the houses got bigger or anything' *People* 5 June 1995.

Samuel Reeves 'sort of disconnected' *Newsday* 18 September 1988.

Rock stars at the Reeves home from *US Magazine* March 1995.

'We never had anyone to play with us' *People* 5 June 1995.

'Keanu and I used to be very famous riders' SJ interview with Shawn Aberle, August 1995.

'He was a fun kid' SJ interview with Donald Mason, August 1995.

'Sometimes I thought she was strange' and following from SJ interview with Shawn Aberle.

'She seemed to know a lot' SJ interview with Alan Powell, August 1995.

Patric ahead of her time from *Sunday Times Magazine* 17 April 1994.

Missing his mom from *Flare* August 1989.

References to Samuel Reeves from *Toronto Sun* 5 July 1987 and *New York Post* 21 May 1987.

'The last time I saw him' *US Magazine* March 1995.

'He isn't anyone I really know' *San Francisco Chronicle* 18 July 1995.

'He's a very angry guy' SJ interview with Alan Powell.

'It wasn't a negative thing' SJ interview with Paul Robert, August 1995.

Keanu's obsession with acting from *Maclean's* 23 January 1995.

Keanu booted out of drama school from *People* 5 June 1995.

'He was a very funny guy' SJ interview with Scott Barber, December 1995.

'The ladies sure loved him' SJ interview with Dick Butti, August 1995.

Keanu in *The Crucible* from *Rolling Stone* 9 March 1989.

'Keanu was all ready to go' SJ interview with Scott Barber.

'He was very engaging and charismatic' SJ interview with Rose Dubin, August 1995.

'We were both arrested by him' SJ interview with Tom Diamond, September 1995.

'We'd all been studying there for quite some time' SJ interview with Tirzah Lea Tward, August 1995.

'I didn't think he was serious' SJ interview with Alan Powell.

'Everyone had learned these cheesy prepared monologues' SJ interview with Shael Risman, August 1995.

'I don't know if we're talking a great actor here' *Maclean's* 23 January 1995.

'I sent him out on a lot of casting calls' and following from SJ interview with Tracey Moore, November 1995.

'He was not the tidiest of people' *ibid.*

'At that time, people didn't dress that way' SJ interview with Rose Dubin.

'He always looked like this kid who lived out of a knapsack' SJ interview with Lucinda Sill, November 1995.

Keanu's dares from SJ interview with Shael Risman.

'There were memories of laughter and fun' SJ interview with Alan Powell.

'He could really put you on the spot' SJ interview with Diane Flacks, October 1995.

'That's not bad, but it's not quite a metre' SJ interview with Alan Powell.

'I was just loaded' SJ interview with Shael Risman.

'He's not a committed person' *ibid.*

'He was a very private guy' and following from SJ interview with Alan Powell.

'One of the jokes about Keanu' SJ interview with Tirzah Lea Tward.

2   A Babe in Hollywood

'It was not too memorable as a play' SJ interview with Rose Dubin, August 1995.

'It was terrible' SJ interview with Shael Risman, August 1995.

'About the survival of love' *Toronto Sun* 5 April 1984.

'I asked around and put ads' and following from SJ interview with John Palmer, August 1995.

Shooting the publicity stills for *Wolfboy* from SJ interview with David Hlynsky, July 1995.

'A real howler' *Toronto Globe and Mail* 5 April 1984.

'Bloody Awful, Awful Bloody' *Toronto Sun* 6 April 1984.

'The first couple of performances we had leather boys comin' out' *Interview* September 1990.

Unsuccessful *Breakfast Club* audition from SJ interview with Alan Powell, August 1995.

'He seemed like a real natural' and following from SJ interview with Peter Markle, September 1995.

Reviews of *Youngblood* from *Variety* 15 January 1986, *New York Post* 31 January 1986, *New York Times* 31 January 1986, *Boston Globe* 31 January 1986 and *Los Angeles Times* 31 January 1986.

Keanu on *Youngblood* from *If You're Talking To Me Your Career Must Be In Trouble* by Joe Queenan, Picador, 1994.

'It was a toss-up between two actors' and following from SJ interview with Paul Lynch, November 1995.

Reviews of *Flying* from *Variety* 21 May 1986, *Toronto Globe and Mail* 12 December 1986, *Toronto Star* 12 December 1986 and *Toronto Sun* 16 December 1986.

'Most of the kids coming in' SJ interview with Lewis Baumander, August 1995.

'He was so committed to that role' SJ interview with Shael Risman.

'For his age he was a brilliant Mercutio' SJ interview with Rose Dubin.

'There was something essential about himself' *Maclean's* 23 January 1995.

Casting of Keanu in *Young Again* from SJ interviews with Tirzah Lea Tward, August 1995 and Steven H. Stern, September 1995.

'That freaked me out completely' *US Magazine* March 1995.

'It was actually more intriguing' SJ interview with Tracey Moore, November 1995.

'Keanu is not the all-American boy' SJ interview with Lucinda Sill, November 1995.

'Trick is that teenager K. C. Reeves steps in' *Variety* 14 May 1986.

Having a good time in Toronto from *US Magazine* March 1995.

Career frustrations in Toronto from *Philadelphia Inquirer* 31 August 1989 and *Toronto Star* 10 April 1990.

'Roles don't open up for hometown boys' SJ interview with Lucinda Sill.

'In twenty minutes I was crazy about him' *Vanity Fair* August 1995.

'He used to call me every three months' SJ interview wth Alan Powell.

Reviews of *Under the Influence* from *Hollywood Reporter* 29 September 1986, *Variety* 15 October 1986 and *Los Angeles Times* 27 September 1986.

'It's hard to act in the morning' *US Magazine* March 1995.

'I was the second guy ever to kill Charles Bronson' from *New York Daily News* 14 September 1988.

'It was just a cough-and-spit' and following from SJ interview with John Mackenzie, March 1996.

Under the Influence reviews from *New York Times* 29 April 1986 and *Variety* 23 April 1986.

'I was just bad in it' *USA Today* 20 May 1987.

'What's missing is any real understanding' *Los Angeles Times* 17 May 1986.

'It was terribly difficult to cast that part' and following from SJ interview with Clive Donner, December 1995.

Drew Barrymore drunk at Rod Stewart concert from *Little Girl Lost*, Drew Barrymore with Jeff Gold, Pocket Books, 1990.

Reviews of *Babes in Toyland* from *New York Times* 12 December 1986, *USA Today* 19 December 1986 and *Los Angeles Times* 19 December 1986.

3   Excellent Adventures

Birth of Bill and Ted from *Starburst* May 1990, *Cinefantastique* August 1991 and *Premiere* (US) March 1992.

'We did an enormous talent search' and following from SJ interview with Scott Kroopf, January 1996.

The troubles of *Bill and Ted's Excellent Adventure* from *Starburst* May 1990 and *Cinefantastique* November 1989.

The Night Before having 'Hollywood technical difficulties' from *Toronto Sun* 5 July 1987 and *USA Today* 20 May 1987.

Review of *The Night Before* from *Variety* 27 April 1988.

Genesis of *River's Edge* from *Rolling Stone* 9 April 1987, *New York Times* 6 June 1987 and *Guardian* 1 October 1987.

Reviews of *River's Edge* from *New Yorker* 15 June 1987, *New York* 18 May 1987, *New York Times* 8 May 1987, *Village Voice* 12 May 1987, *Chicago Tribune* 29 May 1987, *People* 1 June 1987 and *Time* 1 June 1987.

Keanu promoting *River's Edge* from *New York Post* 21 May 1987.

Review of *Moving Day* from *Variety* 2 December 1987.

Frank Mancuso Jnr and Marisa Silver on *Permanent Record* from Paramount publicity notes.

Reviews of *Permanent Record* from *New York Times* 22 April 1988, *Variety* 20 April 1988, *Los Angeles Times* 22 April 1988, *Boston Globe* 22 April 1988, *Boston Herald* 22 April 1988 and *Philadelphia Inquirer* 22 April 1988.

Ron Nyswaner on casting Keanu in *The Prince of Pennsylvania* from New Line publicity notes and *Los Angeles Times* 1 October 1988.

Keanu's hair from *Sky* March 1989 and SJ interview with Scott Kroopf.

'A bit pathetic' *Newsday* 18 September 1988.

'When I do a gig' *Toronto Globe and Mail* 12 July 1991.

Reviews of *The Prince of Pennsylvania* from *Village Voice* 20 September 1988, *Variety* 18 May 1988 and *New York Times* 16 September 1988.

Keanu rejecting role in *The Fly II* from *Variety* 27 February 1995.

Genesis of *Dangerous Liaisons* from *Dangerous Liaisons, The Film*, Christopher Hampton, Faber and Faber, 1989, *American Film* December 1988, *Village Voice* 27 December 1988, *Films and Filming* March 1989 and *Independent on Sunday* 25 April 1993.

Keanu's audition from *Playboy* September 1988, *LA Style* December 1989 and *If You're Talking To Me Your Career Must Be In Trouble*, Joe Queenan, Picador, 1994.

Keanu mistaken for motorbike messenger from SJ interview with David Parfitt, June 1996.

'His first appearance in the film' SJ interview with Christopher Hampton, February 1997.

Keanu offered title role of *Nostromo* from SJ interview with Hugh Hudson, October 1996.

Keanu's bike rides from *Details* February 1989, *Rolling Stone* 9 March 1989 and *Independent on Sunday* 22 August 1993.

'I don't cry much on cue' *Rolling Stone* 9 March 1989.

Reviews of *Dangerous Liaisons* from *New York* 9 January 1989, *Newsweek* 26 December 1988, *New Yorker* 9 January 1989, *New*

York Post 21 December 1989, *Los Angeles Times* 21 December 1989 and *Variety* 21 December 1989.

'My Darceny, if you compare it to the book' from *If You're Talking To Me Your Career Must Be In Trouble,* Joe Queenan, Picador, 1994.

4   An Actor Prepares

Reviews of *Bill and Ted's Excellent Adventure* from *Village Voice* 28 March 1989, *New York Times* 17 February 1989 and 19 March 1989, *Los Angeles Times* 17 February 1989, *Hollywood Reporter* 17 February 1989 and *Variety* 22 February 1989.

'I don't think either one came before the other' and following from SJ interview with Alex Winter, June 1995.

'It's like the difference between *The Goodies* and *Monty Python*' SJ interview with Peter Hewitt, December 1995.

'Keanu has a dreamier side to him' and following from SJ interview with Scott Kroopf, January 1996.

'When I first played Ted it changed my life' *London (Ontario) Free Press* 9 July 1991.

'How do I play stupid people?' *Calgary Herald* 11 April 1990.

'Keanu is really well-read' *US Magazine* March 1995.

'What always struck me' SJ interview with Robert Mark Kamen, August 1995.

'I've never played stupid' *Vanity Fair* August 1995.

Keanu on acting his age from *New York Daily News* 14 September 1988.

'An adolescent in a one-parent household' *New York Times* 30 October 1988.

'One night my mother grounds me' *LA Style* December 1989.

Reviews of *Life Under Water* from *Los Angeles Times* 12 April 1989, *Newsday* 12 April 1989 and *New York Times* 12 April 1989.

Keanu wrestling with the media from *If You're Talking To Me Your Career Must Be In Trouble,* Joe Queenan, Picador, 1994.

Casting Keanu in *Parenthood* from *American Film* July 1990.

Reviews of *Parenthood* from *Variety* 2 August 1989, *New York Times* 2 August 1989, *Village Voice* 8 August 1989 and *Rolling Stone* 24 August 1989.

'Keanu flew out to LA' SJ interview with Lawrence Kasdan, July 1995.

'I was really awed at first' *Premiere* (US) May 1990.

'He's a real serious, tense guy' from *If You're Talking To Me Your Career Must Be In Trouble*, Joe Queenan, Picador, 1994 and *Calgary Herald* 11 April 1990.

'Marlon is not the swiftest person in the world' *LA Style* December 1988.

'I liked the guy, I wanted to work with him' *Interview* November 1991.

'It is the most fun I ever had on a movie' SJ interview with Kevin Kline, July 1995.

'It was really trippy' *Premiere* (US) May 1990.

The sneak previews of *I Love You To Death* from 'Kasdan on Kasdan' in *Projections 3*, edited by John Boorman and Walter Donohue, Faber and Faber, 1994.

Reviews of *I Love You To Death* from *Variety* 4 April 1990, *Rolling Stone* 3 May 1990 and *Los Angeles Times* 6 April 1990.

'That part of the film moves at its own pace' SJ interview with Lawrence Kasdan.

Keanu's Shakespearean ambitions from SJ interview with Kevin Kline.

Review of *The Tempest* from *Boston Globe* 11 July 1989.

Keanu's LA lifestyle from *Flare* August 1989.

Genesis of *Aunt Julia and the Scriptwriter* from *Time Out* 9 October 1991 and *Sunday Telegraph* 6 October 1991.

'Most of the kids he plays' *What's On In London* 16 October 1991.

Keanu's audition from SJ interview with Jon Amiel, November 1995, *London Evening Standard* 7 November 1991 and *New York Times* 21 October 1990.

Keanu's accent from *New York Times* 21 October 1990.

Keanu's love scenes *ibid* and SJ interview with Jon Amiel.

'Keanu is very hard on himself' SJ interview with Jon Amiel.

The film's title change from *Philadelphia Inquirer* 28 October 1990 and *Village Voice* 30 October 1990.

Distribution of *Aunt Julia* from SJ interview with Jon Amiel.

Reviews of *Aunt Julia* from *Hollywood Reporter* 18 September 1990,

Village Voice 30 October 1990, *New York Times* 26 October 1990, *Variety* 3 September 1990, *Los Angeles Times* 26 October 1990, *Wall Street Journal* 25 October 1990 and *Entertainment Weekly* 9 November 1990.

Keanu on *Aunt Julia* from *Attitude* September 1995.

5   Young, Dumb and Full of Cum

Kathryn Bigelow on Keanu's screen presence from Largo publicity notes for *Point Break*.

'Convincing everybody he was the right person' and following from SJ interview with Kathryn Bigelow, October 1995.

Keanu's surfing and skydiving *ibid* and *Toronto Globe and Mail* 12 July 1991.

'My character is a total control freak' *Movies USA* July 1991.

Point Break's homoeroticism from SJ interviews with Kathryn Bigelow and Patrick Swayze, November 1995.

Reviews of *Point Break* from *Variety* 15 July 1991, *Washington Post* 12 July 1991, *Los Angeles Times* 12 July 1991, *Newsday* 12 July 1991 and *Village Voice* 23 July 1991.

'I finished *Point Break* in Hawaii' *Movies USA* July 1991.

Genesis of *My Own Private Idaho* from *Even Cowgirls Get The Blues and My Own Private Idaho* (screenplays, with introduction), Gus Van Sant, Faber and Faber, 1993.

Casting Keanu and River Phoenix from SJ interview with Gus Van Sant, July 1995.

'Hurt my *image*?' *Interview* November 1991.

Phoenix being won over from *River Phoenix: The Biography*, John Glatt, Piatkus, 1995.

'We were driving in a car' *Interview* November 1991.

'I would not have done it if River hadn't done it' *Studio* (France) December 1993.

'They were very interested themselves' SJ interview with Gus Van Sant.

New Line's resistance to the Shakespearean scenes from *Even Cowgirls Get The Blues and My Own Private Idaho* (screenplays, with introduction), Gus Van Sant, Faber and Faber, 1993.

Keanu and River on Vaseline Alley from *River Phoenix: The Biography*, John Glatt, Piatkus, 1995.

'I hung out with Keanu more' interview by John Glatt with Scott Green, May 1994.

The jam sessions at Van Sant's house from *River Phoenix: The Biography*, John Glatt, Piatkus, 1995.

Keanu and River as Romeo and Juliet from *Interview* November 1991.

'They were pretty close' SJ interview with Gus Van Sant.

'River is diplomatic' *Gay Times* April 1992.

'*Idaho* is the story of a rich boy' *Interview* November 1991.

'Well, he's probably me' *Even Cowgirls Get The Blues and My Own Private Idaho* (screenplays, with introduction), Gus Van Sant, Faber and Faber, 1993.

'If I sent him a book' and following from SJ interview with Gus Van Sant.

'He has this kind of Mozart quality' *Elle* (US) October 1991.

'He pulled out all the stops' *River Phoenix: The Biography*, John Glatt, Piatkus, 1995.

Phoenix's changes to the campfire scene from *Even Cowgirls Get The Blues and My Own Private Idaho* (screenplays, with introduction), Gus Van Sant, Faber and Faber, 1993, and *Sight and Sound* January 1992.

'River thought his character loved Keanu' interview by John Glatt with Scott Green.

Scott Favor's effeminacy from 'Freewheelin', Gus Van Sant converses with Derek Jarman' in *Projections 2*, edited by John Boorman and Walter Donohue, Faber and Faber, 1993.

'There was always the question of why Scott Favor hangs on the street' SJ interview with Gus Van Sant and *Even Cowgirls Get The Blues and My Own Private Idaho* (screenplays, with introduction), Gus Van Sant, Faber and Faber, 1993.

Filming the three-way sex scene from *Interview* November 1991.

Keanu's comments on his character's sexuality from *New York Daily News* 17 July 1991 and *City Limits* 23 January 1992.

Keanu seen as geisha girl in *Vanity Fair* October 1991; his publicists' displeasure from *New York Post* 30 August 1991.

'Every actor has his own battles' *Movieline* November 1992.

'I used to be into alcohol and drugs' SJ interview with Alan Powell, August 1995.

'I want to be on speed!' *Interview* September 1990.

'Keanu had some trouble' from John Glatt interview with Scott Green.

Keanu 'strange and confused' from SJ interview with Peter Hewitt, December 1995.

River and Keanu on set from *Interview* November 1991 and *US Magazine* November 1991.

'In the Shakespeare world' *Interview* November 1991.

River's 'sublime performance' praised in *Film Comment* September/October 1991.

Keanu criticized in *Village Voice* 1 October 1991.

6   Bogus Journeys

Genesis of *Bill and Ted's Bogus Journey* from *Cinefantastique* August 1991.

'We were dying to make a better movie' SJ interview with Alex Winter, June 1995.

'Basically Ted is a lot dumber this time' *Los Angeles Times* 17 July 1991.

'Keanu and I' SJ interview with Alex Winter.

'Keanu and Alex were terribly helpful to us' SJ interview with Scott Kroopf, January 1996.

'It definitely brought a different perspective' SJ interview with Alex Winter.

'Often Keanu and Alex would sit around' *What's On In London* 15 January 1992.

'While we were filming he would seem' and following from SJ interview with Peter Hewitt, December 1995.

'To some degree the people who represent him' SJ interview with Scott Kroopf.

Keanu pushing himself too hard and pressures of filming from SJ interview with Peter Hewitt.

Ted Hair from SJ interview with Scott Kroopf.

'It was a very bold and interesting move' and following from SJ interview with Peter Hewitt.

'Keanu-nunus' from *Philadelphia Inquirer* 12 July 1991.

'I have seen Keanu Reeves in vastly different roles' *New York Daily News* 19 July 1991.

'Mr Reeves displays considerable discipline and range' *New York Times* 12 July 1991.

Keanu's appearance on the interview trail from *Toronto Star* 10 July 1991, *Winnipeg Free Press* 19 July 1991 and *Los Angeles Times* 17 July 1991.

Spitting on stage at the New York Film Festival from *Newsweek* 13 June 1994.

Keanu on the *Bill and Ted* merchandising from *London (Ontario) Free Press* 9 July 1991.

Keanu on the *Bill and Ted* sequel from *USA Today* 9 June 1994.

'I suppose it wasn't supported' SJ interview with Peter Hewitt.

'Keanu doesn't like promoting films, ever' SJ interview with Alex Winter.

Hailing an interview from *Details* February 1989.

'I'm a basket case, man' *Los Angeles Times* 17 July 1991.

Genesis of *Dracula* from *Bram Stoker's Dracula – The Film and The Legend*, Francis Ford Coppola and James V. Hart, Pan Books, 1992, *Sunday Telegraph* 24 January 1993 and *Empire* March 1993.

'We're looking for very *deep* emotional relationships' 'Coppola – Journals 1989–1993' in *Projections 3*, edited by John Boorman and Walter Donohue, Faber and Faber, 1994.

Production troubles from *Entertainment Weekly* 20 November 1992 and *Premiere* (US) December 1992.

'I've had some of the best days of my life' *Bram Stoker's Dracula – The Film and the Legend*, Francis Ford Coppola and James V. Hart, Pan Books, 1992.

'That was really one of the worst previews' and following from 'Coppola – Journals 1989–1993' in *Projections 3*, edited by John Boorman and Walter Donohoe, Faber and Faber, 1994.

Success of *Dracula* from *New York Times* 16 November 1992 and *Observer* 21 February 1993.

'My performance was too introverted' *Premiere* (UK) September 1994.

Reviews of *Dracula* from *New York Post* 13 November 1992, *Philadelphia Inquirer* 13 November 1992, *New York Magazine* 16 November 1992 and *Village Voice* 17 November 1992.

'I'll just send them a tape' *Interview* September 1990.

'We weren't expecting a reply' and following from SJ interview with Jean-Paul Rappeneau, November 1995.

Genesis of *Freaked* and following from SJ interview with Alex Winter.

Keanu on Ortiz from *Movieline* November 1992.

'Maybe people don't know who he is' SJ interview with Alex Winter.

Release of *Freaked* from *Wired* June 1995 and *Guardian* 4 June 1995.

7   The Middle Way

Genesis of film from *Much Ado About Nothing* (screenplay, with introduction), Kenneth Branagh, Chatto & Windus, 1993.

'He had nothing specific in mind' and following from SJ interview with Kenneth Branagh, December 1995.

Much Ado test previews from *Variety* 22 January 1996.

'Blow the cobwebs' *Screen International* 7 May 1993.

'I made a couple of trips' SJ interview with Kenneth Branagh.

'I'm an unresolved character' *Independent Magazine* 21 August 1993.

'It's a strange relationship' SJ interview with Kenneth Branagh.

Keanu's leather trousers from *Independent Magazine* 21 August 1993.

Keanu's massage scene from SJ interview with Kenneth Branagh.

'Do you prefer sex to Shakespeare?' *Independent on Sunday* 22 August 1993.

Keanu smitten with Kate Beckinsale from *Ken and Em*, Ian Shuttleworth, Headline, 1995.

'It amazed me' SJ interview with Kenneth Branagh.

'We had a place to eat' *Empire* September 1993.

Genesis of *Even Cowgirls Get The Blues* from *Rolling Stone* 18 February 1992, *Premiere* (US) November 1992 and PolyGram publicity notes.

Casting of Keanu from SJ interview with Gus Van Sant, July 1995.

Script changes to *Cowgirls* from *Even Cowgirls Get the Blues and My Own Private Idaho* (screenplays, with introduction), Gus Van Sant, Faber and Faber, 1993 and PolyGram publicity notes.

Postponement of *Cowgirls* release from *Sight and Sound* December 1993.

'Basically an increasingly dull series of riffs' *Village Voice* 31 May 1994.

'You are experiencing things' *Even Cowgirls Get the Blues and My Own Private Idaho* (screenplays, with introduction), Gus Van Sant, Faber and Faber, 1993.

'I saw he was trying' *Guardian* 4 January 1995.

Casting of Keanu in *Little Buddha* from SJ interview with Bernardo Bertolucci, January 1996, *Los Angeles Times* 5 June 1994 and Buena Vista publicity notes.

'I shouted with joy' *Studio* (France) December 1993.

'It was a terribly difficult and long decision' SJ interview with Jeremy Thomas, June 1995.

'I remember that when I was going through Bangkok' *Studio* (France) December 1993.

Local resistance to the film from SJ interview with Jeremy Thomas.

'The place we were staying in' SJ interview with Chris Auty, January 1996.

'He took their breath away' SJ interview with Bernardo Bertolucci.

Keanu's fasting from *Los Angeles Times* 5 June 1994.

Keanu's accent from *Time Out* 12 May 1993.

The cremation from *Studio* (France) December 1993.

'I realized that in order to continue being an actor' *Empire* June 1994.

'When I come out of the gates' *Empire* December 1995.

Keanu's enlightenment scene from SJ interview with Chris Auty.

'It was a dangerous role for him' SJ interview with Jeremy Thomas.

Reviews of *Little Buddha* from *Variety* 13 December 1993 and *Time* 4 July 1994.

Little Buddha marketing campaign from *Los Angeles Times* 31 July 1994.

8 In the Fast Lane

The abortive attempt to make *Drop Zone* from an interview by Nigel Andrews with Jan De Bont, December 1994 (this interview appeared in a different form in the *Financial Times* 14 January 1995).

Keanu as 'Apollo, Dionysus and Bacchus' from *Independent on Sunday* 22 August 1993.

Ray Liotta on taking on an action role from *Vogue* (US) July 1994.

Speed's druggy connotations from *Studio* (France) September 1994.

Keanu on De Bont's visual style from *Premiere* (UK) September 1994.

'Beautiful warrior master' *Entertainment Weekly* 10 June 1994.

'What makes him stand out' *Independent on Sunday* 9 October 1994 and *Today* 1 July 1994.

'Keanu was not at that time a big star' interview by Nigel Andrews with Jan De Bont.

'Keanu's heard too many times' *ibid* and *Chicago Tribune* 26 June 1994.

Keanu's buzzcut from *USA Today* 9 June 1994.

Keanu's weights training from *Washington Times* 19 June 1994.

'He became very quiet' *Entertainment Weekly* 10 June 1994.

'He said it was a good idea to keep working' *New York Times* 12 June 1994.

Reactions to Phoenix's death from *Independent on Sunday* 5 December 1993.

'I think of it as an accident' *USA Today* 9 June 1994.

'I still have people asking about River' *Attitude* September 1995.

No signs of drug abuse on movie sets from *USA Today* 9 June 1994.

'I know there was a lot of smoking' SJ interview with Clive Donner, December 1995.

'Keanu was as wild as anybody' *People* 5 June 1995.

'There were a lot of people hanging around Keanu' SJ interview with Donald Mason, August 1995.

'Heroin goes in and out of fashion' *USA Today* 1 August 1996.

'I wanted to give my character of Jack Traven' *Calgary Herald* 8 June 1994.

'Jan didn't want gratuitous violence' *Los Angeles Times* 5 June 1994.

'People always say you have to know the character's background' *Independent on Sunday* 9 October 1994.

'They thought it was going to be a tiny little B-movie' and following from interview by Nigel Andrews with Jan De Bont.

Samuel Reeves' arrest and conviction from *Honolulu Advertiser* 24 June 1994 and *Mail on Sunday* 20 November 1994.

'Who the hell needs this?' *ibid.*

'I'm not very proud of myself' *Daily Mirror* 30 August 1994.

'A lot of who I am is a reaction against his actions' *US Magazine* March 1995.

Keanu's arrest from *Mugshots: Celebrities Under Arrest*, George Seminara, St Martin's Press, 1996.

Keanu denying knowledge of his father's arrest from *Vanity Fair* August 1995.

Speed exit polls from *Los Angeles Times* 12 July 1994.

Reviews of *Speed* from *Variety* 6 June 1994 and the *New Yorker* 13 June 1994.

Bernardo Bertolucci on *Speed* from interview with SJ, January 1996.

'To me it's not a hero piece' *Plain Dealer* 20 June 1994.

'Doesn't it seem like a lifetime ago since you did *Bill and Ted*?' *ibid.*

Keanu on his lifestyle from *Vanity Fair* August 1995.

Keanu fixing motorbike from SJ interview with Robert Mark Kamen, August 1995.

'When it comes down to it' SJ interview with Alan Powell, August 1995.

'He'd say, "You live on a day to day basis"' SJ interview with Shael Risman, August 1995.

'He's got something at the back of the eyes' *Independent Magazine* 21 August 1993.

'Take the money and run' *Premiere* (UK) September 1994.

Without Remorse and other offers from *Variety* 11 July 1994.

Genesis of *Hamlet* project from *Toronto Star* 22 October 1994,

Maclean's 23 January 1995 and SJ interview with Lewis Baumander, August 1995.

'The play's the thing, man' *Winnipeg Free Press* 10 March 1994.

'He came to see the *Hamlet* that I did' SJ interview with Kenneth
Branagh, December 1995.

'He arrived having learned it from beginning to end' SJ interview
with Richard Hurst, November 1995.

'We met, each of us' SJ interview with Lewis Baumander.

'Sometimes Lewis would find himself' SJ interview with Richard
Hurst.

'I've always hated those passive, morose Hamlets' SJ interview with
Lewis Baumander.

'I guess the first thing that drew me to Hamlet' *Premiere* (UK)
September 1994.

'His take on *Hamlet*' SJ interview with Richard Hurst.

'Keanu Krazy' from *Winnipeg Free Press* 8 December 1994 and 16
December 1994 and *People* 6 February 1995.

'It was incredibly cold' SJ interview with Richard Hurst.

'The difference between stage craft and film craft' *ibid.*

'There's a level of honesty that he wants to play' SJ interview with
Lewis Baumander.

Nightmares about drying up on stage from *Chicago Tribune* 26
June 1994.

'One of the things people are not banking on' *Toronto Star* 22
October 1994.

'Deal justly with me' SJ interview with Lewis Baumander.

Comments from Keanu's fellow-actors in *Guardian* 14 January
1995, *Montreal Gazette* 11 January 1995 and *People* 6 February
1995.

'We ended up being so protective of him' SJ interview with Richard
Hurst.

Hamlet reviews from *Winnipeg Free Press* 14 January 1995, *Sunday
Times* 22 January 1995, *Vancouver Sun* 14 January 1995, *Toronto
Star* 14 January 1995 and *Guardian* 14 January 1995.

Keanu on his own performance from *Vanity Fair* August 1995,
USA Today 27 July 1995 and *Toronto Star* 1 August
1995.

'I'll say one thing about our production' *Empire* December 1995.

'When I left town at the end of the first week' SJ interview with Lewis Baumander.

'He was absolutely spectacular' and following from SJ interview with Richard Hurst.

'Perhaps it was just opening night nerves' *Maclean's* 23 January 1995.

'These are the remarks of a media' SJ interview with Lewis Baumander.

'One can't fault Reeves for his ambition and guts' *Vanity Fair* March 1995.

9   The Coolest Head in Town

'The stories may or may not be true' and following from SJ interview with Keith Mayerson, December 1995.

'Sleaze Trips of Hollywood Hell-Raiser' *Daily Star* 27 October 1994.

Keanu's love play with Sharon Stone from *Daily Mirror* 30 July 1994.

Keanu at Barney's from *Daily Mirror* 30 August 1994.

Reports of the Reeves–Geffen marriage from *Voici* (France) 14 December 1994 and *Hollywood Reporter* 27 December 1994.

'Sources close to Geffen' *Boston Herald* 21 January 1995.

'Hidden desire, New Age ceremony and conspicuous consumption' *Attitude* September 1995.

The Keanu Stomp and 'Are you gay?' from *Interview* September 1990.

'If you don't have relationships' *City Limits* 23 January 1992.

Keanu's girlfriends from *People* 5 June 1995 and *Vanity Fair* August 1995.

A case of mistaken identity from *Buzz* May 1995.

'On our summer camping trip' SJ interview with Shawn Aberle, August 1995.

'When I knew him? Not a chance' SJ interview with Alan Powell, August 1995.

'He seems pretty heterosexual to me' SJ interview with Gus Van Sant, July 1995.

'I hear that I'm supposed to be married to Keanu Reeves' *Time* 27 March 1995.

Keanu on Geffen from *Out* July/August 1995.

Tim Allis on Keanu from *USA Today* 24 May 1995.

'I've never had a male sexual experience' SJ interview with Michael Shnayerson, October 1995.

'He's really smart' SJ interview with John Palmer, August 1995.

'He understands what mystery is' SJ interview with David Hlynsky, July 1995.

Geffen's visits to Winnipeg from *Toronto Star* 28 May 1995; Keanu dating a ballet dancer from *Vancouver Sun* 14 January 1995 and *Gay Times* June 1995.

Keanu and Amanda De Cadenet from *Sunday Mirror* 22 October 1995 and *Daily Mirror* 23 October 1995.

'This has taken longer' SJ interview with William Gibson, May 1994.

Critics on 'Robert Long-Ago' from *Los Angeles Times* 21 May 1995.

'We were going around' and 'Because Robert and I were both outsiders' from SJ interview with William Gibson.

Johnny Mnemonic production history from *Hollywood Reporter* (Special Issue) August 1994, *Screen International* 2 June 1995 and *Premiere* (US) June 1995.

Val Kilmer acting badly *ibid.*

The script in Keanu's front yard *ibid.*

'He asked me just what the character of Johnny was all about' *Hollywood Reporter* (Special Issue) August 1994.

'In the beginning he's a slick, superficial asshole' *Premiere* (US) June 1995.

Keanu on his role from *Seventeen* December 1994 and *US Magazine* March 1995.

'At times this film feels like *Blade Runner* directed by Fellini' *Los Angeles Times* 21 May 1995.

Reactions of the film crew to Longo from *Premiere* (US) June 1995 and *Hollywood Reporter* (Special Issue) August 1994.

Johnny Mnemonic reviews from *New York Times* 26 May 1995, *New York Post* 26 May 1995, *Hollywood Reporter* 23 May 1995, *Variety* 22 May 1995, *Village Voice* 6 June 1995 and *Washington Post* 27 May 1995.

'Our film has soul' SJ interview with William Gibson.

'It's not the vision' *Empire* December 1995.

A Walk in the Clouds production history from *Premiere* (US) August 1995 and *Dallas Morning News* 12 August 1995.

Keanu preparing for the role from *US Magazine* March 1995.

Keanu's shyness in love scenes from *Vanity Fair* August 1995, *USA Today* 14 August 1995 and *Premiere* (US) August 1995.

Snogging technique and split lip from *Observer* 11 June 1995, *Entertainment Weekly* 24 March 1995 and *Today* 10 October 1995.

Arau's good karma from *US Magazine* March 1995, *Preview* May/June 1995 and *Premiere* (US) August 1995.

Keanu as wine buff from SJ interview with Kenneth Branagh, December 1995.

'When we saw it with an audience' SJ interview with Robert Mark Kamen, August 1995.

Reviews of *A Walk in the Clouds* from *Chicago Tribune* 11 August 1995, *Newsday* 11 August 1995, *Los Angeles Times* 11 August 1995 and *Washington Post* 11 August 1995.

Kamen's trip to Mexico from Twentieth Century-Fox publicity notes.

Martha Stewart wet dream from *Premiere* (US) August 1995.

Critics on Keanu from *Boston Globe* 11 August 1995, *San Francisco Chronicle* 11 August 1995, *New York Times* 11 August 1995 and *USA Today* 11 August 1995.

'That's a private question' *San Diego Union-Tribune* 10 August 1995.

Keanu on the film from *San Francisco Chronicle* 18 July 1995, *USA Today* 27 July 1995 and *Vanity Fair* August 1995

'Listen, I was an actor' *ibid.*

10   The Leap from the Bridge

'I don't talk about his work as acting' SJ interview with Stephen Prina, October 1995.

'The same values underlie a huge amount' SJ interview with Clive Donner, December 1995.

'He's a very honest actor' SJ interview with Alex Winter, June 1995.

'His first appearance in the film' SJ interview with Christopher Hampton, February 1996.

'What seemed to me very clear' SJ interview with Jon Amiel, November 1995.

'No, man, not after *Johnny Mnemonic*' *USA Today* 27 July 1995.

'We played bass together' SJ interview with Alex Winter.

'He and Alex would jam on bass' SJ interview with Scott Kroopf, January 1996.

'He was lousy, we were all lousy' SJ interview with Peter Hewitt, December 1995.

Origins of Dogstar from *Houston Chronicle* 18 July 1995 and *Baltimore Sun* 21 July 1995.

Dogstar 'not a good band' from *San Francisco Chronicle* 24 July 1993.

Keanu as 'a confused puppy' from *San Diego Union-Tribune* 5 November 1994.

'It's just some fun and some free beer with friends' *Sunday Times* 23 October 1994.

Keanu on stage from *USA Today* 27 July 1995 and *New York Post* 28 July 1995.

Reviews of 1995 Dogstar tour from *Houston Chronicle* 18 July 1995, *Orlando Sentinel Tribune* 20 July 1995 and *Observer* (London) 17 September 1995.

'Anybody who has ever played music' *New York Post* 28 July 1995.

Bon Jovi concert review from *Los Angeles Times* 2 October 1995.

Dogstar mockumentary from *Variety* 12 June 1995.

'I don't really have the feeling I exist' *Studio* (France) December 1993.

'He's got a ton of energy' SJ interview with Scott Kroopf.

'It evoked a feeling in me' and following from SJ interview with Steven Baigelman, January 1996.

Stars working in low-budget movies from *Variety* 27 February 1995.

'My film gave him room to be strong' SJ interview with Steven Baigelman.

'These are two really hot people' *Movieline* March 1996.

'The film has a very real look' SJ interview with Steven Baigelman.

Reviews of *Feeling Minnesota* from *Variety* 16 September 1996 and *Village Voice* 17 September 1996.

Keanu's involvement with *Voyeur: A Divine Comedy* from SJ interviews with Rupert Wyatt, November 1995 and May 1996.

Fat Keanu from *Sun* 22 September 1995 and *Premiere* (US) June 1996; discomfort at having to smoke from *San Francisco Chronicle* 18 July 1995.

Keanu, science whizz from *Premiere* (US) August 1996 and *New York Post* 18 August 1996.

'The speed and grace of someone in snowshoes' *Los Angeles Times* 2 August 1996.

'I wanted to look kind of heavy' *USA Today* 1 August 1996.

Reviews of *Chain Reaction ibid* and *Variety* 29 July 1996.

Review of *The Last Time I Committed Suicide* from *Variety* 27 January 1997.

'I didn't fight that hard for Keanu' and following from SJ interview with Jan De Bont, June 1996.

Reviews of 1996 Dogstar tour from *Guardian* 16 July 1996, *Observer* 21 July 1996 and *Daily Telegraph Magazine* 14 September 1996.

'I love him and miss him greatly' *OK! Weekly* 8 September 1996.

'He's going through a difficult time' SJ interview with Jan De Bont.

Industry comment on *Speed 2* from *Los Angeles Times* 7 June 1996.

'I become morally suspect' *USA Today* 1 August 1996.

Keanu's character as Superman and friction on set from *Premiere* (US) March 1997.

'I'd work with him again in a second' from SJ interview with Lawrence Kasdan, July 1995.

'It's hard to stick close to one's actors' SJ interview with Jon Amiel.

'I guess I just deal with my own behaviour' *Toronto Sun* 24 May 1993.

'Lying in bed with my lover' *Movieline* November 1992.

'Did you ever want to jump off a bridge?' *ibid.*

'The way Keanu has run his career' SJ interview with Lawrence Kasdan.

'Rob Lowe had quite a long run' SJ interview with Alex Winter.
'Perhaps in a way' SJ interview with Clive Donner.
'I can't say that I *have* been totally different' *Premiere* (UK)
     September 1994.
'I'd say he's far better' SJ interview with Alex Winter.

INDEX

DANIEL DAY-LEWIS: The Fire Within

GARRY JENKINS

£4.99

Oscar-winning Daniel Day-Lewis is the most brilliant young star of his generation – a romantic screen icon for the 90s but also a complex, mysterious and enigmatic man.

The first biography of the life and work of this chameleon actor draws on interviews with family, friends and colleagues, looking behind his myriad masks and painting an intimate portrait from troubled boyhood to matinée idol manhood. It reveals the fires burning within the most passionate actor of our time.

0 330 33896 X

ANTHONY HOPKINS: In Darkness and Light

MICHAEL FEENEY CALLAN

£5.99

Anthony Hopkins has always wrestled with a dual personality, part dedicated craftsman, part wildboy. From the highs and lows of his roller-coaster career he has finally emerged as an international star for his roles in such films as *The Silence of the Lambs* and *Howards End*.

Michael Feeney Callan has written the first in-depth biography of this remarkable man who is, arguably, one of the finest British actors of his generation.

'vividly portrays a hell-raiser tortured by his own demons' *The Times*

0 330 32889 1

PAN

50 YEARS

NEVER FADE AWAY: The Kurt Cobain Story

DAVE THOMPSON

£4.99

KURT COBAIN 1967–1994

From the basement of Seattle's grunge scene, to his meteoric rise to fame as lead singer of Nirvana, to his tragic suicide at the age of 27, he was brilliant, tortured and destined to never fade away.

0 330 33965 6

PAN

50 YEARS

All Pan Books are available at your local bookshop or newsagent, or can be ordered direct from the publisher. Indicate the number of copies required and fill in the form below.

Send to: Macmillan General Books C.S.
               Book Service By Post
               PO Box 29, Douglas I-O-M
               IM99 1BQ

or phone: 01624 675137, quoting title, author and credit card number.

or fax: 01624 670923, quoting title, author, and credit card number.

or Internet: http://www.bookpost.co.uk

Please enclose a remittance* to the value of the cover price plus 75 pence per book for post and packing. Overseas customers please allow £1.00 per copy for post and packing.

*Payment may be made in sterling by UK personal cheque, Eurocheque, postal order, sterling draft or international money order, made payable to Book Service By Post.

Alternatively by Access/Visa/MasterCard

Card No.   ☐☐☐☐☐☐☐☐☐☐☐☐☐☐☐☐☐☐

Expiry Date   ☐☐☐☐☐☐☐☐☐☐☐☐☐☐☐☐☐☐

Signature   _____

Applicable only in the UK and BFPO addresses.

While every effort is made to keep prices low, it is sometimes necessary to increase prices at short notice. Pan Books reserve the right to show on covers and charge new retail prices which may differ from those advertised in the text or elsewhere.

NAME AND ADDRESS IN BLOCK CAPITAL LETTERS PLEASE

Name _____

Address _____

_____

_____

_____

8/95

Please allow 28 days for delivery.
Please tick box if you do not wish to receive any additional information.   ☐